Praise for *New Jersey Noir*

"In *New Jersey Noir* Joe Bilby uses his encyclopedic knowledge of New Jersey history, a keen eye for a good story, and a gift for telling those stories to create a book that will be an enjoyable read for those within New Jersey and beyond."
- **John Zinn**, Chair of the New Jersey Civil War 150th Anniversary Committee

"New Jersey may be happily known as 'The Garden State,' but it is a garden that also hides some very dark secrets. Historian Joseph G. Bilby has done a wonderful job scouring the records and inviting us to peer with him into the wonderfully odd, macabre, and downright bizarre corners of New Jersey history. Presented with all the requisite literary swagger, *New Jersey Noir* demonstrates how truth can not only be stranger than fiction, but a lot more entertaining!"
- **Gordon Bond**, who runs the website www.GardenStateLegacy.com, is the author of *Wicked Woodbridge & Crazy Carteret: Vice in New Jersey's Oldest Township*

"New Jersey license plates have included its 'Garden State' nickname since 1954, but after reading these action-packed crime tales, readers may start thinking that Bruce Springsteen was closer to the truth when he referred to his home state as 'Jungleland.' From Civil War veteran/tabloid scandal sheet publisher William Mann 'robbing the Robber Barons' to twenty-two-year old Brooklyn Dodger pitcher Billy Loes, involved in a paternity suit in 1956, Joe Bilby's solidly researched, two-fisted crime tales pull back the curtains on the 'good old days' to expose an amazing landscape of damaged World War I veterans, bootleggers, crime bosses, and run-of-the-mill grifters, crooks, and killers playing out their dramas on the Jersey stage. Whether you savor them one at a time or binge read a dozen at a time, these twenty-seven stories will keep you riveted. As the saying goes, 'You can't make this stuff up!'"
- **Joe Bordonaro**, USAF veteran, retired teacher, long time living history presenter and current correspondent for the "Civil War News"

"Lending a historian's sensibility to the seamy underbelly of mid-20th century crime in the Garden State, Joe Bilby delivers the best of both worlds 'only in Jersey' stories that are both tantalizingly juicy and rigorously researched. New Jersey Noir reveals the fascinating stories of madmen, murderous beauty queens, and even a defenestrated congressman, just to name a few. With so many questionable urban legends making the rounds, Noir proves definitively that the truth is indeed stranger and more interesting than fiction."
- **Sue Kaufmann**, New Jersey historian and writer/editor of HiddenNJ.com

NEW JERSEY NOIR

Bizarre Tales of the Garden State
from 1921 to 1952

Joseph G. Bilby

AMERICAN HISTORY PRESS
STAUNTON VIRGINIA

Copyright © 2017 Joseph G. Bilby

All rights reserved. No part of this book may be transmitted in any form by any means electronic, mechanical or otherwise using devices now existing or yet to be invented without prior written permission from the publisher and copyright holder.

American History Press

Staunton, Virginia
(888) 521-1789
Visit us on the Internet at:
www.Americanhistorypress.com

First Printing November 2017

To schedule an event with the author or to inquire about bulk discount sales please contact American History Press.

Library of Congress Cataloging-in-Publication Data
Names: Bilby, Joseph G., author.
Title: New Jersey noir : bizarre tales of the Garden State from 1921 to 1952 / Joseph G. Bilby.
Description: Staunton, Virginia : American History Press, [2017] | Includes bibliographical references.
Identifiers: LCCN 2017045039 | ISBN 9781939995261 (pbk. : alk. paper)
Subjects: LCSH: Crime--New Jersey--History--20th century.
Classification: LCC HV6793.N4 B55 2017 | DDC 364.109749/09041--dc23
LC record available at https://lccn.loc.gov/2017045039

Cover photograph: Police investigating the scene of Dutch Schultz's death (author's collection).

Manufactured in the United States of America on acid-free paper. This book exceeds all ANSO standards for archival quality.

*To my grandchildren, Anna Feldman, Angelica Bilby and Joseph Bilby—
may they carry on a love of New Jersey history for yet another generation.*

Contents

Introduction vii

1. 1921 – The Mad Mann of Morristown 1
2. 1922 – Who Shot Honest John? 7
3. 1923 – High School Flappers with "the Wanderlust" ... 19
4. 1925 – The Bloomfield Madman 23
5. 1927 – The "Chicken Fancier" and His Lady Friend 33
6. 1928 – "Lifetime Jake," the Convict's Friend 41
7. 1929 – The "Torch Murderer" from Westfield 48
8. 1930 – "Richie the Boot" Gets Lucky 61
9. 1931 – The "Parade Murderer" 69
10. 1932 – A Classy Con Man 79
11. 1933 – The Strange Case of Bradway Brown 83
       Gallery of Images
12. 1934 – The Strange Case of Millard Edouard 93
13. 1935 – "Old Smokey" 103
14. 1936 – Downfall of a Detective 113
15. 1937 – Joe Fay and the "Big Six" 117
16. 1938 – The Congressman Goes Out the Window 130
17. 1939 – Wealthy Wacko Runs Amuck in Plainfield 138
18. 1940 – The Tax Collector Goes Berserk 145
19. 1941 – The Puppy Love Slaying 154
20. 1943 – Murder in the Pinelands 158

21. 1945 – A Nazi in Newark	160
22. 1946 – A Lower Case Bonnie and Clyde	165
23. 1947 – Alice Would Have Been Embarrassed	168
24. 1948 – The Redhead and the Cop	170
25. 1949 – Mass Murder in Camden	172
26. 1951 – A "Mercy Killing" in Cliffside Park	174
Bibliographical Note	177
About the Author	180
Index	181

Introduction

The modern public is obsessed with and entertained by crime and bizarre behavior stories, from the O. J. Simpson trial to the fictional but Jersey-centric *Sopranos* and *Boardwalk Empire*, but that interest is not a recent phenomenon. The unusual sells, and always did, and the weirder the story or the people involved the better. Back in the era when much of America's home entertainment was provided by reading the newspaper, the post-World War I "Jazz Age" decline in societal mores was exacerbated by the lawlessness that accompanied Prohibition, leaving the American public appalled, but also fascinated, by crimes and bizarre behavior. The subsequent onset of the Depression and advent of a whole new wave of banditry and mayhem and crackpot political movements increased the popularity of cheap newspaper amusement, even with the growth of radio and the film industry, which would, in its own turn, exploit the same topics. That obsession carried through into the post-World War II era and the 1950s, even with the advent of television—and today's "reality shows."

Public fascination with the bizarre translated to revenue for newspapers, who rushed reporters from one story to another and spun local news across the nation. One of the most popular genres of the era was that of mysteriously murdered husbands. Noted fiction writer and celebrity journalist Damon Runyan, covering the story himself, commented that the 1927 trial of forty-year-old Margaret Lilliendahl, an accused husband slayer, and her neighbor, lover and accomplice, fifty-seven-year-old "chicken fancier" Willis Beach, precipitated the "invasion" of May's Landing, New Jersey, by the "H. M. T. L. (Husband Murder Trial Legion)" of reporters and photographers, all eager to provide entertainment, much of it unrelated to the actual murder itself, for people across the country.

This book provides a summary of many of New Jersey's bizarre tales and curious crimes that made the national news between 1922 and 1952, sometimes known as the "Noir" era.

The stories you are about to read include those of William d'Alton Mann, the nineteenth century founder of tabloid journalism, "rum running" and real estate swindling in Nucky Johnson's Atlantic City, the murder of a monkey collecting circus owner by a howling hit man hired by his brother-in-law, the "Hollywood on the Hudson" death of stuntman "Handsome Jack," the career of Trenton's freelance executioner, the creative counterfeiter from Elizabeth, the case of a Klansman literally hammered to death, the murder of a bigamist inventor in the Highlands by a "dwarflike man," the sad fate of the "Radium Girls" of Orange, the bizarre Westfield "torch murderer," a foiled lynching in Asbury Park, the con man founder of "Storybook Land," the ironic end tale of New Jersey's Sherlock Holmes, the Hoboken stamp collector who put his wife up for sale, ghost pretenders on the *Morro Castle*, the death of the "Dutchman" in Newark, the veteran who claimed to be the shortest man in the army, and much, much more.

CHAPTER 1

1921-The Mad Mann of Morristown

William d'Alton Mann was a war hero, an inventor, a politician, a publisher, and a scoundrel. Born in Sandusky, Ohio, in 1839, Mann, like many of his type in the 19th century, eventually made his way to Manhattan—and New Jersey.

At the outbreak of the Civil War Mann joined the 1st Michigan Cavalry, where his charisma won him an election as a captain, even though he had no prior military experience. In 1862 he was promoted to lieutenant colonel of the 1st and then became colonel of the 7th Michigan Cavalry. He commanded the 7th in Brigadier General George Custer's brigade at Gettysburg during the cavalry fight on the battle's third day. In 1863 Colonel Mann designed an innovative set of infantry equipment, with the cartridge box carried in front rather than the side of the soldier, connected to a backpack by a harness. The 15th New Jersey infantry was one of the regiments selected to test Mann equipment in the spring of 1864.

Following the war, Mann moved to Mobile, Alabama, where he consolidated several newspapers into one, *The Register*, and also invested in cottonseed oil production and railroads. He invented a new luxury railroad car, called the "Mann Boudoir Car," which he later sold to the Pullman company. Mann could be considered a "carpetbagger" of sorts, but he ran and was elected to Congress as a Democrat in the election of 1880. His obituary, however, noted that he "never occupied his seat…for the federal authorities denied him a certificate." Unfazed, he continued dabbling in railroad inventions, including a prototype refrigerator car.

After he moved back north to New York City, Mann's cynical assessment of "New York Society," a seemingly unchanging truth, was that it was "inhabited by jackasses, libertines and parvenus." But to Mann it was also a gold mine. He became the editor and publisher of *Town Topics*, a pre-tabloid scandal sheet concentrating on the immoral behavior, real and suspected, of the elite "Four Hundred" of New York, a collection of "old wealth" families and "Robber Baron" parvenus.

Mann would often approach the candidates he was about to expose and suggest that an expensive (up to $10,000, depending on the mark) subscription to his other publication, *Fads and Fancies*, which featured the Four Hundred in a more flattering light, might result in quashing a story. Some, including a rival publication, *Collier's Weekly*, labeled his business methods as "blackmail." In 1905, Mann filed criminal libel charges against *Collier's* editor Norman Hapgood, but failed to prove his case. In return, the next year the New York City District Attorney filed perjury charges against Mann, but the jury in that court case failed to find him guilty, and *Town Topics* continued on into the twentieth century. He also produced several related spinoffs from his original publications, including one titled the *Smart Set*, which was described by one critic of the era as "a raffish publication," and engaged in a number of shady Manhattan real estate deals. Never one to miss a publicity opportunity, Mann, while attending the Gettysburg reunion of 1913, returned a Confederate flag his regiment had captured at Gettysburg, had his photo taken alongside John Clem, the legendary Civil War drummer boy, and complained to the media that the secretary of war had not made him a principal speaker at the commemoration.

Sometime in the 1890s Mann, while continuing to maintain an apartment in New York, bought a home at 146 Madison Ave in Morristown, where he lived until his death in May, 1920 from complications of influenza. Prior to his demise, in his last article in *Town Topics*, the prescient Mann accurately predicted a Republican victory in the presidential election of 1920, an American return to isolationism and a second war with Germany.

Unaccountably, Mann had previously given his birthplace as "Nevada" to a census taker. His will was contested by his wife Sophie, who was half his age, a daughter by a previous marriage and his nephew, and the case dragged on in court for four years before it was finally resolved. Mann's

Morristown address appears to be a parking lot today. He was buried, among a number of other notable eccentrics of the era in Woodlawn Cemetery in the Bronx.

The long, complicated, colorful life of Colonel William d'Alton Mann was detailed in Andy Logan's biography, *The Man Who Robbed the Robber Barons*, in 1965.

A Rum Run to Atlantic City

The Volstead Act, the enforcement legislation of the Eighteenth Amendment to the United States Constitution prohibiting the production, sale, and transport of "intoxicating liquor," was not a popular law in New Jersey. As with elsewhere across the country, speakeasies opened up all over the state as soon as saloons closed. In Atlantic City, liquor was readily available and openly sold, not only in taverns, but in drug stores and some local groceries. Early on the city became a major landing site for smuggled alcoholic beverages.

Violating alcohol sales laws was nothing new in the "City by the Sea." Local saloon owners had openly defied a state regulation, dubbed "the Bishops' Law," prohibiting liquor sales on Sundays, from the date of its inception, with no consequences.

Such a cavalier disregard for the Volstead law drew federal attention, and in the summer of 1921 government agents thought they had solved the mystery of an "elusive pirate ship" that had been spotted at "various times off the New Jersey coast, near Montauk Point and in Long Island Sound" when they raided the *Pokomoke*, docked in Gardner's Basin in the inlet section of Atlantic City, on July 23.

The *Pokomoke* had set out from the old pirate stronghold of Nassau in the Bahamas, allegedly bound for Canada with a load of liquor, but local rumor had it that the booze had instead been delivered to the New Jersey resort city. This was no doubt with the approval of local political boss Enoch "Nucky" Johnson, who took a cut of all illegal liquor sales, along with a slice of the profits from the city's numerous brothels and illegal gambling dens. City workers, all of them vetted by Nucky, were often detailed at night to unload cases of whiskey from small boats which had ferried the contraband in from larger vessels moored offshore.

Although the schooner's manifest detailed an alcohol cargo, there was none to be found on the *Pokomoke* at the time it was seized.

The captain, Canadian J. A. Roy, explained that his ship had sprung a leak off the New Jersey coast on its way to Canada, and that in order to save it from sinking, he had thrown the thousand cases of liquor he was transporting overboard and then set course for Atlantic City for repairs.

No one believed the story, of course, and there was no evidence of any leak in the boat's hull. While Coast Guardsmen took possession of the *Pokomoke*, federal prohibition agents "combed Atlantic City for a trace of Captain Roy's cargo." Unsurprisingly, there is no evidence that they ever found it. It was a successful rum run, and there would be many many more to come.

While Prohibition agents were responsible for enforcing the law on land, the Coast Guard was detailed with the job of stopping smuggling from the sea—but not without harassment from local officials in Atlantic County. In 1924 Atlantic County Prosecutor Louis Repetto had several coastguardsmen arrested for shooting at rum runners, and local law enforcement obstructed federal authorities repeatedly throughout the decade.

The open availability of liquor and other appealing vices made Atlantic City, characterized by one writer of the era as "a glittering monument to the national talent for wholesale amusement," the most popular convention center in America in the 1920s. When the twenties "roared" the City by the Sea smiled from ear to ear.

The "Petticoat Realty Genius"

She made the pages of the *Butcher's Advocate*, the journal of the meat industry, in May 1921, sandwiched between an announcement of the election of officers of the Ye Olde New Yorke branch of the Master Butchers Association and the news that Katzenstein Brothers, the "well known dealers in fat, grease, bones, calfskins and cow hides" had moved from Bergen Avenue to East 135th Street.

The *Butcher's Advocate* was in awe of Mary M. Drischman, wife of Atlantic City, New Jersey, butcher George Drischman, praising her lavishly as "a woman of unusual financial genius" who had "developed almost uncanny foresight in real estate speculation," and who had "garnered for herself a fortune estimated at more than $500,000." Another journalist, while noting that she had "made her first money over a washtub," dubbed Drischman the "petticoat realty genius of Atlantic City, New Jersey."

Mrs. Drischman had just filed the will of Mrs. Alice Gerry Griswold, a "Baltimore social light [sic]" in probate court, and the wealthy Mrs. Griswold had apparently left most of her estate to Drischman, who had become "an intimate" of hers "a few years ago." An image of a smug Mrs. Drischman was "taken in a specially posed picture in her Palatial home in Atlantic City...exclusively for the Atlantic Foto Service," and was published in newspapers across the country.

According to the media of the day, the late Mrs. Griswold was apparently considered some sort of American royalty, at least by proxy. A newspaper explained that she was "the niece of Elbridge Gerry [a descendent of the original Elbridge for whom Gerrymandering was named], related by marriage to the Vanderbilts and allied to the Napoleonic line in America by marriage to Melville Patterson, nephew of Betty Patterson, the wife of Jerome Bonaparte, onetime king of Westphalia. Thrice married, once widowed, once divorced and separated from her last husband, Mrs. Griswold left many unexplained questions to be cleared up in her personal history." To say the least.

An even more complicated story soon began to emerge, however. Mary M. Drischman had been appointed as trustee and manager of Griswold's estate in 1915, when it was valued at $500,000 (around six million dollars in today's money). Following a series of labyrinthine real estate deals and dubious commissions over six years, the value of the estate had dwindled to "$75,000, an electric car and some furniture" by the time of Griswold's death, hardly an endorsement of Drischman's reputation as a "realty genius." The will was contested immediately by Griswold's daughter, the Countess Anna St. Clair de Conturbia of Milan, Italy, who had received a mere $500 bequest.

The case went to trial in October, and Anna and her attorney produced a parade of witnesses to support her claim that her mother, from whom she was estranged, had been held by Drischman as a virtual prisoner in a cottage at Northfield, a mainland town near Atlantic City. Baltimore Attorney David Stewart, Griswold's divorced second husband, testified that she was a drug addict, had nearly died three times from overdoses and "had less mental control as she grew older." Other witnesses, including a Northfield neighbor and a maid, testified that Griswold was controlled by Drischman, dosed with drugs and made to drink a bottle of wine for lunch every day, and that Drischman threatened to put the elderly socialite in an asylum if she "caused trouble."

It appears in retrospect that Griswold may have been bi-polar, as witnesses described her behavior as erratic, giving away jewelry and other goods to her chauffer, Charlie Miller, and Drischman, on one day, and then writing letters to her daughter claiming she was being held as a prisoner on another. Using the jargon of the psychiatrists of the day, popularly called "alienists," Doctor Roy Woolbert declared on the stand that Griswold's brain "was split into two quite separate individualities" and that "she possessed a dual mind. She was a Jekyll-Hyde character in real life." He declared that she would abandon her "true self, faithful to her education and exclusive society training" to hang out with social inferiors like Mrs. Drischman and her servants. This distressing behavior, according to Woolbert, was a result of her excessive consumption of Veronal, a barbiturate, often called a "hypnotic," used to treat sleeplessness and mental illness. Veronal was very addictive, and had originally been prescribed to her by a Doctor Madden of Pleasantville. Another physician, who had attended Griswold between 1915 and 1917, stated that "most of the time she was more or less hazy from drugs."

On the witness stand Drischman was described as "calm under the barrage" during four hours of intense questioning. She denied all accusations of impropriety, including making off with a bucket full of Griswold's jewelry, and accused the witnesses of lying. However, during a questioning session by the countess's attorney she asked him not to "knock her so hard," and then "broke down," admitting to making factual errors in her previous statements, admitting that she had spent $2,000 of Griswold's money for clothes for her husband and nephews. Drischman could not recall how much she had received in commissions or whether or not she had paid income taxes on the money. Her attorney, Carleton Godfrey, former Speaker of the New Jersey State Assembly, accused some witnesses of being paid by Griswold's daughter to testify against his client.

In the end, Judge Robert A. Ingersol set aside the will, ruling that the testimony indeed revealed that Drischman had exercised "undue influence" over Griswold. Although she lost the civil case, Mary Drischman, the entrepreneurial butcher's wife, was never prosecuted on criminal grounds, and continued to live well, largely, no doubt, due to her grifting off the bizarre Mrs. Griswold. In 1930 the "petticoat realty genius" was living in a $125,000 home at 109 Victoria Avenue in Ventnor, just south of Atlantic City.

CHAPTER 2

1922-Who Shot Honest John?

By 7:30 P.M. on the evening of March 10, 1922, "Honest John" Brunen had fed his basement-dwelling monkey collection, and was sitting in a chair in his living room at 508 New Jersey Avenue in Riverside, New Jersey, perusing a *Philadelphia Bulletin* article on the murder of Paramount Pictures film director William Desmond Taylor, Brunen's "boyhood friend," in Hollywood "under mysterious circumstances." And then the shotgun went off, shattering a window pane before the full charge caught the forty-seven-year-old Circus owner in the back of his head. Brunen never had a chance to draw the handgun he habitually carried in his pocket. His wife Doris heard the shot and ran downstairs. She called a doctor, who arrived, found the dead man and called police.

The following day the *New York Times* noted the coincidental parallels between Brunen's murder and those of Taylor and "bridge expert" Joseph B. Elwell of New York City, as each had been "sitting down when shot, caught off his guard by the murderer." The *Times* remarked that, as in the cases of the other two victims, "the probable motive [was] expected to be found in some hidden chamber of the circus man's past." Renowned Burlington County detective Ellis Parker was soon on the job. It was assumed in New Jersey that if anyone could open that chamber, it was Parker.

John Brunen had emigrated from Germany in the late 1880s at age fourteen, found work in a Coney Island shooting gallery and traveled around the country with carnivals, living in Tennessee and Pennsylvania, before he abandoned his first wife Dorothy to marry Doris Mohr, a former Broadway chorus girl whose first husband, an actor, had deserted her and moved to China. Brunen took over Doris' father's carnival, "Mighty Doris," which he combined with a "trained wild animal" circus as the "Mighty Doris and Colonel Francis Ferari Combined Shows." Brunen's carnival/circus toured all over the eastern United States in the first decades of the 20th century, when such traveling shows were a major source of entertainment in small town America. It was a big production, filling thirty railroad cars on the road. He gained the nickname "Honest John" because he "refused to allow any games of chance" to be connected with his shows, not due to any admirable personal traits on his part.

So, who shot "Honest John"—and why? It turned out there were a number of candidates, as he had made a lot of enemies and lived, according to one newspaper account, "with the fear of death hanging over him," and carried a handgun in his pocket. The day he was murdered, Brunen had been chased by unknown men in an automobile when returning from his circus winter quarters in Williamstown, New Jersey. To name a few, his enemies included a Perth Amboy lion tamer named William Parkston, angry that Brunen had his marriage to the circus man's seventeen-year-old daughter Hazel annulled, Gus Werner, a violent roustabout Brunen had recently fired, and Ben Franklin, a Baltimore advance agent he had fired and whose brother he had had arrested for theft.

The family of William Savitski of Mount Carmel, Pennsylvania, certainly had a motive to do Brunen in. In 1916, the circus man refused to allow lighting company workmen to turn off the electricity at the end of his show at Mount Carmel. They insisted, and in what turned into a brawl, Brunen shot and killed Savitski, who had allegedly kicked him in the groin and ran away. There were conflicting accounts, however, with some saying that Savitski was merely a bystander. Charged with murder, Honest John was acquitted on grounds of self-defense.

Ellis Parker, the nationally known and meticulously assiduous Burlington County detective often referred to as "New Jersey's Sherlock Holmes," found significant motives closer to home. Although Doris suggested to Parker that "the New York gambling crowd" might have been responsible, it appeared that the Brunens had a rocky marriage. They had apparently traded shots in a living room duel the previous Christmas during an alleged argument over Hazel's marriage, with one of his bullets lodging in Doris' corset and one of hers in his leg, but the incident was "hushed up" by local authorities. There were also rumors that Doris was having an affair with Doc Ward, the circus superintendent, and Parker uncovered some steamy correspondence between the two. Brunen's sister Elizabeth Jaeske said that she had received a letter from her brother declaring that his wife was "figuring to do away with me." The fact that neighbors had not heard Brunen's dog barking, and that a talking parrot had been removed earlier from the room where he was murdered, led Parker to consider the probability that Brunen was killed by someone he knew.

One account noted that "heel marks from a woman's shoe" had been discovered outside the window through which Brunen was shot. Doris admitted they were hers, as she had walked past the window to access a "hatchway" into the cellar to check on the monkeys prior to her husband's return home on the day of his death. There were a man's shoe tracks there as well, and a neighbor had seen a man running from the Brunen residence following the sound of a shot.

Burlington County Prosecutor J. E. Kelsey announced that he was going to request that the county freeholders and state government offer rewards for Brunen's killer, "dead or alive." New Jersey law authorized the county to offer $500 to $2,000 and the state $500 to $2,500 in rewards. Parker methodically put the pieces together, along with interviewing witnesses who had seen glimpses of the gunman and his getaway car. His suspicions fell upon Doris's brother Harry Mohr, who was a part owner of the circus and stood to gain it all should Brunen die. Parker interviewed Mohr, who was not cooperative and produced an alibi of sorts. He then decided that the weak link, and possible shooter, was Charles M. Powell, a circus employee and associate of Mohr. Powell was living in Camden, and Parker, rather than request that Camden police detain him, sent his own officers to arrest the suspect. In a subsequent interview Parker said that he had "kidnapped" Powell, a term that would come back to haunt him years later.

In custody in Mount Holly, Powell confessed that he had pulled the trigger on Brunen, that Harry Mohr had offered him $1,000 to perform the act and had driven the getaway car. Both Harry and Doris were arrested and charged with Brunen's murder. Parker opined that Doris "instigated" her husband's murder because "Brunen was getting on the women folks' nerves" and that Mohr, with the added financial motive, had engineered the assassination. Both were subsequently indicted for Honest John's murder.

The trial, held in Mount Holly in December 1922, was a nationally reported event that one newspaper declared "furnished thrills" to the public. Harry and Doris claimed innocence and Harry's wife Bessie testified that Powell was a narcotics addict, and hence his statements were worthless. She also noted that Brunen's "terrible temper and brutal arrogance made him thousands of enemies in every circus lot in the United States," and that there were a lot of people who wanted him dead. On the witness stand Doris, "sobbing convulsively," said "I have never in my life talked about killing my husband. I loved him."

Hazel Brunen, Doris's stepdaughter, differed. The "flamboyantly dressed" Hazel testified for the prosecution, claiming that Doris had unemotionally told her that people were out to kill her father and so she should not be surprised if she heard he was shot. The trial got lively. When Hazel pointed at Doris and said: "She murdered my father," Harry Mohr yelled out "you lie" and Bessie Mohr screamed: "You're a liar Hazel. Be careful, you tramp. I picked you up out of the gutter." As she was escorted out of the courtroom Bessie shouted "I'll get her!" In the wake of the outbursts defense attorney Walter S. McKeown, who had been questioning Hazel, almost collapsed and "had to be aided to a neighboring drugstore and given restoratives." It was suggested that Hazel had changed her previously admiring opinion of Doris and Harry to facilitate her claim to the entire estate of her father.

In dramatic contrast, Powell's "mouselike" wife testified that Mohr had showed up several times at her home, gave her husband money and paid the couple's rent in a Camden rooming house at 45 Cooper Street. Her husband's testimony was particularly devastating for Mohr, as the admitted triggerman asserted that Doris' brother had driven him to Philadelphia, gave him the money to purchase a double-barreled shotgun in a pawnshop on Ninth Street and then proceeded to another pawn shop where he bought a single barreled shotgun. Unsure of whether or not Powell could handle the guns properly, Mohr then took him out in the woods to practice. Powell said that they had originally intended to ambush Brunen on the road, but that that plan did not work out.

Powell concluded his testimony by recounting that Mohr had driven him to the Brunen home on the evening of March 10, handed him the double-barreled gun, poured him a shot of whisky and told him to go shoot "Honest John." According to Powell, the pair had disassembled the murder weapon and tossed the parts along the road during their escape. Detective Parker had found several of the parts, including one with a serial number and traced the gun, a Belgian import, through two owners to the pawnshop where it was purchased. A neighbor who saw the assassin's car speed away had recorded the license plate number. It proved to be Mohr's.

In an interesting sidelight, fifteen potential women jurors were not selected for the case by "common consent" of attorneys on both sides. Mrs. Elizabeth Conover of Delran, one of the rejected jurors, told a reporter that "men dreaded a woman's intuition and especially her direct thinking apparatus when it came to judging the innocence or guilt of a member of her own sex." Mrs. W. F. Letford of Palmyra summed it all up by saying "I consider the calling the women here and then dismissing them by mutual agreement of the defense and prosecution rather a farce and a travesty on giving women the vote."

The trial was national news and even caught the attention of humorist Will Rogers, who commented that "The Brunen murder case has shoved the Hall-Mills case [The New Brunswick minister and the choir singer murder] out of the papers and that State [New Jersey] is the hardest place in the world for a man to tell the truth and not be believed. A guy [Powell] comes forward in this Brunen case and admits he did the killing and the courts won't believe him."

In the end, Harry Mohr was convicted of murder and sentenced to life in prison, and Doris was acquitted. Powell, who "barked like a dog" and screamed bizarre things in his jail cell, was sentenced to 20 to 30 years in prison. In February 1923 he was diagnosed as "paranoic" and transferred to the New Jersey State Hospital for the Insane. Mohr appealed his sentence based on technical points and Powell's diagnosis. The New Jersey Supreme Court decided that although Powell was arguably a "lunatic," it was up to the presiding judge to determine if the witness had "sufficient understanding" of the "obligation of an oath" and was "capable of giving a correct account of the matters which he has seen or heard in reference to the issue." The judge had decided, and the appeal was denied.

In the aftermath of the trial Doris Brunen stated that she was going to move to New York or Philadelphia and open a "Mexican tea room." And then she disappeared. Harry appeared on the 1930 census as a prisoner in the New Jersey State Prison in Trenton. He appears to have been paroled at some point, as he was living in Irvington, New Jersey in 1942 and listed his sister Doris, who had apparently resumed using her maiden name, as a resident of Mountainside, New Jersey.

The Taxi Baron of Lakehurst

Early on the morning of August 14, 1922, railroad workers walking home along the tracks in Lakehurst, New Jersey, a "quiet little town" which had seen the passing of the bog iron and charcoal making industries, heard a woman screaming from a second floor apartment and ran up the building's outside stairs to help, opened the kitchen door, which was ajar, and found thirty-eight-year-old Ivy Giberson laying on the floor with her feet bound, a cord fastening her hands partially undone and a gag on the floor. As she was untied, Ivy said "oh my God, Will, my husband," then ran to a closed door, opened it and screamed. Her husband was lying in bed with a bullet through his head.

Ivy told the police that she had heard a noise in the kitchen at 3:00 AM, got up to check and found that two men had entered the apartment. One tied her up while the other went into the bedroom where her husband was still asleep. She heard a gunshot, and the robber tying her up yelled to the other man "Why did you have to shoot him?" According to her they then fled with $700 in cash that William, who owned a taxicab company, had withdrawn from the bank that day to buy another cab.

Local police were flummoxed after a few leads went nowhere, and so they did what New Jersey police departments had done for many years – called in the state's master investigator, Burlington county detective Ellis Parker. Parker and a Lakehurst detective interviewed Mrs. Giberson at her apartment, and, after they left, Parker remarked that he wondered where she hid the gun. The other officer was startled but Parker told him that the man allegedly tying Ivy up could not have seen who fired the shot, and thus her story was a lie. Parker surmised that she probably shot her husband with his own gun.

Parker's subsequent thorough search of the apartment found the hidden gun, a .32 caliber revolver, and then discovered the money withdrawn from the bank stashed in a couch, along with some love letters to Mrs. Giberson from a male friend, Howard Gannon of New York City, who was married with a child. Parker also established that Ivy had bought "mourning clothes" several weeks before her husband was killed. She was arrested and transported to the Ocean County jail in Toms River. Parker told a reporter that it was "a dead open and shut proposition" that Ivy had killed her husband.

As the story unraveled it also revealed that William Giberson was perhaps not only the "taxi baron" of Lakehurst, a business he began during WWI, catering to those coming and going from nearby Camp Dix. Some anonymous sources alleged that he was also a bootlegger who used his cars for night runs of liquor to various local establishments.

Following Mrs. Giberson's arrest, Lakehurst was, according to one journalist, divided into "two camps...the friends of Mrs. Giberson, indignant over her detention, and those who are against her." The pro-Ivy camp told a reporter that she had "taken an active part in work for the betterment morally and politically for her community." Ironically, considering the rumors about her husband's side business, she was considered to have "made herself conspicuous by opposition to illicit liquor traffic here." The story went on to say that Ivy "was a member of the Methodist Church," and had been "active in Red Cross work" and, "since women obtained the vote, she has been a constant worker for better and cleaner politics." One article noted that she was also "able to drive an automobile better than most of the men employed by her husband and had no fear of lonely roads at late hours." Her father, Joe Richmond, claimed she was being framed, ironically "because of her activity against bootlegging."

Ivy maintained her calm demeanor in jail. Described by a reporter as a "fascinating blonde," who was "plump and pretty," she went to trial in October 1922 in Toms River. In what was shaping up to be the most entertaining event in Ocean County in many a year, "nearly a thousand men and women, many of the latter equipped with basket lunches and knitting, struggled for entry into the courtroom." William Giberson's sister, Nellie Bowers of Trenton, testified that her brother had caught Ivy and Gannon in a compromising situation in their apartment and that the subsequent argument had led to his murder. She added a rather fantastical story alleging that Ivy had tricked William out of the house so that she could have assignations with Gannon by telling him she had secured him a job for $3 an hour as a Secret Service detective assigned to snoop around the Mount Holly railroad station looking for a "German spy with a poison gas formula."

Ellis Parker testified, detailing the circumstantial evidence that he had discovered and that had led him to the belief that it proved Mrs. Giberson's guilt. In a surprise move at the end of the trial, County Prosecutor William Jayne produced "the bloodstained pillow on which Giberson's head rested the night he was slain in bed." On the pillow there was "an outline, in grease and grime of a pistol." He then produced the handgun found in the Giberson apartment and claimed it was a perfect fit. In retrospect, this seems a rather dubious bit of evidence.

After four hours of jury deliberation Ivy Giberson was convicted of murder. The jury recommended leniency and she was sentenced to life in prison rather than execution. She was pardoned and freed in June of 1932, by the recommendation of, among others, William Jayne, the attorney who prosecuted her, and the superintendent of the New Jersey women's prison at Clinton, where she had been incarcerated. Ivy returned to Lakehurst, still maintaining her innocence. She was described as "a little grayer, her face bearing a few lines etched by her confinement, but otherwise unchanged," and was greeted by her mother and friends. She said she had been on the phone with a lot of well-wishers, including "U.S. Senator [Hamilton F.] Kean and Tom Mathis, the [New Jersey] Secretary of State."

Ivy Giberson did not evince bitterness, at least publicly, saying "I made many good friends at Clinton. I was in charge of instructing in beauty culture there and was allowed every possible freedom." She also supervised "the making of clothes for those confined on prison farms. Ivy Giberson spent the remainder of her life in Lakehurst, and died there of natural causes in 1957.

"Handsome Jack" was "a Rat"

Back when Hollywood was on the Hudson, and Pauline hung off the Palisades to the horrified delight of moviegoers, there was a stuntman and actor named Jack Bergen. Once a professional vaudeville dancer in New York City, he was hired by George Cline, manager of the Fox Films studio in Fort Lee, who later stated that Bergen "was a corner loafer, but I made a man out of him, making him work and even spending $1,000 to get him out of jail in Atlantic City." Bergen, who subsequently gained a reputation as a "dare-devil of the movies," doubling for actor "Eugene O'Brien and other heroes of the silver screen when especially daring feats were to be done," was also known as "Handsome Jack," a ladies' man who made a pass at anything in a skirt.

A hyperbolic newspaper article portrayed Bergen as "immaculately dressed, trimmed and pruned to the point of femininity, but "with the heart of a rugged two-fisted man." Robert H. Harris, the grandfather of one of Jack's girlfriends, nineteen-year-old Alice Thornton, a file clerk for a New York City bank, characterized Handsome Jack as someone "too dressed up, too careful with his fingernails, too anxious about the cut of his hair...and interested in running after women."

Never one to miss an opportunity to court a lady, Bergen got very friendly with Cline's wife Mary, described as a "small woman with the figure of a boy," and following a trip they all took to Saranac Lake, New York, Mrs. Cline, a twenty-six-year-old mother of two, admitted to her husband that Jack got her drunk and "took advantage of her." Another account, however, related by Alice Thornton, was that she witnessed Bergen and a "tipsy" Mrs. Cline's first assignation in the Cline family kitchen in Edgewater, New Jersey prior to the Saranac Lake trip.

On August 25, 1922, Cline called Bergen and asked him to come to his home at 190 Undercliff Avenue in Edgewater to explain himself. On arrival, Bergen was confronted by Alice Thornton, as well as Mrs. Cline and her brothers Lawrence and Charles Scullion. It was widely believed afterward that the "lighthearted, lithesome" Thornton, called by one reporter "a mysterious blonde," had lured Bergen to the house after having "squealed" to Cline that she had broken up with "Handsome Jack" because of his affair with Mrs. Cline.

Looking around at the gathering, Handsome Jack knew the jig was up, "threw out his chest," and said "I'm a rat and all that. What of it?" Cline pulled a .45 caliber Colt automatic pistol and challenged Bergen to a duel in a darkened room. When Bergen protested that he was unarmed, Charles Scullion went upstairs and returned with a 9 millimeter Luger pistol for him. Bergen tried to leave, but was herded upstairs by Cline. What happened next is unclear, but a few minutes later there were sounds of a struggle, shots rang out and Bergen staggered from the house leaking blood from two bullet holes. A cab driver called the police and a half hour later they found Jack lying dead nearby, with a note in his hand reading "Cline killed me."

It was alleged that another note, apparently penned prior to his arrival at the Cline home, was found in Bergen's pocket. It read: "If by chance

I am shot in the next few weeks, it will be done by a George Cline, alias George Wats, of Edgewater, N. J. For reasons unknown to me he is threatening me. No doubt a German Lueger [sic] caliber .45 [sic] will be used, as it is a favorite of his many guns. I am John Bergen, 214 East 115th Street."

Cline, Charles Scullion and Thornton were arrested on murder charges. The trio went on trial in Hackensack in October 1922. Cline's attorney, State Senator William B. Mackay, claimed that the "unwritten law" of "self-defense and justifiable homicide," justified the shooting. Cline gave two somewhat different accounts of the fight that led to Bergen's death, in one claiming that the stuntman had attacked him once they went upstairs and in another that he had threatened to attack him.

The trial made New Jersey judicial history, in dramatic contrast to the Brunen case, as the first in which a woman, twenty-three-year-old Susan Squire, a stenographer from Ridgefield Park, was chosen as jury forewoman, and five of her fellow jurors were women, even though one of the accused was a woman. Among the witnesses called was Mary Gribben Bergen, Jack's wife and the mother of his daughter Margaret, who he had deserted. She said of him "I can't say a single good thing about my husband. He never did a good day's work in his life" and added that "Mr. Cline is a man, and that is more than I can say for my late husband." Other witnesses quoted Bergen as saying that "all women are bums," and that Mary Cline "was a bum."

The judge, when charging the jury, said that there was no evidence that Cline had acted in self-defense, but that Thornton and Scullion, charged as principals, were, at most, accessories, and were therefore wrongly charged. In the end, all three defendants were acquitted. Forewoman Squire said: "We were convinced the prosecution failed to prove its case." A woman juror was quoted as saying "A man has a right to protect his home. My husband would have done the same thing under similar circumstances."

Trenton's Freelance Executioner

In November 1922 William S. Gilbert of Trenton got bored with his job as a Trenton night watchman at a rubber mill, and decided to take up another, more exciting and lucrative career, "making some easy money." He had some cards printed up that read "William S. Gilbert, Contracting Executioner," and sent them to the wardens of state prisons around the country, "asking that he be given the job of performing the execution of murderers sentenced to die." He told an inquiring reporter that he had been "commissioned to 'do his stuff' at a western prison some time in February."

Gilbert kept track of newspaper accounts of death sentences. In December 1922 an Illinois newspaper reported that he had advised a judge that he was willing to go to that state and perform an impending execution for a fee and travel expenses and "gave the warden of the New Jersey penitentiary as a reference to his ability and dexterity with the noose." Gilbert's efforts were apparently successful, as the "itinerant executioner" whose home base remained in Trenton, was the subject of a profile in a Wisconsin newspaper in December 1926. He was quoted as saying: "I am proud of my record [40 executions]. And I stand ready to snuff 'em out just as fast as the courts convict 'em." He went on to say that capital punishment would be a better deterrent if it were conducted in public: "Many men, if they ever witnessed a hanging, would hesitate longer before 'killing another.'"

Gilbert told the Wisconsin reporter an apocryphal tale of how he got his start in the business, saying that he had been a prison inmate and the warden, reluctant to execute a prisoner, told him that if he would do the job he would be released immediately. According to Gilbert, "that poor fellow asked me to pray for him before I sprung the trap. I got as far as 'Thy Kingdom Come' and then dropped him through. They criticized me for not finishing the prayer, but, being my first job, I was nervous."

Sharp was described in a Lincoln, Nebraska newspaper in October 1928 as "the man who sends death men to their everlasting without blinking an eye." The paper noted that he was on his way from Trenton to execute Frank Sharp, convicted of killing his wife. Gilbert had apparently expanded his skill set, as he was going to pull the switch when Sharp was scheduled to "take the [electric] chair.

In 1929 an Ohio newspaper characterized Gilbert as "a contracting headsman" who was "finishing his 58th job." At the time, he had executed fifty-six men and two women. When he told a reporter that "my latest job was my hardest," he was referring to his electrocution of Sharp, a man "convicted on circumstantial evidence of killing his wife with a hammer," who protested his innocence to the end.

In his travels around the country Gilbert handed out souvenir pocket knives "bearing the announcement 'William S. Gilbert, contracting executioner, Trenton, N. J. That's my business. I execute death penalty in all its forms.'" Stories on Gilbert and his unique occupation disappeared from the press after 1929. He may have taken on a more mundane but secure job. The 1930 census lists a William S. Gilbert living at 176 Ferry Street in Trenton, with occupation as "city policeman."

CHAPTER 3

1923-High School Flappers with "the wanderlust"

The press seemed to think it was a medical condition, perhaps akin to amnesia, and so they said of Virginia Verrier that "fate imbued her with the wanderlust." Virginia and her friend Georgiana Reid, characterized by the newspapers as "high school flappers," who were "daughters of wealthy parents," allegedly decided to "hike around the world," and so left their homes in Irvington, New Jersey on the morning of March 2, 1923. Virginia, the apparent ringleader, supposedly destroyed all photographs of herself before she left home and withdrew $17 (about $240 in today's money) from a bank in Maplewood. The girls then hopped a Lackawanna train for Scranton, Pennsylvania, and hit the road on foot from there, reportedly pretending to be sisters and using the names Charlotte and Mabel Frazer.

By the next morning, their frantic parents had physical descriptions of Virginia and Georgiana sent to police departments and newspapers across the country, and Albright Radio and Electric, a leading company in the infant radio industry, took up the case as well, broadcasting the information to its listeners.

After reaching Scranton by train, the girls hiked and hitchhiked to Wilkes-Barre, where they spent the night in a barn. Moving on, they stayed in a few cheap hotels and a farmhouse before arriving in Lewistown, Pennsylvania, and checked into a Y.W.C.A. hostel, where the matron became suspicious and notified the police, who detained them as they left in the morning of March 7. A local newspaper ran the headline "New Jersey high school maidens found at Lewistown." The police brought the "maidens" to Altoona, where their fathers picked them up and returned them to Irvington. What happened after that has gone unrecorded.

Death Behind the Belmar Gas Works

It started out as a game, but ended in tragedy. Caleb Hubbard, eighteen, his brother William, sixteen, Dick Forman, seventeen, and Charles Spindler, eleven, were heading towards Shark River inlet for a swim on August 16, 1923, when they decided to "play Indian" in a debris-strewn woodlot on the Belmar/Wall Township border near H Street (Today's Route #71) behind the Belmar Maloney Gas Works on 16th Avenue. Caleb and Dick "captured" the other boys and decided to pretend to burn them at the stake as part of the game.

Caleb and Dick tied William and Charles to a maple tree, threw some excelsior near their feet and lit it with a match. The excelsior quickly caught fire, and then so did the surrounding ground, and the ensuing blaze enveloped the two boys, who screamed in pain. Caleb and Dick tried to put the fire out and release the victims and were assisted by Fred Gough, a local man who had heard screams and seen smoke rising from the woods. The two burned boys were bundled into a car and driven a mile down the road to the Ann May Spring Lake Hospital, where they died that evening.

Caleb and Dick were arrested and charged with manslaughter. They went on trial on January 2, 1924. Belmar borough manager Cook Howland testified that during the previous year "an oil tank at the gas plant had overflowed and some 600 gallons of oil ran over the ground, which was described as 'made ground,' or a fill made of cinders." George Bearmore, who lived near the plant, testified that "the land is so pregnated [sic] with oil thereabouts that three years ago when he was burning rubbish in his back yard the fire spread so rapidly that he was frightened and had difficulty in getting it out." The jury deliberated for forty minutes and acquitted the two boys.

The Maloney gas works, established in the 1890s, produced "water gas," a carbon monoxide and hydrogen variant of coal gas produced by passing steam over superheated coal. It was owned by Martin Maloney of Spring Lake and Philadelphia, known locally as the "gas magnate" who was also reportedly involved in buying and selling high end beach front real estate. The plant, later owned by New Jersey Natural Gas, was demolished in 1971. In 2016, New Jersey National Guard SFC Peter Meyer, a lifelong Jersey shore resident, recalled his father telling him that the property was "oil soaked" and had other environmental problems and the land had to be "capped" after the buildings were leveled and before the property was leased to the Borough of Belmar for $1 a year. The site is currently a skating park, and the location of the tragedy a garden apartment complex.

Maloney, the "gas magnate" who owned the deadly property, was an archetype of the nineteenth century rags to riches story. He was born in Ballingarry, Ireland, on November 11, 1847, and emigrated with his parents to Scranton, Pennsylvania, in 1850. Maloney left school to work in a coal mine at the age of twelve, and, through a combination of talent, hard work, ambition, inventive genius and luck, rose in the American industrial world, becoming a founder of the Philadelphia Electric Corporation along with other energy related corporations.

Maloney eventually moved to Spring Lake for the summers, where he built an estate that covered an entire block, bordered by First, Second, Jersey and Morris Avenues, and named it after his ancestral home in Ireland, Ballingarry. Maloney's home is now long gone, replaced by several expensive but smaller houses, but the original iron fence he used to surround the estate still stands.

Well known as a philanthropist, Maloney funded, among many other projects, a hospital in Philadelphia and the construction of Saint Catherine's church in Spring Lake. On the way home from Florida on May 8, 1929 he became ill, and subsequently died in Philadelphia. Maloney was buried in a family crypt under Saint Catherine's, joining his wife, and there he remains to this day. What his reaction was to the deaths of William Hubbard and Charles Spindler is unknown.

The "Wheel Chair Murder"

In 1924, when you were an old guy going for a mug shot, you had to keep it classy and bring along your derby. At least that appears to be what sixty-nine-year-old Martin Wright thought after his arrest in Newark, New Jersey, for what was called the "wheel chair murder." A dapper dude, Wright wore his derby to the police station after his arrest.

Wright had shot and killed twenty-four-year-old Edward Hallock, a telephone lineman and boarder in his home after he "detected signs of too much familiarity" between Hallock and his daughter, thirty-two-year old Mrs. Minnie Egbert, who, along with Hallock, had been living with her parents at 335 Bergen Avenue in Newark after leaving her husband. To add insult to injury, Wright felt that his wife Hannah was ignoring him for Hallock as well, as why else "would a woman get up at half past 5 or 6 o'clock in the morning and make breakfast for a man?" Indeed.

Wright, a former carpenter described as "an arthritic cripple," was an invalid "imprisoned in a wheel chair" who had moved from Basking Ridge to Newark the year before. As one version of the story had it, "life had passed him by" and "he could only sit by, watch and think. He lost an outlook. He had only 'in look'—retrospection, brooding…and then bitterness and jealousy." Wright blamed Hallock for his daughter leaving her husband and that fact added to his barely suppressed anger at the world.

It all came to a head on March 31, 1924. Although Wright was not very mobile, he managed to get out of his bed and into his wheelchair and positioned himself by a door where he knew Hallock would walk by. The old carpenter was apparently a good enough marksman to get the job done, and, although Wright was firing from the wheelchair, "young Hallock was killed by a perfectly aimed shot…as he crossed the threshold of Wright's room." A bullet went through Hallock's heart, and the young man's body fell to the floor in front of Wright's horrified wife. Later that morning, at Newark police headquarters, Wright admitted to officers that he had shot Hallock, and said "I can't see the crime I've done," claiming that he had "relieved my wife and daughter of a scamp." Needless to say, law enforcement disagreed.

Wright was indicted for murder on April 19, 1924, and was assigned a counsel, as he had no money to hire his own attorney. His confession had obviated the need for a jury trial. On June 18, described in a newspaper article as a "pathetic figure," Wright "hobbled into court, laid his crutches down and seated himself before Judge Porter," who sentenced him to ten to twenty years in prison.

CHAPTER 4

1925-The Bloomfield Madman

Frank Martin, a fifty-one-year-old resident of Bloomfield, New Jersey, described as a "residential and industrial extension of Newark," was obviously a deeply disturbed individual. A year or so before he had attacked his wife Martha, the mother of his three children, with a razor, slashing her throat. The assault led to a ten-month sentence in state prison. Martin was released on parole after eight months for having a "defective mentality," although apparently without any conditions to seek a remedy for his problems. When Martin was freed in May, 1925, his wife forgave him and welcomed him back home, where she lived with her daughters Violet and Helen, son Frank Jr. and Violet's husband, A. G. Smith. That decision proved to be a very big, and, in the end, deadly mistake.

On May 23, Martin returned home at around 3:30 in the afternoon, apparently intoxicated, and almost immediately got into a loud argument with his wife and Violet over the presence of Violet's Collie dog in the house. Neighbors called the police and two officers arrived on the scene shortly afterward, but left when neither Violet nor Martha would file a complaint against Frank. Fifteen minutes later Martha called the police to come back. They found Frank trying on a shirt, and Violet dead on the living room floor, "with a number of cuts on her body, apparently made by a hatchet," which was also found on the premises. Frank was arrested and brought to the Bloomfield police station.

Under questioning, Martin stated that his daughter's dog had tried to attack him, and he held it off with a chair until Violet called the animal to her side. He said that subsequently the dog "came at him again" and he ran to the pantry, grabbed the hatchet and threw it at the dog. According to Martin, it missed the dog but hit his daughter in the head and she fell. He went over to her and spoke to her, but she did not answer, so he took the hatchet and hit her a number of times, then sat down and waited for Martha to appear.

There was, needless to say, a back story. Martin, who had been erratically employed as a "silversmith" at a "novelty shop" in Newark in 1910 and a truck driver for a Newark brewery in 1920 before being put out of a job by Prohibition, apparently held a number of grudges against his wife, but even more so against twenty-two-year-old Violet and her husband. Once, in "an argument over religion" he had attacked his son in law, who had responded by roughing him up. After his release from prison and return home, Martin's seemingly omnipresent anger festered. He later admitted that he had seized the chance to "get square for the beating her husband had given him" by striking Violet repeatedly with the hatchet, and, according to a press report, "nearly decapitating her."

Under arrest, Martin "remained calm" but chain smoked and fiddled with his "nervous fingers." Martha, understandably no longer in a forgiving mood, told a reporter that she "would like to see him go to the electric chair" and screamed and fainted in court as he was formally charged. In custody, Martin dropped all pretense that the killing was an accident and reportedly told police that he had no remorse for his actions, and that his only regret was that he "did not get his wife too." He claimed that "he had been persecuted by his wife and family long enough, and that the crime was the inevitable result of it of four years standing."

Martin's wife countered that there had been "family quarrels" due to the fact that he was "incensed because his daughter married Mr. Smith and because Mr. Smith once struck him during a quarrel over religion." She added her opinion that Martin was not insane but that "he had a violent, ungovernable temper and is given to fits of rage."

Frank Martin went to trial for murder in the Essex County Courthouse with a defense of temporary insanity. Changing his story once again, he testified that he "had no grudge whatever against his daughter; that he had never had any harsh words with her." Several defense witnesses, including Martin's sister Amelia Dillon, were called to testify to his "nervous condition." Another sister, Annie Martin, an inmate of the Overbrook Hospital for the Insane, was called as well, to support the argument that he might be suffering from Huntington's Chorea, as were other members of his family, including Annie. The judge said, however, "I am going to rule against the competency of this witness. My observation of her is that she is absolutely unable to control the movements of her body and the twitching, and, in my judgment, I do not think she is a competent witness."

With Annie discounted, several physicians were called to testify to the fact that Huntington's Chorea was "a disease of the brain, hereditary, progressive, absolutely incurable, and, eventually, [resulting in] complete dementia." They also asserted that "wild outbursts of sudden passion" were symptoms of the malady and "that all of the brothers and sisters of the defendant, with the exception of one, were afflicted and suffering from the same disease."

During the trial Martin had what appeared to be "epileptic fits and had a convulsion... which occurred after the day's session was over. The convulsion was of such a character that he had to be carried to his cell and tied down to his cot and kept there for hours before he again became calm."

In the end Frank Martin was convicted of First Degree murder and condemned to death. He appealed his conviction on a number of technicalities, but the appeal was dismissed by the New Jersey Supreme Court in February, 1926. The Court of Pardons, however, commuted his sentence to life imprisonment. When she heard the news of the commutation, Martha wailed: "Why does the law let him live? Why do they let him live, when the electric chair is too good for him? He killed my Violet and they let him live!"

The 1930 census lists Martin as a resident in the New Jersey State Hospital for the Insane in Ewing Township. In the 1940 census he is still at the hospital but listed as a farmhand on the institution's farm.

Elizabeth's Creative Counterfeiter

Frank Weigand had a problem. His jewelry store in Irvington, New Jersey, went bankrupt in 1923, and he was in need of some money. He was a smart guy, so he made some—literally.

Weigand established what was described as a unique counterfeiting operation in his home in Elizabeth, New Jersey. He was finally busted as the result of a dual investigation conducted by U.S. Treasury Agents and the Canadian Royal Mounted Police – much of the money was distributed in Canada. The agents who raided Weigand's home on December 28, 1925, described his operation as "an ingenious photographic method for counterfeiting money" using cameras purchased from Germany. Apparently, the process involved "a method of photographing separately the various colors of each bank note, done in a way not yet fully solved." The "truckload of cameras" confiscated in the raid were shown to the press.

The only flaw in Weigand's phony money was "in the tracing of the silk threads, which had been cleverly done by pen." When interrupted by his arrest, Weigand was experimenting with bleaching a one-dollar bill and then printing a higher denomination on the paper. He also had another project going on in partnership with two crooked New York attorneys, counterfeiting the stock certificates of the Northern Ohio Traction and Light company. Weigand had four men distributing his counterfeit currency in Canada and the United States, but he remained in Elizabeth, printing the cash with the assistance of "his nineteen-year-old son, a cripple." The son was not arrested, but his four associates, all New Yorkers, were.

It was widely assumed that Weigand was but an artistically talented dupe of the "passers" of the money, professional criminals who never gave him the share of the profits he was supposed to get. Even the federal agents who arrested him reportedly sympathized with his plight. Weigand was held in the Essex County Jail until February 25, 1926, when he entered a plea of guilty before a federal judge in Trenton and was remanded to the Mercer County jail to await sentencing.

On March 2, 1926, Frank Weigand was sentenced to ten years in Atlanta Federal Penitentiary. He was no longer a prisoner there in 1930.

A Klansman Gets Hammered

They parked in front of the garage at 218 Pennsylvania Avenue in Hillside, New Jersey at 1:00 AM in the morning of November 3, 1925. Because the main door was locked, jeweler William J. Clark got out of the car, leaving his wife, Mrs. Priscilla Clark, and her mother, Mrs. Caroline Kent, in the vehicle, and walked around to the side door to open the garage from the inside. A few minutes later Clark staggered out, his head covered with blood, and fell on the driveway. The women awoke Mrs. Clark's stepfather and called a doctor and the police, who, after arrival, found a bloodstained five-pound mason's hammer on the floor of the garage. Clark said he did not know who hit him, and then died.

Clark, a Klansman, was laid to rest with a graveside Ku Klux Klan ceremony in Greenwood Cemetery. As he was interred, Klan women scowled at his widow, who had allegedly refused to join the Kamelia, the Klan's women's organization. And then the police arrived at the cemetery and arrested Mrs. Clark as a material witness. She was subsequently released on $2000 bail, but the plot thickened. A police lieutenant who lived nearby and was home on a disability leave had noticed an unfamiliar car parked at the Clark home several times a week for several hours at a time and had taken down the license plate number. After the murder, he handed it to the Hillside chief of police.

The car belonged to Joseph Cowan, a Newark ironworker and alleged Klansman. Within twelve hours of the attack on Clark, Cowan was arrested and "held on suspicion" of committing the murder. When he was searched after his arrest police found a locket with a photo of him and Mrs. Clark inside it. Cowan's attorney tried to get him released based on the fact that he had been arrested on "hearsay" circumstantial evidence, which included the fact that a pair of his shoes fit footprints around the garage and that he had a $2,000 "love account" in a Newark bank to fund an "elopement." The attorney's habeas corpus application was denied. Cowan also had a wife and child he had abandoned in Brooklyn in 1920, and his wife formally filed for divorce following his arrest. Meanwhile, local Klan leaders declared they would launch their own investigation.

It seemed that Mrs. Clark and Cowan had been more than just friends. Interviewed by the press in the presence of her attorney, Mrs. Clark "frequently wept hysterically" and told reporters that she had known Cowan, a friend of her husband, for three years and that on several occasions he had asked her to run away with him to Florida, although she said he "had always laughed and passed it off as a joke." She admitted that Cowan had handed her $500 from the "love account," but Cowan stated that he had just given it to her to hold, and not to provide an elopement fund. Priscilla claimed that her marriage was a genuine "love match" and that she had met Clark before he shipped out to France in World War I, and married him shortly after his discharge from the service. Cowan's brothers suggested that a more reasonable suspect would be "the vegetable man" who came to the Clark home and "offered indignities to Mrs. Clark and tried to put his arm around her" and vowed revenge when he was expelled from the house. Unsurprisingly, the Klan investigation produced nothing.

Cowan went to trial in March, 1926, at the Union County Court of Oyer and Terminer. Although in summing up, the prosecutor characterized Cowan as "a snake in the grass" who was "not an ironworker but a lover," the case fell apart. A cab driver and a gas station owner who said they saw Cowan in Hillside just before the murder failed to pick him out of a lineup. Fingerprints found on the hammer were smudged. The evidence the prosecution offered was not convincing to the jury, which returned a not guilty verdict after an hour and a half of deliberation. The crowd in the courtroom apparently agreed, as they cheered. Cowan blurted out "Thank God" and fainted.

There would be one more weird chapter in the story. In June, 1926, Harry Hobbs of Irwin, Tennessee, walked into an Atlanta, Georgia, police station and confessed to murdering William J. Clark. Police were skeptical, and, although Hobbs was arrested, he quickly changed his story, saying he "had just got it in my mind and I told the police I did it." Hobbs admitted that he had never been in New Jersey and a records check revealed that he was in jail in Nashville at the time of the murder.

Priscilla Clark did not marry Joseph Cowan or run off to Florida with him. In the census of 1940 she is listed as a forty-four-year-old widow living in Irvington. She died there in 1969. The case was never solved.

The Reverend was a Klansman

"Where's Roscoe?" "Ah...um...Texas?" And therein lies a New Jersey tale. In 1924, Methodist minister Roscoe Carl Ziegler was an up and coming Ku Klux Klan recruiter or "Kleagle" in Trenton. Married with two children, and an apparently charismatic speaker, the twenty-eight-year-old clergyman was an excellent example of the iconic native-born white "real American" the Klan sought to glorify, and he was a rising star in the organization. On July 4, 1925, however, Reverend Ziegler disappeared — with $1,000 (more than $13,000 in today's dollars) of Klan money and his next-door neighbor, twenty-two-year-old Margaret "Peggy" Roberts.

Peggy was engaged to be married to William Chamberlain, who worked for the *Trenton Times* newspaper, and her furious fiancé hired a private detective. The Jersey Klan, looking to recover its money, also hired private investigators and sent out flyers to every Kleagle in the country to be on the lookout for the errant minister. The dragnet eventually closed in on the couple in El Paso, Texas, where a local photographer snapped a picture as Roscoe covered his face and Peggy smiled for the camera. Chamberlain and a party of Klansmen traveled to Texas, made a citizen's arrest of sorts and brought the couple back to New Jersey for possible prosecution under the Federal Mann Act – transporting a woman across state lines for "an immoral purpose." Ironically, Ms. Roberts was also liable for Mann Act prosecution as a participant in a conspiracy to violate the law.

Roscoe had other problems as well, of course, as New Jersey Klan Grand Dragon Arthur Bell wanted his $1,000 back, along with an additional $596.96 in expenses incurred during the pursuit. On his return to New Jersey, Ziegler was arraigned for embezzlement in Red Bank and remanded to the Monmouth county jail, where he was held on $10,000 bail. He was released within twenty-four hours, however, when his parents repaid the Klan and Bell dropped the charges. On Roscoe's release, he and Peggy fled to Ziegler's parents' home in Milford, Pennsylvania.

While a reporter was interviewing Peggy's mother at her home on Edgemere Avenue in Trenton, Chief United States Deputy Marshal Woodbury B. Snowden showed up with a warrant for her daughter. When asked if she was at home, Mrs. Roberts answered "You will find her at Milford, Pennsylvania with that scoundrel Ziegler." Snowden visited the Ziegler home in Pennsylvania, although he did not have legal authority to do so, but could not find the elusive duo. State police were deployed in Sussex County along the Pennsylvania border to intercept Reverend Ziegler should he attempt to sneak back into New Jersey.

At the end of August, Ziegler and Roberts voluntarily returned to New Jersey, were arraigned separately in Newark on charges of conspiracy to violate the Mann Act and then released on bail. According to press reports, Roscoe's wife Mary was going to divorce him in an effort to somehow avoid charges against Peggy, and she did file a divorce petition in Chancery Court in Trenton, while denying there was any "collusion" with her husband or others to dodge the Mann Act charges.

In October, a Federal Grand Jury in Trenton, after considering the case for three days, declined to indict the couple. By that time Roscoe and Mary had reconciled and Mrs. Ziegler was quoted as saying that she was "delighted" at the outcome. She continued with "I am awfully glad. He has started working again and a thing like that hovering over him was a big shadow."

The Zieglers reportedly later moved to Virginia, where Roscoe was rumored to have resumed preaching as a Congregational minister. The effect of the incident on the New Jersey Ku Klux Klan was quite damaging, initiating the beginning of a steadily increasing decline in the organization's membership. The New Jersey Klan's strength had once approached 60,000 disaffected white Protestants fearing the erosion of their status due to the increasing number of Catholic and Jewish immigrants and African Americans arriving in their state. It remained a powerful political force as late as 1928, but by a decade later was mostly a memory.

The second incarnation of the Ku Klux Klan was founded in Georgia by traveling salesman William J. Simmons, inspired by the pseudo-historical film *Birth of a Nation* in 1915. In the years following World War I, Edward Y. Clarke and Elizabeth Tyler turned the KKK into a national organization and a profitable business. The Klan's message of anti-immigrant, anti-Catholic and anti-Jewish sentiment, added to its original mission of keeping black people "in their place," appealed to a rural white Protestant American constituency that believed "their America," north and south, was slipping away.

Perhaps surprisingly to modern readers, New Jersey proved a fertile field for Klan expansion, hence Roscoe Ziegler's success as a recruiter. Many of the state's small town and rural inhabitants, anxious about immigrant filled Jersey City, Newark and Trenton (in 1920 20% of New Jerseyans had been born abroad), as well as an influx of African-Americans as the "Great Migration" began, eagerly donned hoods, marched in parades and burned crosses. There were 60,000 Klansmen, mostly "old stock" blue collar and rural folks, in New Jersey in the 1920s, more than in several Southern states. The New Jersey Klan, however, unlike the chapters of the organization in other regions, particularly in the South, was not known as a violent group. There was plenty of cross burning, bluster and race and religious baiting by New Jersey Klansmen, but no lynching or similar violence.

The Klan was not well received in the urban immigrant areas, however, with their concentrations of Catholics and Jews, although the organization was strong in the immediate suburbs of those cities, where native born Anglo Saxon Protestants were still in the majority. The anti-Klan forces were, ironically, more violent in their opposition than the Klan was in its own actions. Thousands of people attacked Klan meetings in Perth Amboy and Bound Brook, and, unlike in other states, like Indiana, where the Republican governor was a Klansman, the Klan never achieved political power in New Jersey. They were widely denounced by political figures, and the mayor of Nucky Johnson's fiefdom of Atlantic City told his policemen to "break your clubs over their heads."

By the mid-1930s, internal squabbling, public ridicule, scandals like Ziegler's, political pressure and the Depression eroded Klan membership. The remnants of the New Jersey Klan held a joint rally with the German American Bund at Camp Nordland in Sussex County in August 1940, which proved the death knell of the organization.

Original New Jersey Klan photos are hard to find these days. The one which appears in this book, which was originally printed in a British newspaper, shows the New Jersey Klan's Grand Dragon, Arthur Hornbui Bell of Bloomfield, addressing members of the Hudson County Konklave's Lodge of Sorrow, at what appears to be an actual, or perhaps symbolic, funeral service. Bell, born in New York in 1891, was a vaudeville performer who became Grand Dragon in 1922 and joined the Bund in 1940. He was investigated by the Dies Congressional Committee, as well as US Military Intelligence in WWII, although never actually charged with anything. Bell apparently mellowed in his later years, advocating "tolerance." He died in Bloomfield in 1973.

A Newark Cop Runs Amok

There were a number of "Roaring 20s" tragedies in Newark, New Jersey's largest city. One of the most notable was the case of twenty-five-year-old Mrs. Madeline Clearwater Montgomery, who had lost her husband, Douglas Montgomery, a World War I army veteran, to the residual effects of poison gas in 1921. Following her loss, Madeline moved to Newark from Pennsylvania to live with her parents. She subsequently met twenty-eight-year-old Anthony Sheridan, a Marine Corps veteran who had served in Saint Croix in the Virgin Islands during the war and was then a Newark police officer stationed at the city's Sixth Precinct. They began to date.

Sheridan and Montgomery soon became engaged to be married, but shortly afterward Madeline broke off the engagement, maintaining that her health was too poor to remarry. She returned Sheridan's ring and he, in turn, promised to never see her again. An angry Sheridan brooded over his rejection for several years, however, before showing up at Madeline's home on Avon Avenue, where she lived with her mother and brother, at 3:00 A.M. on September 15, 1925.

Sheridan, described in one news story as "crazed by an infatuation," banged on his former fiancé's apartment door and yelled "let me in. I want to talk to Maddie." Madeline pleaded with her mother not to let Sheridan in. After more shouting, it became quiet, and it appeared that Sheridan had left the premises. He continued to lurk in the building, however.

When Madeline's brother Gorum Clearwater returned home from his night shift at the Russel Schwartz Cabinetmaking Company around 7:00 AM and began to open the apartment door, Sheridan suddenly reappeared, waving his revolver and yelling "you'll let me in all right." He shoved his way past Gorum and Madeline's mother, barging into the apartment and Madeline's bedroom, ordering her to go to the kitchen, and telling her it was her "last chance." Madeline responded by pulling a blanket over her head and screaming. Sheridan fired five shots at his former fiancée as she lay in bed, wounding her three times, in the neck, chest and arm, before putting his revolver to his head and shooting himself with the final round.

Both were rushed to Newark City Hospital, where Sheridan was pronounced dead, but Madeline Montgomery, initially thought to only "have a slight chance to recover," was actually "not seriously wounded" by Sheridan's three bullets, and survived.

CHAPTER 5

1927-The "Chicken Fancier" and His Lady Friend

Medical doctor A. William Lilliendahl also allegedly had a law degree, so the seventy-year-old physician should have known better, but the Feds caught him prescribing opiates to drug addicts from his offices in Mountain Lakes, New Jersey and New York City, while he was allegedly running an addiction rehabilitation program. In the wake of that incident, the Doctor, scion of a wealthy New York family, gave up his medical license and moved with his forty-year-old wife Margaret and eight-year-old son Alfred to South Vineland, New Jersey, where, over the next two years, Margaret took a fancy to Willis Beach, a nearby fifty-seven-year-old poultry farmer, known locally as a "chicken fancier."

As a neighborly friendship apparently transitioned into a full-blown love affair, Margaret and Willis allegedly plotted to eliminate the doctor. On September 15, 1927, while driving along the Atsion-Hammonton road with her husband as a passenger, Mrs. Lilliendahl unaccountably pulled off on Great Swamp Lane, a sand side road three miles north of Hammonton, and drove 100 feet into the pine woods. A short time later Margaret appeared running down the main road "screaming and disheveled," crying desperately for assistance. Two men driving by in a milk truck stopped to aid her and she led them to a dead Dr. Lilliendahl slumped down in the car, oddly enough in the driver's seat, with three bullets in his head and neck, one through his jugular vein. Margaret told arriving police that "two Negroes" with guns had "jumped from the bushes" onto the car's running board, kidnapped the couple, made them drive off the main road, robbed them of his cash and her jewelry and then shot her husband when he tried to resist. According to Margaret, she then passed out and, when she awakened, the assailants had disappeared.

Police were mobilized all over southern New Jersey in an attempt to capture the alleged murderers, but a preliminary investigation caused local authorities to begin to doubt Mrs. Lilliendahl's account and to look into her possible affair with Beach, a liaison local gossips were well aware of. There were bloodstained bills in her purse and one of her rings lay on the ground, along with a letter to a "Peggy Anderson" apparently from Beach, who was described by journalists as a "raiser of fancy chickens and a rustic playboy," as well as a "rustic Romeo." More letters to "Peggy Anderson," a pseudonym used by Mrs. Lilliendahl, soon appeared and a man fitting Beach's description pawned some of Margaret's allegedly stolen jewelry in Philadelphia.

Neighbors told police that Beach had been a "frequent visitor" to the Lilliendahl home, and that the couple had "frequent quarrels" including a recent one involving Margaret's relationship with Beach. Young Alfred Lilliendahl confirmed his parents' troubled relationship. As police began to dig deeper into the evidence, they found that a road map in the "death car" had an "X" marking the spot where the fatal incident occurred, and that there was a piece of colored cloth tied to a tree at the location as well. A county detective stated that "the only people who could have committed this crime were the two Negroes or the woman." There were, however, no male footprints in the sand around the car. Atlantic County Prosecutor Louis Repetto decided that there was more than enough circumstantial evidence to arrest both apparent perpetrators, who had been out on bail as "material witnesses," four days after the murder.

Under arrest, Mrs. Lilliendahl came up with another scenario for her husband's murder: "I am now convinced that my husband was killed by a drug addict." Referring to his shady opiate distribution past in New York and northern New Jersey, she went on to state that: "My husband dealt with all sorts of people. If I had his books I could show you the names of many gunmen in them. When he closed his New York office he was arrested by government agents for violation of the federal narcotics act, but the case was nolle prossed. [*"To discontinue something by entering a "nolle prosequi," which is an entry in a criminal action denoting that the prosecutor will not prosecute the case further in whole or as to one or more of several counts or one or more of several defendants." Merriam-Webster's Dictionary of Law.*] He gave up his medical practice. Lots of times on our automobile rides we have been followed by desperate looking men. On several occasions the doctor hinted to me that his life had been threatened." She added that any arguments between her late husband and Beach had to do with "how to handle chickens" and that the admitted correspondence with "Peggy Anderson" was about the "chicken fancier's" concern with keeping posted on the doctor's health.

Assistant Prosecutor A. Cameron Hinkle dismissed Margaret's latest storyline and proceeded to have the county grand jury indict both her and Beach. The ensuing trial resulted in the invasion of May's Landing, the Atlantic County seat and future "national capital of the nudists," by the "H. M. T. L. (Husband Murder Trial Legion)" of reporters and photographers, eager to provide entertainment, much of it unrelated to the murder itself, for people across the country. Noted fiction writer and celebrity journalist Damon Runyan, who covered the trial for the Hearst Newspapers, observed that Margaret, dubbed "the Black Widow of South Vineland" by the press, was a "a passionate type of woman" and described Beach as "the hottest man in his home township, even if he is not as young as he used to be." Runyon sat behind Margaret during the trial and observed that "Mrs. Lilliendahl uses a brand of perfume known as Incarnat, made by Piver. I offer this information for the benefit of my lady readers."

Another reporter was puzzled as to why the "tall and stately Mrs. Lilliendahl" was attracted to the "short and dumpy" Beach, who, to the delight of the press, local people oddly regarded as an "ardent Lothario" and the "Don Juan of the countryside." Yet another writer countered that opinion by noting that Margaret's "dominant characteristic" was her "buck teeth." Margaret's demeanor was compared unfavorably with that of Frances Hall, who, also accused of her husband's murder, had taken the stand at the recent Hall-Mills trial in New Brunswick.

Prosecution witness Samuel Bark, "a trick roper and circus man from Oklahoma" testified that Beach had approached him after the murder in Baltimore to borrow money, saying that he was "in a terrible jam" and admitting that he had killed Dr. Lilliendahl in a quarrel over money the doctor owed him. Bark also said that Beach told him that he was running "dope up to New York for Lilliendahl." Conversely, Bark was accused of trying to blackmail Mrs. Lilliendahl's attorney Robert H. McCarter through false testimony, which cast doubt on his admittedly improbable story. Harry F. Sanderson, a traveling aluminum salesman, testified that he saw a man resembling Beach fleeing the scene, although he waffled on the identification under questioning. Other than that, the rest of the evidence against Margaret and Willis was circumstantial.

Three defense witnesses swore they had seen Beach eating lunch at a location twenty-five miles away at the time of the murder, and Beach testified that he had never even known Bark. He denied an affair with Margaret and said that his disagreement with Dr. Lilliendahl was over a remedy to "cure chickens," and denied killing the doctor. Margaret testified, amidst periodic sobbing, that she had nothing to do with her husband's death and that he was indeed murdered by "two Negroes." She said she was aware of neighborhood gossip about her and Beach, but that there was nothing to it. She insisted that she "kept no secrets from my husband."

Hinkle asked for a first-degree murder conviction and the death penalty for Margaret and Willis, and the case went to the jury on December 7, 1927. After numerous ballots over twenty-three hours, the jury of five women and seven men denied the prosecutor's request and convicted the defendants of voluntary manslaughter, arguing that "reasonable doubt" existed since there were no eyewitnesses to the crime. One juror later told a reporter that the initial vote was "9 to 3 for acquittal"

Both defendants were sentenced to ten years in prison, the maximum penalty. The judge was unhappy with the jury's decision, declaring "why the jury brought in that verdict of manslaughter I don't know. The crime was, without question, murder. They were being tried for first degree murder, and since the jury believed them guilty of a criminal homicide, I would not be justified in imposing less than the maximum sentence."

The couple continued to declare their innocence, and allegedly "laughed and chatted" on their ride to the state prison in Trenton. On arrival Beach said "we won't be here long." That turned out to be true for him, albeit probably not in the sense that Beach meant it, as he died of a heart attack at the Bordentown prison farm on October 12, 1930.

Margaret, who shared a cottage at the New Jersey Reformatory for Women in Clinton with Lakehurst's Ivy Giberson, another convicted husband murderer, worked "cutting out garments for use of inmates in other institutions." A model prisoner, she was paroled when it appeared she was "near death" from cancer on June 29, 1934, but prison authorities commented that she could still work "and intended to earn her living by sewing." Margaret Lilliendahl left for Connecticut to rejoin her now fifteen-year-old son, who was in the care of relatives, and was not heard from again, although a 1948 account of the case reported that she had survived her illness and was working as a "housekeeper for a wealthy resident of Connecticut."

Murder in the Highlands by "a dwarflike man"

On November 14, 1927, Elizabeth attorney Peter Olde was on the telephone in his office with his business partner, Highlands, New Jersey inventor Herbert O. Meisterknecht, when he heard a noise, a groan, and the phone went dead. Olde quickly called hardware merchant Frank Siegfried, whose store was 100 feet away from Meisterknecht's Shrewsbury Avenue shop. Siegfried ran over to check on his neighbor, picking up lobsterman Irving Parker on the way. As they approached, a "dwarflike man in a blue suit" ran by them in the opposite direction and entered a waiting car.

Parker said later that the man stopped for a second and handed him a note. There were various reports on what that note said. One version reported that it announced that: "I have shot my brother-in-law." There were several other versions of what was written on the paper, however, including: "Alexander Schreiber, Everton Avenue, Cleveland, Ohio. It might be necessary to call the police soon, and if they want me I can be found at this address." Siegfried and Parker caught a glimpse of the license plate on the getaway car, but only enough to discern that it was registered in Essex County, New Jersey. Entering the shop, they found Meisterknecht dead on the floor, shot once in the head and three times in the body. Siegfried called the police.

The "dwarflike man" was the apparently short in stature Alexander Schreiber, who indeed was Meisterknecht's brother in law, and was known as a mentally unstable religious fanatic, who, ironically, also ran a speakeasy in Cleveland. Parker recalled that Schreiber approached him and Meisterknecht several days before, belligerently shouting at Parker: "Do you know this fellow Meisterknecht? He has been impersonating a navy officer and has committed bigamy." Schreiber yelled that Meisterknecht had "a wife and kids in Yonkers" and had been treating his sister Sophie "like a dog." Parker left as the two men argued. Meisterknecht later asked the lobsterman: "What did you make of that duck? A little off his nut, wouldn't you say?"

It turned out that Meisterknecht, who had met and married Sophie Schreiber while on a business trip to Cleveland the year before, was indeed previously married and had apparently never filed for divorce from his first spouse, Susan. She did, however, refuse to sign a statement saying that she was Meisterknecht's housekeeper, rather than his wife. Susan was aware of her husband's bigamy, but he sent her support money to keep her quiet and she later said "I did not object to his association with the other woman. What was the use?" She told a reporter that she had last seen her husband at the funeral of their son, who had died in an accident in September, 1927, and that he had hinted at a possible reconciliation. She added that a private detective who said he had been hired by Schreiber had contacted her in New York and quizzed her on her marital status.

Meisterknecht was another of those eccentric and elusive characters who seemed to proliferate in the late nineteenth and early twentieth centuries. Born in Germany in 1883, he emigrated to the United States in 1909, became a naturalized citizen, and in 1920 was a shipyard mechanic in New York, although he had claimed to be a mechanical engineer on his draft registration card in 1918. Meisterknecht met Peter Olde while working on Olde's boat and convinced the attorney that he was actually an engineer and inventor developing an innovative "gauge for gasoline pumps" that would measure flow more accurately than those in service at the time, as well as "a new type of internal combustion engine."

Olde, convinced he had met a "mechanical genius," agreed to finance Meisterknecht's work as a partner in "Emmo Manufacturing" and the inventor moved to Highlands, where he had previously lived some years before. Most of Meisterknecht's time seems to have been spent developing his allegedly revolutionary gasoline gauge. The partners wanted to sell the rights to the invention to Standard Oil, which had reportedly expressed considerable interest in the device, and they traveled to Cleveland several times to negotiate a possible deal with the company.

Police all over the state of New Jersey and beyond were soon searching for the thirty-seven-year-old Shreiber, who continued to elude them. A man resembling him was arrested at a Trenton gas station, but released. Another report had him boarding a train in Newark for Cleveland, but when state troopers reached the city with a murder warrant, there was no sign of him. Rumors that he was hiding in Newark or New York City also turned out to be dead ends. The case was further complicated by the discovery by Monmouth County detectives of correspondence between Olde and Meisterknecht indicating that Olde intended to break up the partnership, and that Meisterknecht had previously turned down a significant offer from Standard Oil for his invention. Olde denied that that had been his intention.

Meanwhile, funeral preparations for Meisterknecht proceeded, with one complication. Susan and her daughter came down from Yonkers, accompanied by an attorney, and, in an emotionally charged confrontation during the services, claimed Meisterknecht's body. As both wives, "who alternately sobbed and ridiculed each others' grief" stood by, Meisterknecht was stashed in a "receiving vault" at Fairview Cemetery in Middletown until things were sorted out. The first Mrs. Meisterknecht prevailed and the murdered inventor's body was eventually granted to Susan and transported to Yonkers for burial. Susan also inherited Meisterknecht's patent rights. In death, as in life, Meisterknecht remained a man of mystery. Although his coffin was covered by a flag at the Fairview temporary interment, the inventor's claim to have been a United States Navy officer in World War I seems somewhat dubious, to say the least, with no extant records reflecting such service, although someone from Ohio with the same name served as an enlisted man in the Army's Corps of Engineers in World War I.

It appeared that the elusive Schreiber had committed the perfect crime, escaping to parts unknown. On April 13, 1928, however, a Keyport clam digger working in shallow water along the shore of Raritan Bay came upon a decomposed body, which "in many respects resembled the missing Alex Schreiber, murderer of Herbert O. Meisterknecht, Highlands inventor." Relatives were unable to definitively identify the badly decomposed corpse, however, which was buried in a local "Potter's Field." The police told the press that "the search for him is going to continue, for some time at least."

It turned out to be far more than "some time." The case remains officially open to this day, although the fact that Schreiber was never heard from again makes it distinctly possible that the corpse found floating in Raritan bay was him. Despite that possibility, rumors of Schreiber sightings circulated for many years. He was back in Cleveland, he had fled to Germany, he was sighted in Miami, and he was hiding in Lakewood, New

Jersey. On one occasion in 1934 the Highlands Police were notified that New Jersey State Police had detained a man named Alexander Schreiber in Pennsauken. Accompanied by a Highlands policeman, Irving Parker traveled to Pennsauken, but could not provide a positive identification, saying that although the man resembled Schreiber, he had only glimpsed him briefly years before. Over two decades later a newspaper article on the case noted that there was still a murder warrant out for the "dwarflike man."

A 1949 interview with Monmouth County Detective William S. Mustoe disclosed that Mustoe, who was involved in the initial investigation, believed Schreiber had "a combination of motives," and that "a group of Cleveland men sought one of Meisterknecht's inventions and inflamed the emotionally unstable Schreiber, then the operator of a Cleveland speakeasy, to kill the inventor because of the fake marriage."

Around 1960, young Leslie Layton and his father were visiting his uncle Irving Parker, the lobsterman who was at the scene of the murder, at the Highlands sewer plant, which Irving had managed for many years. While they were there, a man walked in and asked the sewer manager some questions about the Meisterknecht murder. Irving told him "that about a week after the murder, two men drove up in a black car and asked him some questions, and then one opened his coat and showed a revolver, said "be careful" and drove away." Leslie later asked his father who the men in the car they were talking about were, and was answered with two words: "Standard Oil."

CHAPTER 6

1928-"Lifetime Jake," the Convict's Friend

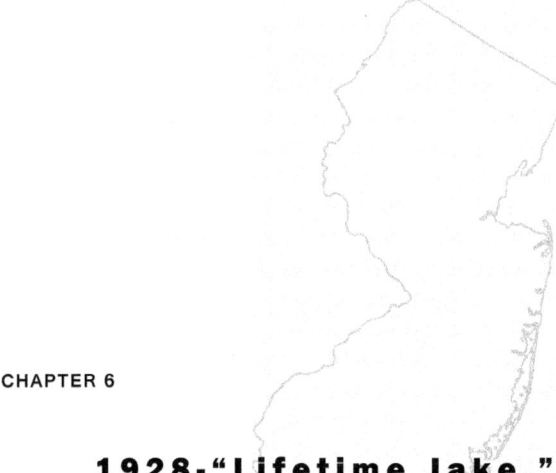

When "Lifetime Jake" Pensendorfer was pardoned by Governor Gifford Pinchot and walked out of Eastern State Prison in Pennsylvania in December, 1926 after serving twenty-five years, his jailers and fellow inmate presented him with "a watch, a chain and a penknife of white gold and a purse of $400." He promised he would not forget them. And he did not.

In 1901, Pensendorfer had shot and killed his father in law, who did not approve of his daughter's marriage. According to Pensendorfer, his wife's father beat her and tried to shoot her mother. Pensendorfer caught up with him and gunned him down on a Philadelphia Street. He claimed self-defense, but was found guilty of murder and sentenced to death. Two days before he was scheduled to hang, Pensendorfer's sentence was commuted to life imprisonment.

While at Eastern State, Pensendorfer taught himself woodworking "and became a master of carving and intricate inlay." He also "patented woodworking devices and watched his income pile up." He became the manager of the prison woodworking shop, with a number of other prisoners working for him.

While in prison, Pensendorfer earned enough royalty money from his inventions to buy his elderly mother a home and build a $50,000 bank account. After his release, he moved to West Berlin, New Jersey, where he opened a woodworking factory. By 1928 he had fifteen employees "turning out radio cabinets, ship models and such."

Pensendorfer, photographed with his mother for a news story in 1928, kept his promise to his fellow inmates, and hired only ex-convicts, on the condition that they "keep straight and never touch liquor." His factory superintendent was a pardoned murderer and his chief draftsman a former bank teller who had served ten years for embezzlement. Pensendorfer told a reporter that he could use more skilled woodworkers, and knew where he could find some, but "unfortunately they are being detained by the authorities."

The Freehold Bungler

Steve Demick of Freehold was not the smartest murderer in New Jersey history. When you plan to kill your neighbor over the affections of a woman, telling someone to "watch the papers for something interesting" is probably not advisable. The thirty-year-old Demick was feuding with his neighbor, thirty-nine-year-old Russian violinist Nikita Evanenko, over the affections of Mrs. Eva Petroski, once Demick's housekeeper, who had moved from his home to an apartment on Main Street. A newspaper subsequently reported that "both Demick and Evanenko were frequent visitors to the apartment."

On March 28, 1928, Demick, a Russian immigrant himself who came to America in 1914, broke into Evanenko's house on Throckmorton Street to lay in wait and ambush the violinist on his return home. Demick surprised Evanenko, and hit him repeatedly with an iron pipe as he tried to flee, leaving a gruesome blood trail throughout the house. Once Evanenko was dead, Demick wrapped his bloody body in a bedsheet and quilt, put it in his car and drove thirty-five miles to Rancocas, where he deposited the corpse in a roadside ditch, where it was discovered the following day by Benjamin Seippel of Camden, "a roving junk man on the lookout for bits of iron and other junk by the side of the road."

Over 600 locals viewed the battered corpse in an attempt to identify it, but to no avail, although one said he thought he had seen him once before, but did not know his name. Evanenko was finally identified through fingerprints on file with the Philadelphia police, who had arrested him in 1920 for bootlegging. The famed Ellis Parker, Chief of Burlington County

Detectives, opined that "the man had been beaten to death elsewhere."

The police, who described the murder as "a variety of the 'eternal triangle' so dear to the hearts of novelists and playwrights" searched the murdered man's home, talked to Mrs. Petroski's estranged husband John, who Demick had advised to check out the *Asbury Park Press*, discovered blood in Demick's car and on his pants and other clues and quickly arrested him.

Under relentless interrogation, Demick confessed to killing Evanenko, and was charged with first degree murder. The police investigation produced evidence that the murdered man was also, as he had been in Philadelphia, a small-time bootlegger as well as a musician, as there was a whiskey still in his cellar. Ironically, Eva Petroski, whose affections had inspired Demick's violent act, had left Freehold with her son Eugene and sailed to France allegedly on her way to visit relatives in the Soviet Union four days before the murder. She did not return.

Demick later claimed that his confession was "wrung from him to prevent bodily harm from the officers of the law" and pleaded not guilty to the first-degree murder charge lodged against him. He then changed his plea to guilty of second degree murder, which was accepted by the prosecution. Demick went before Judge Jacob Steinbach Jr. in Freehold for sentencing on March 5, 1929. Harold A. McDermott, Demick's attorney, "stated that the defendant has always borne a good reputation in the community in which he lived, with the exception of the one incident, but that the deceased did not bear such a reputation. He pointed out that Demick was in fear of his life, after being beaten up at the instigation of the man he killed, and that he took his rival's life in self-defense." Steve Demick was sentenced to thirty years in prison at hard labor for the "one incident." The 1930 census listed him as an inmate of Trenton State Prison employed in the prison machine shop.

The Radium Girls

They called them the "Radium Girls," and it was not a joke. They were the young women who worked with "Undark" radium paint at the United States Radium Corporation's factory at 422 Alden Street in Orange, New Jersey, beginning in 1917. Although the owners of United States Radium and other companies dealing with the substance around the country, and the chemists they employed, took care to avoid direct contact with radium, and even advised the medical profession of the inherent danger of the substance, they did not provide any protection or guidance for their young female employees.

The women were employed painting luminous dials on watches with the radium paint which, they were assured, was harmless. Production was accelerated with the entry of the United States into World War I as luminous watches were in demand for military use. The work was delicate, and workers were advised by management to lick their brushes to create a fine point and so speed up production. On breaks, some painted their nails with the supposedly harmless luminous substance for entertainment. As the years went by, the watch face painters began to develop a number of illnesses, including anemia, brittle bones and "radium jaw," a grotesque deterioration of the jawbone. In 1925, some of the victims began to conclude that their condition was due to their work with radium. As six of the women died, United States Radium denied the allegations that the deaths were due to working with radium, paid doctors to keep quiet about the problem, spread rumors that the women were afflicted by syphilis and then hired Harvard physiology professor Cecil Drinker to examine the factory. His report, that it was an unhealthy and dangerous place, was altered to reflect the opposite view when the company sent it to the New Jersey Department of Labor. When he discovered the fraudulent manipulation of his work, Drinker published it, despite threats of legal action from United States Radium.

Grace Fryer, one of the afflicted, attempted to find an advocate to handle her case against the influential company, which used its power to discourage attorneys. It took several years, but she and four other workers found a Newark lawyer, Raymond Berry, to file a complaint against the company in the Newark circuit court in 1927. The case moved slowly, but got nationwide headlines. An attempt by the corporation to claim that the statute of limitations in the case had expired was denied by the court and the body of Amelia Faggia, an employee who had died several years prior to the suit, was exhumed. An autopsy report on Ms. Faggia concluded that her body contained "radioactive substances in large quantities in the upper and lower jaws and the lumbar vertebrae."

In the end, the case was arbitrated out of court, and each of the five women received $10,000 cash, payment of all medical bills due to their illnesses and a $600 a month annuity for the rest of their lives, which were not long. The last New Jersey "radium girl" died in the mid-1930s.

Their effort, however, made history by establishing a precedent for such suits, making occupational diseases liable to compensation by employers and reinforcing the call for regulation legislation requiring labor safety standards, which was eventually passed.

United States Radium's Orange facility was closed in 1927, as the case against the company proceeded in court. The site had not only produced the radium watch dials, but was used to process 1,000 pounds of radioactive ore a day, with a total of 160,000 tons of residue dumped on the property. In 1983 it was declared a Superfund Site. Beginning in 1997, remediation began on the site and a massive amount of debris and earth was removed. The project was declared finished in 2009 and the site is now a vacant lot. Unfortunately, none of the executives of the Radium Corporation ever faced criminal charges for their duplicity. They certainly should have.

The End of the "Jersey Kid"

On October 15, 1928, five bandits robbed the Public Service Coordinated Transport Company payroll of $2,500 on Lake Street at the company's Bloomfield Avenue garage. It was their second strike in Newark, as they had robbed the Alderney Dairy Company's Orange Street payroll office several weeks earlier. The Public Service cashier, twenty-six-year-old George B. Lee, picked up his telephone, shouted "call police – holdup" and was shot to death by twenty-eight-year-old "Jersey Kid" James McBrien, whose gang included Victor Giampietro, Frank Orlando, Louis Malanga and Joseph Rado. Giampietro and Malanga were captured in Lackawanna, New York, over the winter and Orlando was killed in a shootout with the Chicago police after a holdup in December, 1928. His body was identified through fingerprints sent out across the country by the New Jersey state police.

Rado was arrested on August 28, 1929 by sharp eyed New Jersey State trooper David Reid of the Malaga substation, who spotted him at the Iona Lake Hotel in Gloucester County. The "Jersey Kid," who was also wanted in Monmouth County for killing a bank messenger in a Bradley Beach holdup, and by Philadelphia police for a series of armed robberies in that city, was finally captured in December 1929 in a raid on a New York City apartment he was sharing with Mabel Davis, who was held as a material witness. After the arrest, New York City police noted that McBrien had a tattoo reading "death before dishonor" on his forearm.

McBrien was extradited to Essex County and all four of the robbers went on trial in Newark on January 13, 1930. McBrien testified in his own defense, admitting that the robbery was planned in the High Street apartment of Mrs. Margaret Rosenthal, who supplied the gang with pillowcases to carry the loot. McBrien said that on arrival at the Public Service facility "he called on Lee to come out" of his office and "as he came out I pushed my gun [a .32 caliber Colt automatic pistol] toward him and it went off." He claimed the shooting was an accident and that he simply pushed Lee and, after the cashier was shot, asked "are you hurt buddy?" and "called for aid" for the dying man before leaving the office.

Malanga's testimony supported McBrien's. He said that he heard a shot, ran into the room and saw McBrien "leaning over the prostrate form of the cashier and tearing at his shirt." According to Malanga, McBrien said "to hell with the money this poor guy is dying. I'm going to call the cops. Gee buddy, are you hurt?" Neither judge nor jury bought the defendants' stories. Although McBrien was the actual trigger man, all were found guilty and sentenced to death by electric chair at Trenton State Prison. When the judge set the execution date for March 9, McBrien yelled out "can't you make it sooner Judge."

The execution was actually delayed until July 22 by failed appeals. It made the record books as only the second time in New Jersey history when four men were executed on one day. (The previous such event was July 15, 1924.) Giampietro, tagged as a stool pigeon by the others, as he had cooperated with prosecutors, expected a last-minute reprieve, but it was not forthcoming, and he was the first to take a final seat in "Old Smokey." He was followed by McBrien, Malanga and Rado. Malanga and Rado bid McBrien goodbye as he walked by their cells on his way to the chair puffing a cigar and sporting a red carnation pinned to his shirt, and the "Jersey Kid" responded with a cheery "OK boys." Robert Elliott, "executioner of many years," made short work of the criminal quartet, "and turned the death wheel on the four men within half an hour." Elliott, who was paid $600 for his night's work, "killed them as fast as they were strapped in and the cathodes attached. Then he went home to sleep."

The Body in a Barrel

Young Robert Woodward and a friend were playing down by the Delaware River near Washington Park Pier in Westville, New Jersey on

December 4, 1928. When they noticed a barrel float into shore they went down to inspect it. What they found, a "headless, armless and legless body," terrified them. The boys ran away as fast as they could and told fifteen-year-old Arthur Fox about their traumatic discovery. Fox quickly notified the local police.

Apparently this sort of thing had happened before, as the press noted that it was yet "another torso murder." The Westville police brought the mutilated corpse to the Borough Hall, where a local physician, Dr. Ralph K. Hollinshead, examined it and concluded that "the body was that of a woman," but that "chloride of lime had virtually destroyed all the flesh." The police sought the missing limbs in the area where the barrel came in to land, but without any success. They examined the barrel itself, found a tag bearing the address of "a wholesale meat company from Philadelphia," and notified the "Philadelphia murder squad." Further investigation established that the victim was "5 feet four inches tall and weighed about 125 pounds." It was discovered that the barrel had originally held pork to be used as food by the crew of the *New Orleans*, a government dredge working the river, and police questioned the crew, who said the container was apparently tossed overboard after the original contents were consumed. It was repurposed by persons unknown.

It appears the identity of the victim, dubbed by the press "the pork barrel woman," was never discovered and the case was never solved.

CHAPTER 7

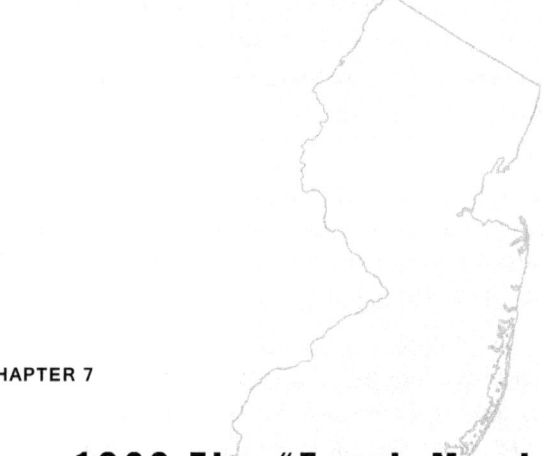

1929-The "Torch Murderer" from Westfield

Sixty-year-old Doctor Richard Campbell, also known as Henry Colin Campbell, among many other aliases, met Mildred Mowry, a fifty-nine-year-old widow living in Greenville, Pennsylvania, through a "matrimonial agency," the 1920s version of a modern dating website, where he had entered his preference in women as for "widows with no children." Richard and Mildred, who was a nurse, connected, and in the summer of 1928 he took her to Elkton, Maryland, and married her, providing the address of a lot he owned in Baltimore as his residence. Campbell convinced his new bride to transfer her $1,000 life savings to a joint bank account in New Brunswick, then told her he had to go to California on business and left. The immediate problem was that he had another wife, Rosalie, and four children, in New Jersey -- and there was much more. Mildred returned to Greenville, and when she did not hear from him after a few letters professing undying love, sent him this letter:

"Why, oh, why have you deserted me? I, who need you so. And only two days after you married me! You told me you were rich; but you have nothing. Are you not going to live with me? I must have an understanding. What have you done with my money? If you do not return it to me I shall commit suicide. But first I will let everyone know what you have done to me. I cannot let you get away!" When she got no response by February 15, 1929, Mildred set out to track Campbell down.

Campbell had been gradually draining Mildred's cash from the bank for his own uses. He finally agreed to meet her at the Broad Street train station in Philadelphia on February 22. They drove to Dover, Delaware and spent the night there and drove to New Jersey the following day. By three o'clock in the morning the couple arrived in Cranford, New Jersey, and an increasingly desperate Campbell did not know what to do. Mildred wanted to go someplace where she could sleep in a bed, and began to doze in the car. Campbell reached into his pocket and took out the handgun he habitually carried when he drove at night and shot her in the head. He drove on another three or four hundred yards, stopped, dragged her body out of the car, rolled it into a ditch, poured gasoline from a container he kept in the car over the corpse, then lit it with a match. He then drove home to Westfield and tossed her luggage bag in the house coal furnace.

On the morning of February 23, a delivery truck driver saw a "blazing bundle" in a ditch alongside Kenilworth Boulevard near the intersection with Springfield Avenue in Cranford and told the Cranford police. When they investigated, they found Mildred's body, burned beyond recognition. It took some time to identify her, but Greenville police, her neighbors and dentist visited the Union County morgue and identified her as Mildred Mowry, now known as Mrs. Mildred Campbell, who had been declared missing. The newspapers reported that she had been "shot in the head, doused with gasoline and 'torched.'"

Campbell was actually not a doctor, but a civil engineer and failed real estate entrepreneur. He had on occasion practiced medicine without a license, had "picked up a superficial knowledge" of medical procedures by pretending to be a physician in Mexico "amid illiterate peons," and had also worked as a public relations manager and a salesman. Police, following a trail from Pennsylvania to Maryland and back, came to the conclusion that he was their man, and Campbell was arrested on April 29, 1929 and charged with murder. Arresting officers found a gun, morphine tablets and a syringe in Campbell's Elizabeth apartment, where he had moved his wife and three children from his spacious house in Westfield, "a prosperous suburban town with substantial homes" immediately after the murder.

Campbell initially told police that he had met with Mowry to repay her the $1,000 he had swindled her out of and then drove around with her trying to collect money owed him, apparently taking drugs on the ride, and then could not remember what happened until he awoke at home. Under extensive questioning at Elizabeth Police Headquarters he admitted that Mildred had "kept pestering me to turn the car around and stop somewhere for the night. I suddenly decided to get rid of her because I could not afford two homes. She was dozing in the seat and I shot her in the back of the head." He signed a typewritten confession statement in which he affirmed that: "I did not intend to marry this woman originally, but I married her thinking it might relieve me of some of my financial difficulties. I had been in financial difficulties for the last two years or more."

Campbell's back story was considerable, and confusing, as he had several personas. It appears he was born as Henry C. Close somewhere in the Midwest, married three women without divorcing any of them, abandoning one with a small child, and then moved to Montclair, New Jersey, where he claimed to be a physician named H. C. Close and opened a sanitarium on Willard Place. One day in 1903 he disappeared, apparently to go to work in New York City, where he embezzled $10,000 from an employer in 1905, absconded, was captured in Mexico and spent seven years in New York's Sing Sing prison. At some point, he had engaged in real estate speculation in Maryland. How his present wife and children fit into the storyline remained unclear.

Apparently his current wife of fifteen years, mother of his three daughters, had married him without knowing that he had at least one other wife whom he had not divorced. She claimed to be totally bewildered by the whole affair, stating that: "I know no one will believe me. I don't know what it's all about. But he was always so fine, in all the 15 years we were married he never used a cross word to me. I don't know what happened to him. I don't think I'll ever know. He won't help himself. He doesn't care."

Detectives conducting a systematic search of Campbell's small Elizabeth apartment found an assortment of interesting material. A press account noted that "what they found gave them a picture not only of the Jekyll-Hyde existence his confession had revealed, but also of an eccentric, esoteric personality that defied their understanding." The detectives discovered that Campbell was "a lover of strange dolls. In his room dolls were strewn everywhere. A strong box he owned was forced open and it was filled with dolls." They also found considerable correspondence "with matrimonial agencies and the 'lonely hearts' columns of newspapers. For years, apparently, he had been baiting a secret matrimonial hook, seeking to entice women with money."

The Somerset county prosecutor, seeing striking similarity between the cases, sought to charge the bigamist swindler with the murder of Margaret Brown, a governess who had withdrawn her $5,000 life savings from the bank, married a mysterious "doctor" and whose burned body was found alongside a road in Bernardsville prior to the discovery of Mildred's, but the evidence was not deemed conclusive enough to bring to a grand jury.

Although one account noted that he led "a dual life so complex as to astound the most experienced psycho-pathologists," psychiatrists pronounced Campbell/Close legally sane, if indeed "disturbed," and he was indicted and brought to trial by Union County prosecutor Abe David for the Mowry murder. His defense attorney claimed that his client was "mentally deranged," citing a history of "toxic poisons, narcotic drugs and heredity," concluding that "we, as rational men, must realize that something must have happened to a mind that would commit that crime." Despite that defense, the "torch murderer" was found guilty of first degree murder on June 13, 1929.

Campbell's attorney appealed his conviction. While not arguing that Campbell was innocent of killing Mildred, he maintained that diminished responsibility, because his client "suffered from prostration of the mind ...to that degree which made it incapable of forming the deliberate intention to commit murder," made the crime of a lesser degree than that of first degree. In evidence, he offered a whole host of Campbell's physical problems, ranging from a "bad heart" to "pyorrhea" and noted his apparent addiction to narcotics. The New Jersey Supreme Court disagreed, citing one doctor who examined Campbell and said that he "was a psychopathic personality with psychoses and that he was sane." The court held that there could be an argument for diminished responsibility if Campbell was drunk, but he was not.

Campbell was a quiet prisoner on death row in the New Jersey State Prison in Trenton, where he received news that his appeals to higher courts were denied, had numerous visits from his wife, ate regular prison food for his last meal and "desired no spiritual comfort in his last hours." On April 17, 1930, Campbell "walked calmly and slowly into the death chamber, a guard on each side of him" to take a seat in "Old Smokey." He was pronounced dead of 8:06 PM. He had been scheduled for execution on April 16 but "because of an unwritten rule that no executions be made on Good Friday" the date was advanced a day.

A Bootlegger's Fate

They found twenty-two-year-old Michael Cicero, of Pitman, New Jersey, slumped over the steering wheel in his mud and blood spattered car on Green Tree Road in Glassboro on April 30, 1929. Cicero, variously described as a race car driver and a mechanic, had been shot in the head three times, and it appeared that the shooter was likely sitting behind him in the car. Subsequently, after discovering "numerous clues," the county prosecutor charged Cicero's twenty-nine-year-old brother Patrick "Patsy" Cicero, of Woodbury, with Michael's murder. The brothers had allegedly "quarreled over a girl."

Michael's other two brothers, Anthony and Dominic, told County Under-Sheriff Jacob K. Tryon that their sibling was wanted by New York City police for killing an officer several years before. According to his brothers, Michael had been driving a truck for a bootlegger in the city and, when stopped, had engaged in a shootout with a police officer, killing him and then escaping back to southern New Jersey.

Although there was no further confirmation of the New York Story, the case against Patsy went to trial in Woodbury in December, 1929. He was acquitted after the jury deliberated for two and a half hours. The case was never solved, but Michael Cicero's connection to New York bootleggers may well have had something to do with his fate.

Trouble in Belmar

In March, 1929, Margaret Kugler left her husband George and their Briarwood Terrace home in South Belmar, New Jersey and, taking her three children with her, moved to a three-room bungalow on Greenwood Terrace in nearby West Belmar owned by her alleged lover, William Studeman. She subsequently sent her two sons, Raymond and Arthur, back to George but kept her four-year-old daughter Marjorie with her.

George Kugler filed charges against his wife and Studeman alleging that they were exposing Marjorie to "unnecessary mental and physical strain that tended to injure her moral well being." In response to the charges, Constable John Solly of South Belmar and three "special officers" raided the Woodland Terrace address, where they discovered Margaret Kugler in a nightgown and bathrobe and Studeman in "shirt sleeves." They arrested the couple, who were arraigned in Belmar on April 22.

A hearing on the charges was held in Belmar Borough Hall before Justice of the Peace Sigmund Eiseman of Glendola. John L. Montgomery, "head of the Monmouth County Office of Social Service" aided the prosecution. Studeman, who maintained a residence at 913 Curtis Avenue in West Belmar, admitted owning the bungalow, which he said he rented to Mrs. Kugler for ten dollars a month. He added that he did not live there, and was never there late at night. When asked what he was doing there at 1:00 AM on the night of the raid, his response was that he was walking by and saw the light on and "Mrs. Kugler said 'come on in.' So I went in and had some eats and then the officers came" George Kugler, on the other hand, said he had gone to the house several times to get his daughter, but that Margaret had threatened to have him arrested. He also noted that he had seen Studeman run out the back door on these occasions.

Montgomery had the courtroom cleared and questioned Marjorie in front of her mother and Studeman. Although her mother claimed it "untrue," the child told Montgomery that "mother slept with Bill." Justice Eiseman castigated the defendants, mentioned that this was not the first time Studeman had been arrested on a morals charge, said that they were "not providing the child with a proper home" and sentenced them to fines of $100 and a year in the county jail, under the provisions of the state's Child Welfare Act. Margaret collapsed "in a fit of semi-hysteria" and had to be revived by the Belmar First Aid and Safety Squad.

Kugler and Studeman would not be in jail long. Both were released on parole for health reasons within two weeks of their incarceration. Margaret returned to the "pathetic little shack" on Greenwood Terrace where she had lived after leaving her husband, although it appears that her children were back in her custody, or at least Raymond was in the house in early December, when Studeman visited. Shortly afterward George Kugler arrived. What transpired next is unclear, but Studeman apparently got into an altercation with Kugler and began to beat him with an axe handle. It did not end well for Studeman, however, and he was soon dead on the ground with stab wounds inflicted by a Boy Scout pocket knife in his neck. A neighbor told arriving police officers that Margaret was kneeling next to Studeman crying "I will hang for this." Her husband fled the scene.

The police arrived and Margaret told them she stabbed Studeman to save George from being beaten to death, but she was arrested and remanded to the Monmouth County Jail in Freehold. In subsequent days, her son Raymond came forward and said that he had actually stabbed Studeman with his knife to save his father, offering blood stains on his "knickers" where he wiped the knife clean, in evidence. Margaret then stated that she had confessed to the killing to save her son. Initially skeptical that the boy could have reached the six-foot Studeman's neck, after intensive questioning Monmouth County Prosecutor John J. Quinn came to believe that the boy was telling the truth. In the end, the Grand Jury did not indict either Margaret or Raymond, on the grounds that they acted in self-defense.

A Fife, A Drum, and a Gun

The story traveled all across the country, and one newspaper headlined it as "The Tooter and the Shooter." It wasn't quite so humorous for those involved. It all started in Alloway, New Jersey, in May, 1929, where twenty-nine-year old Lillian Fleming, as one story put it, citing a popular aphorism of the era, "seems to have taken seriously the various jests about shooting the neighborhood saxophone player."

There was no saxophone player, but there was a musical annoyance that sparked the journalist's use of the cliché nonetheless. Fleming, from nearby Carney's Point, near a large Dupont gunpowder plant, was visiting her sister, who lived near the town hall, where Alloway's newly formed fife and drum corps was practicing. Apparently driven wild by the noise, Fleming and her sister went over to the hall and "threw insults at the musicians." The corps' leader, forty-five-year-old Lewis Collier, who was also the town's postmaster, responded by leaving and returning with "the sheriff, a constable and a warrant." At that point, Fleming pulled a revolver from her purse and shot Collier in the chest. She was immediately arrested and he was taken to a local hospital.

Collier survived his wound and, in November, Fleming was

convicted of atrocious assault and battery. The judge did not sentence her to jail, but assessed a $1,000 fine. And the band played on.

The Ambitious Mayor

Ohio-born Clarence Hetrick moved with his family to Neptune, New Jersey, in 1887, where he became the first Monmouth County student to win an academic scholarship to Rutgers University, graduating in 1895. Politically active early on, Hetrick gained a reputation as a budget computing whiz while tax collector of Neptune Township and, in 1906, treasurer of Asbury Park. He was elected as Monmouth county sheriff in 1907, despite rumors that, although married into an old county family, he had a mistress who worked at the Keystone Laundry.

In 1911, Sheriff Hetrick prevented the lynching and proved the innocence of a black man framed on a murder charge, gaining the gratitude of Asbury Park's African-American community – and their votes. He was elected mayor in 1915. A Progressive Republican who was a Teddy Roosevelt Bull Moose Party supporter, Hetrick built a new high school, appointed the first woman as city clerk, promoted women's suffrage, and hired African Americans, Italians and Jews as city employees for the first time.

Hetrick was a "wet Republican" who opposed prohibition and incurred the ire of the Anti-Saloon league and, in the 1920s, the revived Ku Klux Klan. In the mid- 1920s the Klan, allied with a Methodist minister, charged Hetrick and his associates with holding an orgy at a nearby Ocean Township speakeasy, where a naked woman sat on the mayor's lap and apparently did other favors for the assembled politicians. The charges were dismissed by a grand jury and Hetrick ran for reelection in 1927 with a public anti-Klan stance and won overwhelmingly.

As a political boss akin to Enoch "Nucky" Johnson, who he viewed as a rival, Hetrick came to the conclusion that his own junior grade city by the sea had to compete seriously with Johnson's Atlantic City to the south for the crown of top year-round tourism center of the Jersey Shore. Although the possibility of Hetrick winning this competition was nil, he could still bring more cash into Asbury Park to capture at least some of the offseason market if he could attract the then-growing convention business. These gatherings included large national multiday meetings of business, fraternal and veterans' organizations and were invariably scheduled for a venue that would prove attractive, aside from any business transacted, to the membership of those groups, as well as the families that often accompanied them. In 1905, the National Education Association had held its convention in Asbury Park and Ocean Grove, and the mayor envisioned a steady stream of such events in the future. He realized, however, that he needed to do a lot of modernizing work in his city to make that happen with regularity. That work would take longer than he thought.

In 1929, Hetrick pointed out in an *Asbury Park Press* article that Atlantic City had outstripped Asbury Park in the number of its construction projects during the "Roaring '20s" and, most notably, had a huge new convention center on the planning boards. Coincidentally, at about the same time that Hetrick renewed his push for a modernization of Asbury's municipal facilities, mysterious fires "of undetermined origin" destroyed both the Fifth Avenue Pavilion, which dated from 1905, located at the north end of the boardwalk, and the Casino building, constructed in 1903 at the south end of the boardwalk. The city council agreed with the mayor that these structures had to be replaced and rapidly approved a special bond issue to pay for new construction at both locations. That May, when Hetrick judged the baby parade on the boardwalk, he was at the top of his game. The world, or at least the Monmouth County part of it, seemed his oyster.

Mayor Hetrick entered into no-bid contracts with Architect Whitney Warren of New York City and his partner, attorney Charles Wetmore. Warren designed Asbury Park's Convention Hall complex, with a 3,200-seat capacity, as a Beaux-Arts gem that spanned the boardwalk with a graceful "Grand Concourse" arch with skylights and included an auditorium, as well as the 1,600-seat Paramount Theater on the west side of the boardwalk, later administered by famed theater impresario Walter Reade. The Paramount's grand opening in 1930 drew a number of Hollywood stars of the era, including the Marx brothers and Ginger Rogers.

The new Warren-designed Casino, constructed of concrete and steel, was indeed a far superior structure to its wooden-frame predecessor and a perfect mate for Convention Hall to the north. The building's solid extension over the beach served as a venue for trade shows, concerts and convention-oriented affairs. A boardwalk arcade was spanned by an arched roof that connected to another semicircular section that housed amusements and refreshment stands and also boasted an attached circular merry-go-round building with a stylish copper roof. The wooden carousel horses were provided by the Philadelphia Toboggan Company and were delivered in 1932.

Unfortunately, Hetrick's massive projects quite literally broke the bank for Asbury Park. Taking on bond debt of over $4 million on the eve of the Depression subsequently staggered the city. The still-rich went elsewhere for vacations, and the vacationing middle class went broke. The only bright spot in Asbury Park's financial picture during the Depression was provided by the macabre appearance of the burned-out *Morro Castle* ocean liner on the beach by Convention Hall. During the six months that the blackened ghost ship remained near the beach, an estimated 250,000 visitors came to Asbury Park to see it, and merchants took advantage of the public's morbid curiosity to offer food and entertainment to the crowds.

The popular mayor developed a dark side during the 1930s though, and became a rich man without any apparent outside employment. He was then hired as "confidential advisor" to a wealthy executive, became a lobbyist with apartments in New York and Washington, and was connected to a number of sleazy deals. Hetrick lost the election of 1933, but was returned to office and remained mayor until his death in 1941.

Voodoo in Atlantic County

Voodoo in Atlantic County — and Nucky Johnson was not involved! When fifty-eight-year-old James London was burned to death on June 27, 1929 in his Conovertown home near Atlantic City, where he lived with his twenty-nine-year-old wife Flossie, it was at first thought to be an accident. According to Fire Chief Charles M. Kessler of Absecon, "London's charred body had been found in the basement of the house lying on his neatly folded coat and trousers." Initial investigators had concluded that London had "fallen asleep with a cigarette in his mouth and had been burned with his bed."

Within days, however, Aaron London, James' son by his first marriage, was accusing his stepmother, who had gone to visit her brother in Philadelphia at the time of the fire, with either committing or arranging for James' murder. Aaron told authorities that Flossie's motive was to collect a $25,000 insurance policy, and he demanded that police conduct a thorough investigation of the circumstances surrounding his father's death.

When interrogated, Flossie told police a strange and seemingly irrelevant tale. She stated that Otto Martin, an African-American house painter from Absecon, "had cast evil spells over her and her husband" and that "it was only through antidotal voodoo rites that she was able to free herself from Martin's will." The press reported that Martin's "mother hails from a Virginia settlement of Negroes where voodooism is practiced, they say."

Flossie explained her "antidotal voodoo" remedy thusly: "I went to a voodoo practitioner last year. Under the orders of that practitioner I made a magic potion from tree bark mixed with water and sprinkled it over my hair. That magic dose brought immediate relief. I felt that Martin's spell over me was broken. When Martin next came to call upon me I ordered him from my house. That was last August. He has never returned." Although she did not say so directly, she no doubt intended to shift suspicion for her husband's death to Martin.

Needless to say, Martin denied the story, although admitting that he knew James London, a former bread truck driver and lately a golf course caddy, and had had a quarrel with him over a business matter a year prior to London's death. In the end, despite Aaron London's claims, there was no substantive evidence produced that his father was murdered, and despite Flossie's implying that voodoo may have something to do with his demise, the New Jersey judicial code no longer had provisions for prosecution under witchcraft ordinances.

Three Lads on a Spree

It was December, 1929. The stock market had crashed on October 24, but there is no indication that that was of any concern to twenty-one-year-old Harold George, of Brooklyn, New York, whose wedding day was planned for December 20, and who no doubt had plans for Christmas as well. Perhaps Harold and his friends Frank "Bunk" Warren and Bernard Toner thought the spree they were about to set out on would be a kind of bachelor party. Harold and Bernard would later say that it was all Frank's idea. Frank had indeed assumed a leadership role, reportedly "through his domineering attitude."

When you are seeking to stage a road trip party, the first thing you need is a car, so the trio stole one in Queens. You also need some gas money, so on December 11, they robbed a grocery store, netting $250, and drove to Paterson, New Jersey, where they rented a hotel room under false names. The following day they drove to Scranton, Pennsylvania and then to Port Jervis, New York. On December 13, they came back through Scranton to Wilkes Barre, where they robbed three more stores (they specialized in A&Ps) of $800 and proceeded on to Harrisburg, taking a room in a hotel there for the night. After staging three holdups in Harrisburg and York on the following day they drove to Baltimore and then Washington, where they visited a friend in a hospital. On December 16, returning to Baltimore, they robbed three more stores of $300 and proceeded on to Philadelphia.

The bandits took a break in the City of Brotherly Love and "Bunk" proposed a recreational dice game, each putting up money from his share of the loot. The crap shoot resulted in Warren winning the better part of his buddies' ill-gotten gains. After staying overnight in Philly, Warren and Toner decided to upgrade their armament and bought six guns at a South Philadelphia gun store. They went on to rob two stores in Darby, netting $275, turned around and returned to the gun store, robbing it of $400 and eight more guns, raising their arms cache to sixteen weapons.

On December 18, the bandit trio crossed over into New Jersey, driving through New Brunswick and arriving at Paterson, taking a room in the same hotel from which they had launched their multi state adventure. That evening they hit three stores in Passaic and a gas station in Glen Rock, for a total of $350, caught a movie in Paterson, drove down to Red Bank and then up to Linden.

George and Toner had been comparing notes and had come to the conclusion that Bunk had cheated in the crap game, and so when they reached Linden they shot him in the back of his head and dumped his body beside the road. Warren may have been a "domineering" personality, and he may well have loaded the dice, but it quickly became apparent that he was clearly the brains of the outfit. He may also have been their lucky charm.

After disposing of their erstwhile leader, the two surviving bandits abandoned their car, which got stuck in mud, and hijacked a milk truck, forcing the driver to bring them into Elizabeth, where they stopped to rob Stout's Gas Station. Meanwhile a state trooper had found Warren's body alongside the road and alerted local police, who had also been contacted by local witnesses who saw the hijacking. The saga ended at

Stout's where Elizabeth cops closed in and surprised the duo as they were rifling the cash register after tying up the attendant and "hammered the pair unconscious with revolver butts and fists." A photographer took a picture of Bernard Toner, described by a reporter as "a dopey looking gangster," in the Elizabeth police station after his arrest. It was December 20, George's intended wedding day.

While the two bandits were held at Elizabeth, witnesses appeared at police headquarters to link them to a number of their crimes. They included Henry Boederman of 227 Putnam Avenue in Brooklyn, whose car the trio stole to start the spree. Boederman picked George and Toner out of a lineup. Alice Keller, George's fiancée, also came down from Brooklyn with her friend Theodora Finkelstein. She said George had told her he would "give up his life of crime" after their marriage, but that he "went on the last trip to get the money for our wedding." She also said that he told her that Warren "was a rat and no good." On December 28 Toner's girlfriend, eighteen-year-old Ruth Orlosky, was arrested for robbing a dress shop in Brooklyn. Alice Keller was arrested along with her and charged with vagrancy.

At their subsequent trial for murder at the Union County Court of Oyer and Terminer in Elizabeth, Toner and George, who claimed Warren had led them into crime, were found guilty, but the jury recommended mercy. On February 7, 1930, Judge Alfred A. Stein sentenced them to life in prison. Toner asked the judge: "Does that mean there is no chance of parole?" Stein replied "You have heard the sentence." The census of 1930 records both as inmates of Trenton State Prison, but by the census of 1940 they had apparently been released.

CHAPTER 8

1930-"Richie the Boot" Gets Lucky

He was the guy who ultimately received the envelopes that my barber used to put the cash in -- Ruggerio "Ritchie the Boot" Boiardo. Born in Naples in 1890, Boiardo arrived in Newark, New Jersey, in 1910. Starting out as a bookmaker whose role model was Al Capone, he rose in the ranks of organized crime, assisted by Prohibition, until he was in charge of illegal activities in Newark's North Ward. Boiardo ruled over his criminal domain from the Vittoria Castle, a restaurant he owned in Newark's "Little Italy."

In 1930, Ritchie had a feud with another Newark gangster, Abner "Longy" Zwillman, whose organization dominated the city's Central Ward, but Charles "Lucky" Luciano came over from New York in November of that year to negotiate a peace. Shortly afterward, on November 26, Boiardo was ambushed by shotgun wielding assailants who peppered him with buckshot, seriously wounding him as he stepped out of his bullet proof car. A news report on the incident characterized Boiardo as a "widely known gang leader and dabbler in the policy, wine and alcohol rackets." Some thought Zwillman the ultimate culprit, but the gangsters behind the attack were two rivals from Boiardo's own neighborhood seeking to take over his operation. Ritchie had them both eliminated shortly afterward. Ironically, Newark police officers who arrived on the scene discovered that Boiardo had a revolver and he was charged with carrying a concealed weapon without a license and served twenty-two months in jail. It was the only time he was ever incarcerated in his long criminal career.

Among Boiardo's varied interests was the dubious diamond trade, and he reportedly personally provided Joe DiMaggio with an engagement ring for his first wife, Dorothy Arnold. On Zwillman's death, allegedly by suicide, in 1959, Boiardo became the sole boss in Newark. In addition to his New Jersey enterprises, he also had interests in casinos and hotels in Havana and Florida and perhaps Las Vegas. In 1979 he was federally charged with gangster activities, including extortion, racketeering and murder conspiracy in connection with his alleged ownership, along with other gangsters, of the Jolley Trolley casino in Nevada, but was dropped from the case due to a decision that he was "physically and mentally unfit to stand trial."

Boiardo's fortress-like mansion in Livingston, built in 1941 in a style described jokingly as "Transylvanian traditional," included a long driveway lined with statues of members of his family. It still stands. Ruggiero Boiardo lived to die of natural causes in 1984, at the age of ninety-three. The HBO series *The Sopranos* was reportedly inspired by his story.

"Hard Boiled" Golding Stages a Raid in Newark

On March 20, 1930, "a squad of Prohibition agents armed with pistols, shotguns, axes and heavy trucks which were used as battering rams raided the old Hensler Brewery in Newark and confiscated some seven thousand barrels of beer. The bootleggers who were running the place had a pipe line running across the street from the brewery to an old garage where they filled their barrels with the banned beverage "at the rate of five barrels at a clip." The garage was owned by one T. B. Plunkett, who later claimed ignorance of the beer line into his property, a claim a judge would later dismiss.

The raid was led by Albany, New York, based Captain George E. "Hard Boiled" Golding, the "ace of undercover men in the Prohibition service," who was known for employing "rough house and strong arm methods in enforcing the dry law." In 1951 a Chicago reporter remembered that Golding had come to town in 1928 with an entourage of thirty agents, "most of them young and untrained," and some "seemed overeager to use the submachine guns with which they were equipped." After several raids, during which Golding's trigger happy agents shot several citizens, including an insurance agent who happened to be walking by a raided premises, and even raided a police station where a janitor had obtained a bottle of bourbon for a prisoner, there were a number of unflattering news stories and Golding was transferred, allegedly at the request of a US senator, to Baltimore.

If Golding learned anything from his Chicago experience, it did not seem to stick. By 1930, as leader of a special detachment, he apparently had carte blanche to travel around the country making raids, but was a continued source of complaints filed by citizens and local law enforcement. One journalist writing about the Newark operation noted that Golding "popped up one day with a dozen agents armed like cowboys and raided the Hensler Brewery, getting 7,000 barrels of beer – the largest single seizure in Jersey. It was done without the aid or knowledge of the regular Prohibition unit stationed in that territory." In addition to confiscating the beer, Golding's team arrested thirty-six men and women on the premises of the brewery and garage. Within a short period of time the brewery was back in action under the name of Superior Manufacturing Company, however, and was raided once again in November 1931.

The Hensler Brewery, founded by Joseph Hensler in 1860, was one of twenty-seven breweries that once called Newark home. It occupied a large building at 73 Wilson Avenue in the "down neck" or "ironbound" section of the city. Wilson Avenue was formerly known as Hamburg Place, but was renamed Wilson Avenue during the anti-German hysteria of World War I.

With the advent of Prohibition, breweries across the nation closed. Some quickly reopened, however, "repurposed" to blend more innocuous beverages like "near beer" or soda or as ice houses and similar businesses. For some, however, that new life was merely a mask for the continued production of beer. The Hensler Brewery reopened legally at the end of Prohibition in 1933 and produced what the company advertising dubbed as "A Whale of a Beer," with a publicity truck representing a whale, until it closed in 1958.

And Captain Golding? Oh, yes. In July, 1930, Golding was "relieved of his duties" as a result of "charges being filed with Washington by a young woman," who turned out to be "a stenographer in Golding's office." He was dismissed in November, but the bureau never revealed the exact reason. One can guess.

"Plenty the Matter" in East Orange

In the early morning hours of April 13, 1930, forty-five-year-old Frank Demarest Crawford dialed the East Orange Police Department and said there was "plenty the matter" at his apartment at 5 Harvard Street. When two officers arrived, Crawford met them in the hall and then led them to his bedroom, where his forty-two-year-old wife Louise was sprawled on the bed, dead. He remarked, in a matter of fact manner, "I choked her to death." They arrested him.

At East Orange police headquarters, Crawford, who the press described as a "real estate operator" and the owner of East Orange's Regent theater, signed a confession "in which he blamed jealousy for his act." He went on to say that he had killed Louise after asking her "about rumors he had heard that she was accepting the attentions of another man." Crawford found her answers to be unsatisfactory, and things went downhill from there. His questions about that allegation had ignited a loud argument which woke up his fifteen-year-old son, Frank Jr., who yelled "stop fighting dad," to no avail. He said that Louise's replies, which were not detailed, "infuriated him…and he seized her by the throat."

Despite his confession, Crawford, who had later amended his description of Louise's conduct to say that he had "accused her of intimacy with four prominent East Orange men," pleaded not guilty when he was charged with first degree murder in the court of Oyer and Terminer in Newark on May 16. He subsequently agreed to plead guilty to a charge of second degree murder.

When Crawford appeared for sentencing before Judge Walter D. Van Riper, though, the judge downgraded the charge to manslaughter and sentenced him to six years in prison. In justifying his sentence, Van Riper said that "Crawford was shocked when he learned of the things that had been going on in his home, and the killing was done in the heat of passion. According to the judge, Crawford "had been inflamed with jealousy by the stories of his nineteen-year-old daughter Kathryn, who told him her mother frequently went around with other men and came home intoxicated."

By 1938, Crawford was out of prison and living in Newark at 187 North 7th Street. He was still living there in 1941, with his then married daughter, Kathryn Crawford Biringer and listed himself as "unemployed." The house, built in 1910, still stands.

A Scoundrel in Atlantic City

Harry Kendall Thaw worked hard, and planned well. He was an entrepreneur's entrepreneur. It was not easy to arrange being born into a wealthy family in 1871, but he did it. And, like almost every other hard working con man of the late 19th and early 20th centuries, he ended up spending a lot of time in his later years in Enoch "Nucky" Johnson's Atlantic City. There were brothels, booze, illegal gambling and the beach in the city by the sea. What more could a rich ne'er do well want?

Being an Atlantic City beach bum was not what Harry was principally known for, however. Early on Thaw had attacked family servants, often while babbling "baby talk," even into adolescence. As he grew older he lavishly expended family money on drugs, "loose women" and assorted other vices, and the family had spent as lavishly on attorneys and bribes to cover up his excesses.

Thaw attended the University of Pittsburgh before transferring to Harvard, where his privileged status gained him immediate entry. After a record of academic indifference coupled with a devotion to cockfighting, drinking, gambling and threatening faculty and other students with violence, capped off by chasing a cab driver who he claimed shortchanged him with a shotgun, young Harry was expelled from Harvard for vaguely referenced "immoral practices." He was given three hours to get off campus and out of town.

On Harry's father's death in 1893, his allowance of $2,500 a month was raised to $8,000 ($200,000 today) a month. He took off for Europe, where he lured an English hotel bellboy into his room, beat him, stripped him naked, tied him up and tossed him in a bathtub. After paying $5,000 to get that incident swept under the rug, Thaw left for France, where he gained a reputation for patronizing S&M brothels and held massive parties.

Once back in the United States, Thaw began to spend a lot of time in New York City, where he became a rival of noted eccentric architect Stanford White for the affections of Evelyn Nesbitt, a supermodel and famous showgirl of the era. Nesbitt, who had been seduced by White, and who it is safe to say made poor choices in men, married Thaw on April 4, 1905. The couple moved to Pittsburgh, where Harry became obsessed with the idea that White had hired New York gangsters to kill him. In response, he traveled back to Manhattan and, on June 25, 1905, shot and killed White at the conclusion of a show on the roof of Madison Square Garden, a murder that hit front pages all over the nation. In jail, Thaw's customized cell had a brass bed, his table a tablecloth and he dined on catered meals, washed down with expensive wine. The story of the murder and its aftermath has been told a number of times, most notably in the film The *Girl in the Red Velvet Swing* as well as the novel and film "Ragtime."

Thaw, unsurprisingly, was represented by the best legal talent available at his January, 1907, murder trial, which ended with a deadlocked jury. In a second trial, the jury found him insane and he was sentenced to the Matteawan asylum for life. On October 25, 1910, Evelyn gave birth to a son, Russell William Thaw, who she claimed had been conceived during a conjugal visit to Harry, although Thaw claimed he was not the father. Nesbitt divorced Harry K. Thaw in 1915.

Appeals went on for years, and in 1913 Harry, who was a privileged inmate, escaped by walking out the door of the asylum. Recaptured, he was subjected to a new trial that found him sane again and hence innocent, and he was released. In 1916, Thaw was charged with the kidnapping, whipping and sexual assault of nineteen-year-old Frederick Gump of Kansas City. Arrested, he was confined again in an asylum in Philadelphia, but released as cured in 1924.

In later life Harry seems to have calmed down a bit, but remained a shyster, refusing to pay writers he had hired in an abortive film production business. He was a popular guy in Atlantic City, however, where he was a frequent visitor, and where his photo was taken in August, 1930. The Atlantic City lifeguards allegedly found Thaw to be "a great favorite, as many times he aids them in the launching of their boats and in the rescue of a drowning bather." Evelyn reportedly performed in Atlantic City while Harry was in town, and the two reputedly met for lunch. Harry K. Thaw died in Miami, Florida in 1947 and was buried in Pittsburgh.

Beware the "evils of present day whoopee"

At her sentencing in April, 1931, nineteen-year-old Mary McClyment of Camden warned other young women about the "evils of present day whoopee." On the evening of October 7, 1930, Mary had hopped in her roadster to attend a "Whoopee Party," at the farm of sixty-seven-year-old

Joseph Van Dexter in the Blenheim section of Gloucester Township. Six hours later she was in jail, charged with the murder of Edward Nicholson, another guest at the affair. A newspaper reported that initially "no one seemed to have a clear recollection as to just what had happened. Memories had been vague. There had been drinks and more drinks, words, song. Perhaps a shot had been fired, perhaps not."

If anything, things got more confusing. The prosecutor said Mary had confessed, and, as his alcohol induced haze cleared, Van Dexter stated that Mary had indeed shot Nicholson. Mary denied that she had confessed, but said that she had indeed fired three shots into the ground to make Van Dexter and Nicholson stop fighting. They could not find a bullet in Nicholson's body, and old man Van Dexter had apparently been waving a cane sword around, which was later found in a closet along with a dark stained rag. Mary's attorney tried to prove, unsuccessfully, that Nicholson's fatal wound was inflicted by a sword or spear. Eddie Sims, a seventeen-year old boy who was at the party, testified that he had seen Mary fire the revolver at Nicholson. When questioned by the defense, Sims admitted that the prosecutor had offered him a job, but denied that the offer had had any influence on his testimony.

The jury found Mary guilty of manslaughter and she was sentenced to three years in prison at the State Reformatory for Women in Clinton. A moralizing reporter concluded that she had ignored potential dangers, seeking "life," but that "life, she had learned, consisted, in this enlightened age of mad jazz, in the gin tempo. She knows better now." Mary agreed, and in her closing statement went on to say that although she still maintained her innocence, she looked on her two to three-year sentence as "swift retribution for attendance at a whoopee party." She concluded with: "If I could speak to all the young girls in America today I would say: 'Think of me. Think of poor Eddie Nicholson, when you get an invitation to a whoopee party.'"

Sad as her story was, and contrite as she appeared, Mary's lifestyle before and after the whoopee party suggests that perhaps she might not have been completely sincere. In 1926 she had eloped with thirty-six-year-old Herschel Lake to Elkton, Maryland, where they were married, although the marriage was apparently quickly annulled. She was paroled after two years in prison following her manslaughter conviction, but in February, 1933, was arrested in Dauphin County, Pennsylvania along with her younger brother and her prison friend Anna Roland, for breaking and entering and auto theft. Mary was returned to prison to finish out her sentence for violation of parole.

In 1935, free once more, Mary had an altercation with her mother Myrtle at a "drinking party" and Myrtle stabbed her in the abdomen with a kitchen knife. Foggy recollections of alcohol induced violence might have been a family tradition, as Myrtle stated "I stabbed her, but I don't know how I did it. I had been drinking and I don't remember much." Although Mary was, according to a newspaper account, "near death," she recovered. In 1940 she was living with her mother and other relatives at 523 Williams Street in Camden, although now calling herself Mary Lake, apparently in reference to her quickie marriage back in 1926.

One would think that with such a record Mary McClyment would not have survived to a ripe old age, but she did. Mary passed away on December 19, 2001 in Cape May, New Jersey, at the age of ninety. She is buried in Cold Spring Presbyterian Cemetery.

CHAPTER 9

1931-The "Parade Murderer"

The press of the 1930s, as with today's media, loved a colorful crime story, and so when they came up with a case in which the "principals [were] colorless" and they had to have "results fantastic" to sell papers, they looked for an angle, and a catchy title. And so it was with the murder of Phoebe Stader, a "personable young hairdresser" in Rahway, by her lover William Frazer. The newspapers turned "a crime of the ordinary run" into what they called a "parade murder."

The leading characters in this drama were married, but not to each other. The "unhappily married and childless Mrs. Stader's" affair with "one-time restaurant manager and World War veteran Frazer" who had a wife and two children, had cooled after he ran through his $25,000 inheritance. According to one account, "Frazer's infatuation with the dark-haired buxom Mrs. Stader led to extravagances on her behalf. There were 'parties'; wild gayety; night clubs. The inheritance burned up."

On February 18, 1931, while they were sitting in his car, parked on the road between Newburgh and Walden, New York, Phoebe told William their relationship was over. His response was to shoot her in the head with a .22 caliber rifle and drive off, with the mortally wounded Phoebe still in the front seat. It was calculated that she did not actually die until they reached Elizabeth "by the Durant automobile plant," thus making her murder technically a Garden State crime. And thus began the story of New Jersey's "first parade murder," as Frazer continued to drive around the state with his former lover's dead body "propped up in the front seat" of his car. It would be, according to one press account, "the longest 'ride' a bullet victim ever took."

Frazer's first stop was in the early morning of February 18 in his mother's driveway at 67 Cherry Street in Rahway, where he met his twenty-year-old cousin Ira Jensen, who was living there as a ward of Mrs. Frazer, and asked him if he wanted to meet his girlfriend. Jensen later recalled that he "thought she was bashful. Then I saw she was dead." The duo then drove over to see Frazer's estranged wife Hilda at 519 Jefferson Avenue, who, when she was apprised of the situation, told them to go to the police.

Fraser had no intention of going to the police, and as the cousins left to ride around town with the late Mrs. Stader again, he suggested to Jensen that he was thinking of committing suicide, then pulled in to an Iselin golf course and left the car with his rifle in hand. A few minutes later he returned, said he could not do it and asked Jensen to shoot him, but the younger man declined. The two put Phoebe's body in the rear seat, covered it with a blanket and drove back to Cherry Street, where Frazer locked the car and went to bed.

The following day Frazer, with Phoebe's body still in his car, drove south, stopping in Philadelphia to mail a letter to Phoebe's sister stating that the couple was heading to California. He left a note instructing Jensen to bring him money at the Sir Walter Hotel in Raleigh, North Carolina, and Jensen showed up there two days later with $260. In succeeding weeks Frazer, knowing Jensen was due to receive a $3,000 inheritance, asked him to bring more money.

Meanwhile Frazer's wife told her father, Lloyd Madden, that her estranged spouse and his cousin had showed up at her home with a body in their car, and Madden reported the incident to the Rahway police, who had been looking for the missing Mrs. Stader. Jensen was questioned and revealed Frazer's location and a warrant was filed for his arrest.

And what became of Mrs. Stader's body? The parade had ended for her in Virginia. A man "plodding down a Highway between Washington and Richmond took note of buzzards hovering over a wooded piece of land," and investigated the area, near Bowling Green. He found "the body of a woman, divested of clothing and partly decomposed." After dumping Phoebe's corpse, Frazer had halted to burn her clothes near South Hill, Virginia. Her body was identified by her husband and returned to

Elizabeth where an autopsy was performed and it was determined that "she died of a bullet wound in the head, the bullet entering one inch to the left and one inch above the occipital protuberance."

Frazer, arrested in North Carolina that same day, confessed that he had killed Phoebe, and disposed of her corpse in Virginia, but maintained that his gun had discharged accidentally. He said that the rifle was in the back seat of his car and that he had reached for it and that "in some manner it had exploded. The bullet buried itself in her head. He feared he would be blamed, so he disposed of the body."

He was extradited to New Jersey, and stood trial for first degree murder in Elizabeth. The fact that he had purchased a box of .22 caliber ammunition at a Walden, New York store the day before the shooting was posited as proof of premeditation. In addition, there was testimony indicating that Frazer's story of an accidental discharge was, to be kind, unlikely. The rifle could not have been fired as Frazer described due to lack of room in the car, and the prosecutor's contention was that "the proofs demonstrate further that the woman must have been shot while the murderer stood on the side of the road and took deliberate aim." Frazer was convicted of first degree murder and sentenced to death. An appeal based on technicalities of Phoebe's actual death location, and the fact that Frazer was drinking apple brandy before the murder, which mitigated his responsibility, was rejected by the New Jersey Supreme Court. The court held that mere drinking was not evidence of intoxication, which might be used to justify a conviction on a lesser charge.

Last minute attempts to secure a commutation to a life sentence from Governor A. Harry Moore by Frazer's "war comrades" from the Fourth Division, who contended that the veteran's "intellect had been impaired by war service," which, in retrospect, may well have been true, failed. On April 1, 1932, William Frazer walked down death row at the New Jersey State Prison in Trenton and sat down in the electric chair, seemingly "a passive but interested spectator" to his impending execution. Robert Elliott, the ever-assiduous state executioner, "adjusted the straps" and, five minutes later Frazer was pronounced dead by Dr. Wellington Crane.

"Too Beautiful to be Bad"

In 1923 the contest was not yet called the "Miss America Pageant," but went under the name of the "Atlantic City Beauty Pageant." Charlotte

Isabel Nash was a contestant that year as "Miss Saint Louis," and she came close to winning. She was definitely a winner with one of the judges, Philadelphia and Atlantic City theater mogul forty-five-year-old Fred Nixon-Nordlinger, who became smitten with the eighteen-year-old Charlotte and proposed marriage. She accepted, and after completing a course at a finishing school where Nirdlinger sent her to smooth her rough edges, they were married in Hagerstown, Maryland on February 3, 1924.

Fred Nixon-Nirdlinger had a checkered romantic past. His first marriage, to actress Tessie Burke, with whom he had two sons, had ended in divorce in 1908. He married again, to Lura McKenna, in 1909, but the time and place that marriage ended was rather hazy. One account stated that the divorce was granted in France, where Nirdlinger was a frequent visitor, but that is not clear. In 1922 Franz Voelker, Secretary of the Atlantic City Board of Taxation, had sued Nirdlinger for $150,000 for "alienation of the affections of his wife." The jury awarded Voelker six cents in damages.

Unsurprisingly, Fred and Charlotte's marriage was rather rocky. The couple maintained a home at 25 South Laclede Place in Atlantic City, but were often in Paris or Nice. Fred apparently not only had a wandering eye, but was insanely jealous with a tendency towards violence. Although neither fault was specified publicly, Charlotte successfully sued for divorce from the theater baron in 1926, but remarried him in 1928. Over the course of their two marriages, the couple had two children, Fred Jr. and Charlotte.

In March, 1931, the Nirdlingers were in their apartment in Nice when Fred charged that Charlotte's attempts to learn Italian and her perusal of an Italian newspaper proved she had an Italian lover, which she vigorously denied. He put his hands around her throat and began to choke her and she pulled out a revolver she had stowed under a pillow, perhaps anticipating his erratic behavior, and shot him twice, killing him. Charlotte called the police immediately afterward and when they arrived they took her into custody. She was charged with manslaughter.

The trial, held in May, was a circus. The French police had to keep the crowds of the curious away from the courtroom and "Riviera playboys and girls" established a betting line on the outcome. The odds in favor of acquittal were twenty to one.

Charlotte appeared on the witness stand dressed in mourning for the husband she had shot. Although the judge sharply questioned her about an alleged affair with a swimming instructor, which she emphatically denied, the prosecution was far from vigorous, with one correspondent reporting that it sounded more like a defense. The Nirdlinger children's nursemaid testified that Charlotte was "never out alone" and that her husband read every letter she sent or received. Fred's friend and attorney Charles Loeb testified that Fred had suffered severely from "the disease of jealousy."

In summing up, Charlotte's defense attorney declared that "she is too beautiful to be bad." The jury agreed, and acquitted her in fifteen minutes. Charlotte returned to the United States and Atlantic City, where she resided until she sold the Atlantic City home two years later. It still stands and was up for sale recently.

The Camden Boat Murder

After the freighter SS *Helen* docked at Camden, New Jersey on April 1, 1931 with a load of sugar from Puerto Rico, the crew hopped off for a night of shore leave on the town. There were plenty of speakeasies in Camden, so it wasn't hard to find a drink. What the quality of the bootleg hootch the boys imbibed was, however, open to question

Second Engineer Claude McCroy and Oilers Wilfred Moller and William Coughlin drank until late at night in Camden, and as the trio staggered back aboard the *Helen*, McCroy and Moller argued and McCroy punched Moller. They disengaged and went to bed

The following morning a hung-over Moller got out of his bunk and began to dress, and, as Coughlin later testified, "He felt his jaw and said: 'How did my face get so sore.' I told him the second engineer had hit him." Moller was incensed at what he perceived as a gross indignity.

Just then McCroy walked past the two men, and Moller approached him and said "So, you're the guy who hit me?" McCroy's response was to pull out a gun and shoot Moller and then Coughlin and, finally, put the gun to his head and shoot himself. Both Moller and McCroy died at the scene, but Coughlin was removed from the ship and rushed for treatment to a Camden Hospital. He survived.

A "Thrill Killer" in West Orange

"Hey, is youse guys still lookin' for dat Knapp guy? I hoid he was in

Joisey—in West Orange." Well, it didn't really go down that way, but it could have. Phillip Knox Knapp, scion of a wealthy Syracuse, New York, family and Cornell University dropout, had joined the US Army Air Corps and was stationed at Mitchel field when he murdered Hempstead, Long Island, cab driver Louis Panella on July 4, 1925, in a quest for the "supreme thrill" of killing a human being.

Knapp fled to New York City, where he sold Panella's cab for $100 and disappeared. Listed as a deserter by the army, he changed his name to Alan K. Phillips, married and went to work as a mechanic, first for the US Coast Guard on Staten Island and then for the Public Service Company in Newark, New Jersey, while a nationwide search went on for him, resulting in several arrests of people who resembled him and were released. The police interrogated Ruth Peggy Stark, Knapp's former fiancée, who told them that she had not heard from him in months and had broken off the engagement.

Detectives even followed leads to Canada, to no avail. But they did not give up. A reporter noted that the "similarity to the Leopold-Loeb Case was cited and it was observed that Knapp had many tendencies in common with the Chicago slayers, who considered always as right what they wanted to do." Today this would be described as a classic case of narcissistic psychopathy.

In October 1930, Knapp moved to 35 Ridgehurst Road in West Orange, New Jersey. Over the next several months, Nassau County detectives received some tips from relatives that he might be living in West Orange as Phillips. They contacted the West Orange police, and, early on the morning of June 2, 1931, along with West Orange officers, raided the home and arrested Knapp, who, on arrival at local police headquarters, confessed as to who he was and what he had done. Later, when on trial for murder in Mineola, Long Island, Knapp claimed the shooting was an accident. He was eventually sentenced to twenty years in prison. He was sent up the Hudson River to Sing Sing, where he became an instructor in the prison's automobile repair school.

A Kidnapping Planned in Newark

It was complicated. It all started on August 11, 1931, when "youthful broker" Charles M. Rosenthal was hanging out in a Harlem speakeasy. There he met "a mulatto girl" named Betty Green, who, most likely in the interest of upper class white sensibilities of the era, was later described in the newspapers as someone who "would pass for a white woman." Rosenthal later stated that Betty "invited him to a party," but instead delivered the twenty-three-year-old to three thugs who held him in for ransom in an apartment at 42 Hamilton Terrace while conducting secret negotiations with his family for a ransom to release him. After seventeen days, the Rosenthal family paid the kidnappers $50,000, half of their initial demand, placing the money in a bag left at the Hotel Vendig, at 20 West 47th Street in Manhattan, and he was freed to resume his pillaging career on Wall Street.

The police recorded the serial numbers on the ransom bills prior to paying the kidnappers and, in late August, arrested Marcus Blumenthal, alias "Jack Markham," after Blumenthal, who the press described as a "college-bred black sheep of a wealthy family," tried to break one of the $100 ransom bills in a local bank. Once in custody, Blumenthal led police to two of his partners in crime, Theodore Adinolfi, alias "Harry King," and Albert Sileo, alias "John Rocco," who had plotted the kidnapping in their West Market Street saloon in Newark, New Jersey, and were sharing an apartment in the New Jersey city. When Newark detectives arrested the pair, they found them "attired in silk dressing gowns and possessing $12,500 in cash which they claimed they won by gambling."

Then things got confusing. Law enforcement officers proceeded to Atlantic City, where they arrested Betty Green, also known as Bettine Green and Betty Stewart, and an African-American hotel waiter named Clarence Green. Clarence was described in the press as the gang's "ringleader" and Betty's husband. It turned out, however, that the real ringleader was actually Nick Rutigliano, a bootlegger who also owned the Hotel Vendig, who used the alias "Nick Green," and who was apparently with Betty Green in Atlantic City. Waiter Clarence Green was quickly released, but not after posing for a bewildered looking mugshot. It is doubtful that Betty, described as a member of an elite African-American social circle in Philadelphia, would have been married to a waiter. Clarence was just at the wrong place at the wrong time, with the wrong last name.

Rutigliano, who the other kidnappers called "the chief," apparently conceived the plot because the income from his bootlegging business was off due to the Depression. Ironically, his arrest might have saved him from a worse fate. It turned out that although he collected the full $50,000 ransom and promised an equal division of the loot, Rutigliano took $25,000 for himself before giving his three cohorts the remainder.

They later read of the full amount of the ransom in the newspapers and the two arrested in Newark remarked to reporters that they "wanted to take him[Rutigliano] for a ride, and that "they were sorry they had not had time to put about 40 bullets in the chief."

All five of the accused were indicted in New York City September, 1931, and went to trial in October. The four men were convicted and Betty Green, who insisted that she had no idea what they had in mind, and did not get any of the ransom money, was acquitted. Adinolfi, Sileo, Rutigliano and Blumenthal received sentences of sixty years in Sing Sing prison. A review of the 1940 census found all of them still incarcerated, but housed in separate facilities, no doubt due to the personal conflicts among them.

The Death of "Mickey Duffy"

Mickey Duffy was born in Philadelphia in 1888 as William Michael Cusick. A career criminal, Cusick, whose parents were Polish, changed his name to Duffy to better fit in with the Irish mobsters in his neighborhood during the early twentieth century. He "started out in life as a hoodlum" in the Gray's Ferry District in Southwest Philadelphia, quickly establishing a record as a petty criminal and thief and being incarcerated a number of times. Duffy's criminal career blossomed with Prohibition, when he, like many other minor gangsters of the era, "became a big shot in the beer racket" and made large amounts of money as a bootlegger as well as a numbers racketeer.

Duffy expanded his territory into New Jersey, where he owned the Rising Sun Brewery in Elizabeth and operated a number of other bootlegging enterprises around the state. Duffy aggressively expanded his crime empire throughout the 1920s and made local history of a sort when he was shot by rival gangsters in 1927 in what was described as the first use of a Thompson submachine gun in Philadelphia. He survived the attack and subsequently spent a lot of his time in Atlantic City.

As he became wealthy, Duffy reportedly "began to shed the manners of the hoodlum" and "began to associate with more polished people and learned to acquire polish himself." Duffy and his wife gave money to charities and churches, but the liquor business of the day was a dangerous one, and he finally met his end at the Ambassador Hotel in

Atlantic City on August 31, 1931 when he was shot to death in his bed.

In the immediate aftermath of Duffy's murder, a number of gangsters were sought for the crime and some were actually arrested, including New Yorker Paul Corbo, also known as "Dago Frankie," and his "cabaret dancer" girlfriend "Vivian Lee" whose real name was Ophelia Malfatto. Corbo's alibi, which apparently held up, was "that he had been under treatment for his nose in a hospital" at the time of Duffy's death. Herman Cohen and Albert Hodkinson, suspected of being the actual triggermen for a time, were arrested after a police motorcycle chase in Toms River. The case was never solved but there was speculation that some of Duffy's own gang members might have done the deed. The Philadelphia police department reported that Duffy associates "Sammy Grossman and Albert Skale, wanted for questioning in the murder, had offered to surrender to Atlantic City police if they were released on bail to attend Duffy's funeral." You gotta pay respect – even if you done it.

Mickey's cronies planned a great sendoff for the bootlegger. Members of his organization reportedly charged numbers racket winners an eight percent fee to pay for his funeral, which was held at his widow Edith's "$150,000 modernistic villa" in the Philadelphia suburb of Overbrook. Edith, a "former hat check girl in a Philadelphia Hotel," had made the most out of her marriage to Mickey. A reporter described the Duffy estate as having "…grounds elaborately landscaped; two big parrots occupy gilded cages on the stone ledges of the patio and make such inane comments as 'Hello Polly' to visitors who happen to pass by. A species of butler, immaculate in black, answers the doorbell. Virginia creepers hang from pottery jars on the third-floor window sills. Everything is all very elegant."

In the end the sendoff from the elegant estate was seriously curtailed, with over 200 Philadelphia and local police keeping curious crowds away from the ceremonies, and limiting attendance to relatives and close friends. Philadelphia police chief Lemuel B. Schofield told reporters that "no parade of gangsters will be permitted for a common thief," and his men "strongarmed" journalists and photographers who tried to cover the event. Duffy was buried in Mount Moriah Cemetery in Philadelphia, and a newspaper noted that his final resting place was "near the grave of Betsey Ross, maker of the first known American flag."

Mickey Duffy was the inspiration for the character "Mickey Doyle" in the HBO series *Boardwalk Empire*. Doyle was portrayed as a Polish American bootlegger from Philadelphia who adopted an Irish name.

Oops, There Goes the Still

The massive explosion "shook the countryside for miles around" Woodstown, New Jersey, on December 2, 1931, and sent a three-ton boiler through the wall of the barn where the still was located and flying off through the air. The boiler hit the nearby farmhouse of Fred Danner, driving a ten-foot-wide hole through the home before it landed in a field. Local firemen and citizens quickly put out the fire which the explosion had started in the barn. State police later reported that "the still was an elaborate affair, made for large scale production."

Danner, his wife and their seven children were tossed out of bed when the boiler hit their house, and the children were hit with debris as it passed in front of their bedrooms. Fortunately, they were only slightly injured. The same was not true for the men tending the still, which had a 10,000-gallon capacity. Both were killed, and one was tossed 450 feet away from the barn. They were "mangled beyond recognition" and remained unidentified. Authorities had little to work with. One corpse had a gold ring marked "R. G." and there were some "laundry marks" on their clothing. Woodstown police chief William Pennel posited that the boiler "probably went dry with an exceedingly hot fire under it and the accumulated heat caused the explosion."

Prohibition agents from Camden arrested Danner, and told reporters they might charge him with manslaughter due to the deaths. He, in turn, said that the two men to whom he had leased the barn, who had not given him their names, said they were going to make tallow in the building and that he had no idea they were distilling alcohol. He was subsequently released.

CHAPTER 10

1932-A Classy Con Man

New Jersey has produced more than its share of bizarre characters over the years, and James Edward Duncan has to rate as one of the most notable. In 1932, Duncan, a twenty-year-old New Jersey rum runner, shot and killed a man who tried to hijack his load of liquor, and was subsequently tried for second degree murder, convicted and sentenced to life in Trenton state prison. While incarcerated, Duncan began a business making plastic costume jewelry pins out of melted down toothbrushes. Sold around the country by the warden, the jewelry made the prison $90,000. During World War II he volunteered as a human guinea pig who contracted sleeping sickness, dengue fever and sand-fly fever so army physicians could study those diseases, and was paroled in 1946 for his contribution to the war effort.

After his release, Duncan left New Jersey and moved to Ketchikan, Alaska, where he became a pressman and then advertising manager of *Alaska Sportsman* magazine. In 1947 Duncan opened the Curb Lunch, a hamburger joint that also sold his costume jewelry and apparently had a back room used for illegal gambling and liaisons with local prostitutes. He was arrested for burglary in 1954, and after the charges were dropped, returned to New Jersey to open "Storybook Land" in Egg Harbor. A restless soul, Duncan moved on in another year to California where he ran a couple of restaurants before returning to Ketchikan, where he became a crab and long line fisherman and rented some rooms above a bar for an illegal gambling operation. Duncan died in Ketchikan in 1983 at the age of sixty-eight, variously remembered as a smooth-talking con artist from New Jersey by some, and a charming mystery man by others.

A Fugitive from a Chain Gang

Robert Elliot Burns was born in Palisades, New Jersey, in 1892. Burns served in World War I as a medic and on his return, was a "shell shocked and war draggled soldier from the front." He could not find a job and, undoubtedly suffering from PTSD, wandered across the country. He was involved in a robbery that netted $5.81 in Georgia in 1922, was arrested, tried, found guilty and sentenced to six to ten years of hard labor on a chain gang.

Burns escaped from the chain gang, traveled to Chicago, became an editor and publisher of *Greater Chicago* magazine and ended up marrying his landlady, who turned him in when he became interested in another woman. He agreed to waive fighting extradition to Georgia when he was promised he would only be imprisoned for ninety days, but ended up back on the chain gang, from which he escaped again in 1930.

Following Burns' second flight he headed back home to New Jersey, where he worked at odd jobs in Newark while writing a book on his experiences. Burns was arrested again in Newark on December 15, 1932. The Georgia State Prison Board demanded that the state's governor ask for Burns' extradition, but New Jersey Governor A. Harry Moore refused to extradite him to "the Goober State," as one newspaper called it. In 1945, Burns received a parole and pardon from the Governor of Georgia. He died in 1955, and is buried in Beverley National Cemetery in New Jersey.

Burns' memoir, *I am a fugitive from a Georgia Chain Gang*, was published as a magazine serial and then as a book in 1932. He was portrayed by Paul Muni in a 1932 film based on the book, and by Val Kilmer in a television movie in 1987.

The Child Slave of Camden

The press called Lena Persiana (aka Persiano) "a 12-year-old slave" and she was indeed confined to the basement of her Camden New Jersey home, where she "made lamp shades for her parents to sell." The story broke on

July 22, 1932, and was carried by newspapers around the country over the next two weeks. When interviewed, Lena "recalled vividly the day her mother chained her when a little more than ten years old. She told reporters that "mother said I was running around with boys and then she put a chain around my ankle. I wasn't out with a boy at all."

It all came out when Lena broke the lock on her chain and ran away in July, 1932 – to the offices of the Camden Society for the Prevention of Cruelty to Children, where she met Mrs. Louise Walsh. Mrs. Walsh soon arranged a court hearing in which Lena's father Anthony, who owned a pool room, defended the chaining by claiming that it was necessary since "the cruelty society wouldn't let us beat her anymore. She just kept running away."

Mrs. Walsh testified that "the Persianas, [who had six other apparently unchained children], evidently believe that Lena should have no amusement at all. They compel her to wrap lamp shades in all her spare time and when school is in session she falls asleep in class." Interestingly she had not complained to her teachers nor had her teachers inquired regarding her problem.

The judge remanded Lena to the custody of the court, until a "private home" with "merciful foster parents" or adoption could be found. The Persianas apparently kept on having children and Lena apparently reconciled with her parents eventually, as she is listed, as Lena Rogers, as a surviving sibling of twelve children when her twenty-year-old brother Frank, at the time a plumber's helper, was killed in a gun battle on a Camden street in May, 1955.

The Petting Party Bandits

In the years after World War I, adults raised in the 1890s and the early years of the new century were appropriately horrified by the conduct of young people of the day. There were short skirts, bobbed hair, drinking and, worst of all, "petting parties" that were spreading across America, in woods and fields and "lovers' lanes" throughout the decade and into the next.

There was hope, though, that some of this apparent reckless behavior could be stifled in New Jersey, or at least that was the message Mrs. Charles A. Prickett conveyed to the New Jersey Federation of Women's Clubs chapter in Pitman, New Jersey, on November 12, 1932. According to Mrs. Prickett, the Jersey Mosquito would enforce proper morality in the state's outdoors. She told the assembled ladies that "Swarms of healthy, ambitious mosquitos will see to it that there never is an epidemic of 'petting' in New Jersey."

Well, not quite. Especially after the first frost. A few weeks before the ladies were assured that petting would not become a Jersey thing, there had been a rather violent outcome of a petting party in a lovers' lane near Clementon, New Jersey, a town better known for melting precious metals over charcoal fires than being a love nest. It seemed that some thugs from Philadelphia had been robbing couples parked in rural areas at gunpoint, and some New Jersey State Police officers at the Berlin Barracks thought they had a solution.

The solution involved Trooper Stanley H. Austin "dressing up as a girl" and then, with Trooper Ray Osborne playing a "boyfriend," parking in a car along a country side road known locally as a lover's lane. Austin was armed with two revolvers and Osborne had a shotgun. Additional insurance was provided by Trooper Eric Hossek, who hid in the nearby brush with another shotgun.

The "petting party bandits" took the bait on October 29, 1932. A car screeched to a halt alongside the "petting" Troopers and two men jumped out with guns and climbed aboard the parked car's running board. One gunman pointed a handgun at Trooper Austin's head and demanded money. Osborne fired his shotgun in the robber's face, killing him instantly. Hossek stepped out of the woods and shot the second bandit. The getaway car immediately took off, with three surviving occupants, towards Camden, drawing fire from the three troopers. While the escaped bandits were not captured, it is probably safe to say that the survivors of the crew thought twice the next time they were considering leaving Philadelphia to prey on New Jersey lovers.

Following the shootout, a news photographer took a picture of State Police officers inspecting the body of one of the foiled robbers shortly after the encounter. Trooper Austin, still dressed in a woman's hat and fur collared coat, can be seen in the photograph.

CHAPTER 11

1933- The Strange Case of Bradway Brown

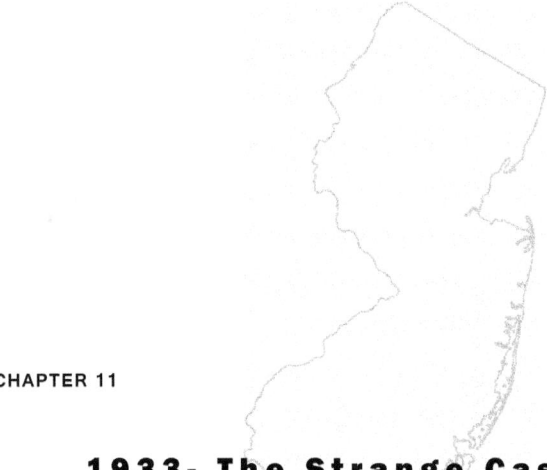

On the night of January 16, 1933, the police, called by neighbors who heard yelling and several shots, found twenty-eight-year-old Bradway Brown, "socially prominent scion of a prominent Moorestown family" and a printing company executive in the family business in Philadelphia, dead in the living room of his house in Cinnaminson. There was a .32 caliber Colt revolver with four empty cartridge cases in its chambers and with its muzzle stuffed with dirt laying nearby.

The police found Brown's car in the garage, with its headlights on and a still warm engine. An initial assessment that Brown's death was a suicide was dismissed after it was discovered that one of his two bullet wounds was in his back, and his own gun was discovered in an upstairs room. The conclusion was that he had been shot in the garage and then dragged into the house.

There was a suggestion in some quarters that some sort of conspiracy was afoot, and, as is usually the case, the conspiracy theorists associated a number of incidents and individuals that would appear seemingly unrelated to a more astute analyst. Among the points raised were that Brown had testified at the inquest into the apparent murder-suicide of two of his friends, Ruth Wilson and Horace Roberts, back in 1929, and had allegedly commented to friends after a few drinks that there was more to the story, and that Brown's father had committed suicide in 1931. Just how these incidents were supposed to be connected was not clear.

In February, 1933, Horace Roberts' father, Horace Roberts Sr., stated that he believed the three deaths were "linked," by a "strong connection," and demanded a new inquest. He said that "thirteen individuals" including police officials, but who he refused to name, had provided him with "information." It was rumored that Horace Sr., who had lost money in the depression, was attempting to collect an insurance policy on his son, which had been invalidated due to the verdict of suicide. The senior Roberts' allegations were eventually dismissed and he subsequently conceded that there was no real evidence to sustain his initial assumption.

Master detective Ellis Parker was on the case however, and he would doggedly pursue all leads until he solved it. Initially, Parker went along publicly with the suicide theory, but later claimed that he had never believed it and merely used it to give the murderer a false sense of security. When he found no expended bullet in the wall of the room where Brown's body was discovered, he concluded that the killing took place outside the house. The bullet was found in an old wooden boat in the garage.

Parker also found two hats in the garage. One was Brown's but the other was not. It was the "Clark Gable model" Adam hat, and it appeared that the owner had blond hair – and dandruff. Although the Colt revolver used to kill Brown had had its serial numbers filed, they were still visible on close inspection and were traced to an Illinois mechanic, who had reported it stolen some time before.

Despite the presence of physical evidence, rumors continued to swirl, and it was not until April of 1934 that the case was finally solved, with the assistance of Pennsylvania authorities and the continual assiduous work of Ellis Parker. It turned out that Brown had apparently surprised two Philadelphians, Edward Adamski and Arthur Szewczak, known as the "after dinner burglars," who had been responsible for a series of similar crimes, and they had shot him. They had escaped from a subsequent burglary, but an associate had been shot and killed by the police, providing clues to the identity of his friends. Adamski was arrested in Newark and brought to Mount Holly, but escaped from the Mount Holly Jail.

The search led to Philadelphia, where both men were captured and then brought to Mount Holly for trial. A mountain of circumstantial evidence compiled by Parker, coupled with the testimony of Solomon

Lutz, a barber who had rented the robbers the getaway car for $5, sealed the case. Lutz had initially been charged as a participant, but further investigation had established his innocence. Adamski pleaded "nolo contendere" and received a twenty-year prison sentence. Szewczak went to trial, was convicted and sentenced to life in prison.

Death due to Socrates

Beatrice La Falcia walked into a Newark police station on February 1, 1933 and told the desk sergeant she had just killed a man and locked his body in her apartment. She then placed a revolver and the key to the apartment on the desk.

La Falcia was taken into custody and detectives proceeded to her residence, where they found the body of thirty-one-year-old pool room proprietor Charles Kermis in the kitchen "shot through the head at close range." There was a note on the kitchen table that read "I, Charles Kermis, the undersigned, at present being in my sane mind and having read this statement do solemnly swear that it is the truth and it is all my fault. I have alienated the affections of Victor La Falcia from his wife Beatrice. I am now signing this statement as true and do so of my own free will." There was no signature and the note was not written by Kermis.

Beatrice had apparently written the "confession" and shot Kermis when he refused to sign it. When asked by police how Kermis had "alienated the affections" of Victor, she said that the pool hall owner was a "student of ancient Greek philosophy and had monopolized all the attentions of her husband by his discussion of Socrates." There may well have been another reason, but if so, it went unsaid.

In 1940, Beatrice La Falcia was listed as an inmate of the New Jersey State Mental Hospital.

The Bootlegger Murders that Come Back to Lindbergh

The rooms were first rate—a suite in the top floor of the Elizabeth Carteret Hotel, leased at $150 a week (about $2,700 in today's money) by an alcohol entrepreneur known as James Feldman, aka Max Hassell, whose real name was Mendel Gassel. On April 12, 1933, they found Feldman/Gassel, a close friend of bootlegger Al Lillien, recently killed in Atlantic Highlands, dead in the doorway of the suite with three bullets in his head. His associate, Joseph, aka "Max" Greenberg, was found "slumped in a chair" with five bullets in him, his hand on a pistol in his pocket that he had not had the time to draw. The motive for the murders was not robbery, as investigating officers found almost $2,000 in Greenberg's pockets. Police and reporters, looking around the apartment in the aftermath of the killings, also discovered "several bottles of liquor, a keg of beer, a quantity of flashy raiment and eight sets of golf clubs."

Irving "Waxey Gordon" Wexler, who was apparently registered in another room as "Mr. Rogers," had apparently just missed the massacre, leaving the apartment after conferring with his two friends and associates on business concerns before the gunmen arrived. No one at the hotel, workers or residents, admitted to seeing or hearing anything, and there were no immediate arrests. Several years later the New York City Police Department arrested notorious gangster Frankie Carbo, allegedly employed by "Murder Incorporated," who was also among those suspected of shooting bootlegger Mickey Duffy in Atlantic City in 1931, on suspicion of being the triggerman. Carbo was never tried for any of the killings, however.

So why were Gassel and Greenberg killed? They controlled a number of illicit breweries in New York and New Jersey, including one in Harrison. Although Prohibition did not end until the formal repeal of the Eighteenth Amendment at the end of the year, on March 22, 1933, President Franklin D. Roosevelt signed an amendment to the Volstead Act permitting the legal production of 3.2% alcohol content beer, which led to the legalization of breweries, some of which had remained in business illegally during Prohibition and were ready to start legal production immediately. Gangsters scrambled to find respectable front men to operate the new businesses, and there was apparently considerable competition among them. One theory holds that Gassel had a contract out on Longy Zwillman, a notable Newark mobster, and that Zwillman had him killed in response, and that Zwillman subsequently took over the dead man's northern New Jersey breweries.

There were a couple of curious footnotes to the Elizabeth Carteret Hotel murders. In the aftermath, the Union county prosecutor discovered that Gassel, Greenberg and Zwillman all had concealed carry handgun permits issued by Asbury Park police chief H. L. Byram. When questioned, Byram defended his actions by saying that he approved their applications because they included references from "reputable citizens," including

"Thomas Fury, former Monmouth County Grand Jury Commissioner," but he promised to be "more careful" in the future. He failed to comment on whether he knew the people he granted the permits to were well known gangsters.

The most bizarre sideshow was the story concocted by Gaston B. Means, perhaps the most notorious swindler and poseur of early 20th century America. Means, who was on trial for swindling a wealthy woman out of ransom money that was supposed to gain the living Lindbergh baby's freedom from captivity, asserted that Gassel and Greenberg had engineered the Lindbergh kidnapping. As was his wont, Means (author of a book accusing President Warren G. Harding's wife of murdering him) spun a labyrinthine story involving a number of people, all conveniently dead, asserting that the Lindbergh baby was alive and well in Juarez, Mexico, had arrived there via South Carolina and El Paso, Texas and that the ransom money could be found in Gassel's safe deposit box at the Elizabethport Banking Company under the name of Max Hassell. Investigators did find $213,500 in cash in the box, but none of it matched the serial numbers of the ransom money bills.

Interestingly, both Waxey Gordon and Gaston B. Means were minor characters in the HBO series *Boardwalk Empire*.

The Missing "Dry Crusader"

Justice of the Peace Charles L. Carslake of Mount Holly, New Jersey, a former postmaster and Prohibition agent, disappeared in the pine woods and cranberry bogs near Chatsworth in June 1933.

In 1925, Carslake had been instrumental in one of the biggest Prohibition busts in New Jersey history, when he discovered between $300,000 and $500,000 worth of liquor on the barge *A. B. Blaters*, docked at Adams Wharf on Rancocas Creek near Bridgeboro, and arranged a raid with the New Jersey state police, with whom he had worked before. There were fifty-five men at the wharf and aboard the barge, some of them heavily armed, but they surrendered readily to Carslake and four state troopers, to whom they offered $15,000 each to forget what they found. The offer was turned down and the bootleggers were arrested and hauled to court in trucks, but quickly released on low bails of $200 to $500 each, paid in cash, and apparently using assumed names, disappeared. The alcohol reportedly mysteriously disappeared as well in the aftermath of the incident. Carslake, a faithful Quaker and an enthusiastic Prohibition agent who claimed that he had been "eased out of the service" because of his refusal to accept bribes, was a private detective at the time. A newspaper report stated that he had been "mysteriously dropped from the dry forces" due to being "framed up" by members of a "rum ring."

The fifty-nine-year-old Carslake had last been seen on June 22, when he bought gasoline at Harry Leek's gas station on the Speedwell-New Gretna Road. His abandoned car was discovered stuck on a lonely sand trail on June 27, with an empty gas tank and an empty pistol holster in the back seat. His hat and several handkerchiefs were found scattered along the road. Locals opined that Carslake may have tried to walk out of the woods after running out of gas and become disoriented, as his family said that he had not been feeling well for several days before he disappeared. Needless to say, considering his background story, others speculated more darkly. One account that characterized Carslake as a "dry crusader" mentioned that he had been "threatened with death by bootleggers" in the wake of the Rancocas Creek raid.

As was usually the case when things went awry in Burlington County back in those days, County Chief of Detectives Ellis Parker was called to the scene. Parker expressed doubt that Carslake would be found alive, considering "the thick underbrush and extensive bogs of the Chatsworth country." A local newspaper reminded readers that "it was in this dense morass that Emilio Carranza, Mexican 'goodwill' flier, crashed five years ago."

Working on the assumption that Carslake was possibly "lying exhausted somewhere among the bogs and pine barrens, in this most desolate part of the county," a massive search was launched. Hundreds of local residents, boy scouts, state troopers, game wardens and Civilian Conservation Corps workers combed the countryside where Carslake vanished, while a blimp from Lakehurst Naval Air Station searched from the air. As the days passed, the sense that the story would not turn out well increased, and a June 30 newspaper noted that searchers were being "guided by the slow circling of buzzards over a certain section of pine forest."

On July 5, Carslake's body was discovered in West Papoose Swamp, two miles from the nearest road and three miles from where his abandoned automobile was found. He was buried in the Columbus Cemetery in Burlington County. A state police investigation declared he had died of natural causes, but the rumors persisted.

A Riot in the Pharmacy

Maybe she caught on that something was afoot when he sprouted that too-cute Hitler moustache. No matter, she had ears, and "there were rumors around town, heads were nodding, tongues were wagging." And so Elizabeth Pfeiffer decided to visit her husband Ernst William Pfeiffer's pharmacy in Cresskill, New Jersey, one Saturday in June, 1933, when the store, and the town, was filled with weekend shoppers.

Elizabeth was suspicious that something was afoot, and, while her husband waited on customers, she walked around the pharmacy, randomly opening doors until she came to the bathroom, which was locked. She went to her husband and asked him "who is in there." His answer, "no one," did not satisfy her, and Elizabeth asked him for the key. He said he didn't have one, but that the merchant next door did. Elizabeth went to get the key and on her return, saw a woman leaving the bathroom and heading rapidly for the front door. It was Gladys Johnson Westervelt, daughter in law of Cresskill's mayor, who was estranged from her husband —and rumored to be Ernst's love interest.

The "plump, buxom, attractive" Gladys weighed in at 200 pounds, but the 110 pound Elizabeth went after her, swinging a belt and hitting her in the eye with the buckle. Gladys fell back screaming for help but Ernst kept on filling prescriptions while the customers stood transfixed by the battle. Elizabeth began to "hurl bottles and jars at her rival. Perfume, lilac, heliotrope and jasmine. Peppermint sticks. Ammonia, witch-hazel, turpentine, cod liver oil." Ernst finally tried to intervene, but was hit in the head with a jar of licorice and fell to the floor. As Gladys took advantage of the diversion to bolt outside, Elizabeth tossed a stamp machine through the front window.

Elizabeth cut her hand on the shattered glass, stopped to bandage it, and then, through the broken window, saw Gladys and her husband running down the street towards the railroad station, where they both boarded a waiting train. A few days later Ernst called her and asked "how is everything?" Elizabeth responded "come home and find out." Perhaps wisely, he didn't. She subsequently filed for child support for her two children.

It was the most exciting thing to happen in Cresskill since they closed Camp Merritt, the huge World War I transit base near the town, in 1920. A short time later a reporter commented that "if there had been a few motion picture cameras grinding in Cresskill, New Jersey, one Saturday not long ago, they could have made a reel of as humorous a comedy as anybody ever paid a quarter to see." Elizabeth Pfeiffer doubtless would not have agreed.

Who Tried to Blow Up the Congressman?

The congressman looks unhappy in the image the newspaper photographer took of him. So would anyone who discovered that a bomb had been hooked up to his car's ignition system. The congressman was Charles A. Eaton of New Jersey's Fifth District. On the morning of June 22, 1933, Joseph Galent, an employee on Eaton's Watchung estate, said that he noticed a wire sticking out from the congressman's car, opened the hood and discovered the bomb, composed of a pipe stuffed with dynamite and nitroglycerine, submerged it in water and called police.

Local and state law enforcement authorities, as well as the Department of Justice, conducted an investigation, and although several men were temporarily detained, with no detailed explanation as to why, no one appears to have ever been charged in the incident, although it made newspapers nationwide. A story in the local *Hopewell Herald* reported that the bomb "weighed 22 pounds and was made of a highly explosive substance with enough power in it to blow Mr. Eaton to atoms and completely destroy the other members of his family and surrounding buildings."

When questioned by journalists, Eaton said, "As I see it there are three possibilities. It may have been placed there by a practical joker. It may have been fixed up by someone who wanted to have a claim on my gratitude by saving my life. And it may have been placed there by someone who thinks our form of government is all wrong and that the best way to change it is to blow up some Congressmen." The fact that Galent allegedly picked up what he perceived as a bomb and submerged it in water in an apparent fearless act may lend some credence to Eaton's second speculation. On November 10, 1933, Eaton filed for bankruptcy, claiming liabilities of $160,924 and assets of $26,499. What this, if anything, had to do with the bomb incident is unknown.

Eaton, born in Nova Scotia in 1868, moved to the United States after he was ordained as a Baptist minister in 1894. He preached in Cleveland and New York and then worked as a journalist before moving to New

Jersey in 1909 and buying a dairy farm. Eaton served in Congress as a Republican from 1925 to 1953. Although an opponent of many New Deal programs, he got along personally with his Democratic colleagues and was often invited to the White House for discussions with Presidents Franklin D. Roosevelt and Harry Truman. Roosevelt appointed Eaton to the committee that drafted the United Nations treaty and he allied himself with Truman as a proponent of the Marshall Plan. Charles A. Eaton died shortly after retiring from Congress and is buried in Hillside Cemetery in Scotch Plains.

He "Landed Her a Wallop," and then...

A cautionary headline read "Tragedy Stalks the Playboys Who Marry Show Girls." There were a lot fewer playboys around in 1934, when the article made the Sunday papers, then there had been before the crash of 1929, but surely those remaining took heed. Perhaps not, though, as the narcissism that comes with the title is a powerful force.

Audrey Smith "was pretty, red-headed, with plenty of rhythm in her voice and walk. She wanted to be a tap and toe dancer." Audrey made a few appearances on stage between films at New York movie theaters and then was selected for the road company of the popular Broadway show, *Rose Marie*. In December, 1925, when *Rose Marie* was playing in Richmond, Virginia, the seventeen-year-old Audrey was introduced to twenty-eight-year-old Sheldon Clark at a speakeasy night club. To say the newly introduced couple had a whirlwind courtship would be an understatement to say the least. They married the next day and she resigned from her role in the show.

Sheldon, originally from Chicago, was the son of Sheldon Clark, vice president of Sinclair Oil. Being the son of the senior Clark seems to have been his career goal, and was certainly his occupation. With plenty of cash at his disposal, Sheldon could live anywhere he wanted, but brought his new bride to Red Bank, New Jersey, where they lived and had two children.

Sheldon became even more wealthy in 1930, due to the hard work it took to be born to a wealthy family. His mother, the former wife of Sheldon senior, was the daughter of the late New Jersey Republican Congressman Henry D. Loudenslager. When the congressman's widow passed away she left a significant estate to Sheldon, which included a mansion in Paulsboro, New Jersey, where the Clark family then moved. Whatever Sheldon wanted, Sheldon got. Shortly after his arrival in Paulsboro, he decided that he wanted to take a sleigh ride, even though it was summer. So he found an old wooden sleigh, hooked it up to his automobile, sat in it and had his chauffer drive him around town. His vanity did not go unnoticed.

On the night of November 20, 1933, Sheldon was playing pool in his basement billiard room with his cousin and a man who was working on his yacht. Audrey came downstairs and asked if he was having dinner with the family, and Sheldon brusquely responded that he was going out for dinner. They had words, and Audrey stormed upstairs. Sheldon followed and "landed her a wallop on the head with his billiard cue," breaking it and inflicting a six-inch wound in her head. She fell to the floor and he went downstairs again, tossed aside the broken cue, picked up a new one and continued to play.

According to Audrey, she grasped a nearby radiator to assist her in getting on her feet and, lo and behold, found one of her husband's guns, a 9-millimeter German Luger, conveniently sitting atop it, apparently with a round in the chamber and the safety off, allegedly positioned there to be readily available in case of a burglary. She later claimed she did not recall what happened next, and that everything was all a blur until she awoke in a hospital bed.

Witnesses, however, said that Audrey staggered to the basement stairs, and that Sheldon was standing at the foot of them. She aimed, pulled the trigger and Sheldon went down. She then screamed "I've shot you!" to which he responded "It's alright hon" as he fell down dead.

In the end, no one wanted Audrey prosecuted. The Gloucester County Grand Jury declined to indict her and, and although the case was to remain open indefinitely due to the fact that there was no statute of limitations on murder, "officials emphasized no action is contemplated." Audrey inherited the Paulsboro mansion and $50,000 (around a million dollars in today's currency), and apparently lived happily ever after.

A newspaper photo of Sheldon and the couple's two children has Audrey officially blanked out.

Gallery

(All photographs are from the author's collection, unless otherwise noted)

William d'Alton Mann (left), had his photo taken alongside John Clem, the legendary Civil War drummer boy, while attending the Gettysburg reunion of 1913. (*Library of Congress*)

The rum runner *Pokomoke* at a dock in Atlantic City.

Coast Guardsmen from the Cape May station aboard a patrol boat assigned to interdict rum runners in 1921.

This image of a smug Mrs. Mary M. Drischman, the "petticoat realty wizard," was "taken in a specially posed picture in her Palatial home in Atlantic City…exclusively for the Atlantic Foto Service."

Mrs. Alice Gerry Griswold, the "Baltimore social light [sic]," in a photo taken in her younger years.

Doris Brunen, wife of the murdered circus owner "Honest John Brunen" accused in his death.

Doris Brunen and her brother, Charles M. Powell, on trial in Mount Holly, New Jersey, for the murder of her husband, "Honest John" Brunen.

"Honest John" Brunen's sister, Elizabeth Jaeske (center), who testified that she had received a letter from him indicating that Doris was planning to murder him, leaving the Brunen home the day of her brother's funeral.

Hazel Brunen, daughter of "Honest John."

The late William Giberson, "taxi baron" and alleged transporter of bootleg booze, of Lakehurst, New Jersey.

Ivy Giberson, accused of murdering her husband.

Ivy Giberson being escorted into court by a Lakehurst detective.

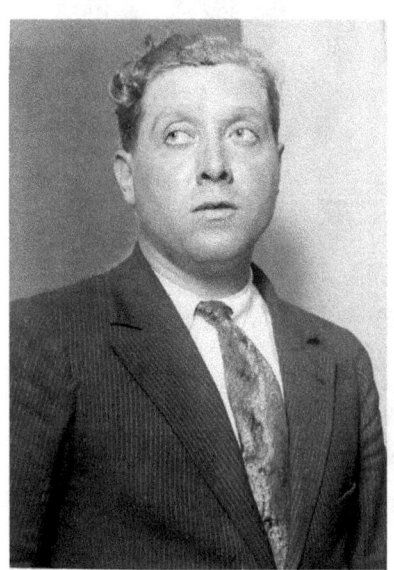

George Cline, the offended husband who shot "Handsome Jack" Bergen for having an affair with his wife.

Mrs. Mary Cline and her brother Charles Scullion. Charles was accused of being an accomplice in the murder of "Handsome Jack Bergen."

Teenaged Alice Thornton, spurned by her boyfriend "Handsome Jack Bergen" once he developed an interest in Mrs. Cline. She was also charged as an accomplice in the murder of "Handsome Jack" as prosecutors alleged she had lured him to the Cline home.

Mrs. Mary Cline being escorted into court by a detective.

"Handsome Jack" Bergen's wife and the mother of his daughter Margaret, whom he had deserted "I can't say a single good thing about my husband. He never did a good day's work in his life."

William S. Gilbert, Trenton's freelance traveling executioner, posing grimly as he began his career in 1922.

Virginia Verrier, the "Wanderlust" girl from Irvington, who, with her friend Georgiana Reid, took off on an attempted world tour. The press referred to the two as "high school flappers."

Caleb Hubbard, whose game of "playing Indian" led to a tragedy involving the deaths of two boys, including his brother, behind the Belmar Gas Works.

"Gas Magnate" Martin Maloney's Spring Lake estate.

Martin Wright, the wheelchair murderer, looking dapper in his derby at Newark police headquarters.

Mrs. Martha Martin, wife of the deranged Bloomfield killer Frank Martin, at the time of his trial.

Federal agents examine Fred Wiegand's sophisticated counterfeiting operation in Elizabeth.

William J. Clark, the jeweler and Ku Klux Klansman who was literally hammered to death in his garage.

William Clark's widow, Mrs. Priscilla Clark, and her mother, Mrs. Caroline Kent.

Mrs. Priscilla Clark, looking appropriately doleful at the trial of Joseph Cowan, her husband's accused murderer.

Roscoe Ziegler and Margaret "Peggy" Roberts, caught by a photographer in El Paso, Texas after they fled New Jersey.

A rare photo of a Klan ceremony in Jersey City in 1939, conducted by New Jersey Grand Dragon Arthur Hornbui Bell.

Madeline Clearwater Montgomery, whose former fiancée Anthony Sheridan shot her in her bed.

Patrolman Anthony Sheridan, the Newark police officer who shot his former fiancée, in his World War I Marine Corps uniform.

Great Swamp Lane, the sandy road where
Dr. A. William Lilliendahl was shot to death.

A police reenactment of the position in his car
in which Dr. Lilliendahl's body was found.

"Chicken fancier" Willis Beach, the accused murderer of Dr. Lilliendahl and lover of his wife, relaxes in court.

A closeup view of Willis Beach.

Margaret Lilliendahl at court during a break in her trial.

Alfred Lilliendahl,
Margaret's son.

Dr. Lilliendahl's brother and
his wife at the trial.

The Meisterknecht widows feuding at Fairview Cemetery in Middletown. The inventor's body was temporarily interred in a Fairview vault until custody could be determined. In the end, his first wife, Susan, received the remains and brought them to Yonkers for burial.

Herbert O. Meisterknecht, the eccentric and mysterious inventor murdered in Highlands.

Susan Meisterknecht, the inventor's first wife, and their daughter.

"Lifetime Jake" and his seventy-nine-year-old mother.

Some of the products of the woodworking factory of "Lifetime Jake."

The Freehold house where violinist Nikita Evanenko was murdered by neighbor and rival Steve Demick.

Eva Petroski, the love interest source of the feud between Evanenko and Demick.

U.S. Radium president Clarence V. Lee and vice president Horace Baker leaving the courthouse in Newark where the case against their corporation's malfeasance was being tried on June 6, 1928.

The U.S. Radium Company factory in Orange as it looked in the early 1990s, before the Super Fund cleanup.

The site of the U.S. Radium factory in 2016.

A mug shot of Joseph Rado, a member of "Jersey Kid" James McBrien's bandit gang that robbed the Public Service Coordinated Transport Company payroll and murdered an employee in Newark in 1928. Four members of the gang, including Rado, were executed on July 22, 1930.

Long time New Jersey executioner Robert Elliott, (center) enters the State Prison in Trenton to go to work.

Robert Woodward, who discovered the barrel murder victim floating in the Delaware River.

"Torch murderer" Henry C. Campbell/Close.

Torch murderer Campbell/Close under arrest and escorted by two Union County detectives.

Torch murder victim Margaret Brown. Campbell/Close was a suspect in this case, but evidence was inconclusive and it was never solved.

Michael Cicero of Pitman, New Jersey, alleged driver for bootleggers, who was murdered in 1929.

The death car where Michael Cicero's body was found.

Raymond Kugler in police custody for questioning after he claimed he killed Studeman.

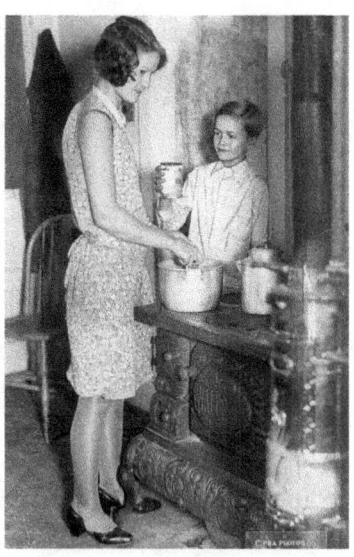

Margaret Kugler after her release from jail following the killing of William Studeman, cooking dinner for her son Raymond.

Alloway New Jersey's postmaster and fife and drum corps leader Lewis Collier, shot by Lillian Fleming because his band was too noisy.

New Jersey Governor A. Harry Moore (l) and Asbury Park mayor Clarence Hetrick (r) greet "Queen Titania" at the Asbury Park Baby Parade in 1929.

The *Morro Castle* on the beach at Asbury Park, September, 1934.

Mayor Hetrick's Convention Hall in the 1930s.

Horace Roberts, perpetrator of the murder-suicide in Moorestown.

Ruth Wilson, murdered by Horace Roberts in Moorestown.

Ruth Wilson in happier days, playing golf.

Flossie London, the self-proclaimed Voodoo victim in Atlantic County.

Bernard Toner, the "dopey looking gangster" in the Elizabeth Police Headquarters.

Ritchie "the Boot" Boiardo in 1930 at the time he was ambushed and wounded.

The garage where the beer was pumped to from the Hensler brewery in Newark after the Prohibition agent raid.

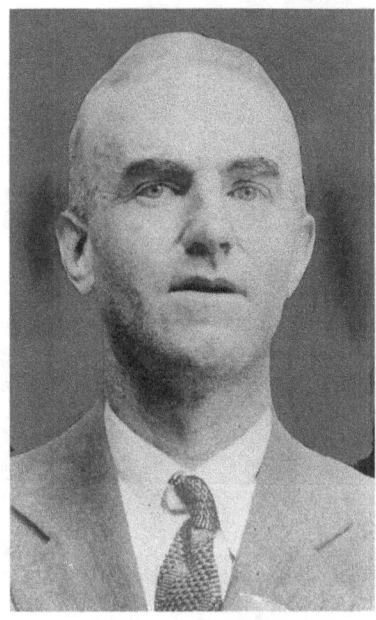

Frank Demarest Crawford, East Orange wife killer.

Harry K. Thaw (l) on the beach in Atlantic City in 1930.

Evelyn Nesbit after her marriage to Harry K. Thaw in 1905. (*Library of Congress*)

Mary McClyment in custody after the shooting of Edward Nicholson at the tragic "Whoopee Party."

Mary McClyment in court at the time of her trial.

William Frazer, perpetrator of the "parade murder."

Phoebe Stader, victim and deceased passenger in the "parade murder."

Ira Jensen, William Frazer's cousin who thought Phoebe was "shy," but then discovered that "she was dead."

William Frazer in custody in North Carolina before his extradition to New Jersey.

Charlotte Nixon-Nirdlinger, nee Charlotte Isabel Nash.

Fred Nixon-Nirdlinger, the insanely jealous husband.

Charlotte, (r) her children and their nursemaid on her return to Atlantic City in 1931.

The Nixon-Nirdlinger home in Atlantic City in 1931.

Ruth Peggy Stark of Syracuse, New York, Phillip Knapp's fiancée until he disappeared.

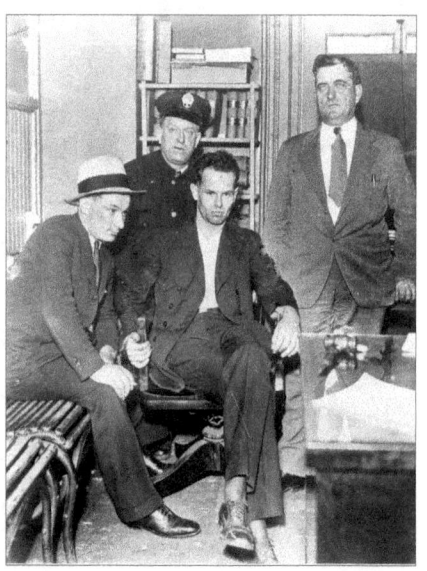

This photo, taken in the West Orange Police Station on July 2, 1931, shows (left to right) Detective Joseph Hixenski, Nassau PD, Patrolman Thomas Higgins of West Orange PD, Phillip Knapp and Lieutenant Heslin of the Nassau County, New York, PD.

Phillip Knapp in custody of Captain Emil Morse of the Nassau County Police.

William Coughlin being removed from a launch to shore
on his way to the hospital in Camden.

Rosenthal kidnappers Theodore Adinolfi (l) and Albert Sileo
in police custody in Newark.

The confused waiter Clarence Green, wrongfully arrested in Atlantic City in the Rosenthal case and Betty Green, acquitted of the crime.

Mickey Duffy, bootlegger and numbers racketeer of Philadelphia and Atlantic City, who met his end in the city by the sea.

Fred Danner's farmhouse, showing the results of the passage of the boiler from the whiskey still explosion that "shook the countryside for miles around" Woodstown, on December 2, 1931.

James Duncan, the eccentric con man.

Robert Elliot Burns after his arrest in Newark in December, 1932.

The December 29, 1932, hearing in the New Jersey Assembly on Georgia's request to extradite Robert Elliot Burns. Governor Moore is identified by the backwards "B" while Burns is identified by the "A."

Robert Elliot Burns' wife and children learn of his 1945 pardon by the governor of Georgia from a phone call by a *Newark Evening News* reporter.

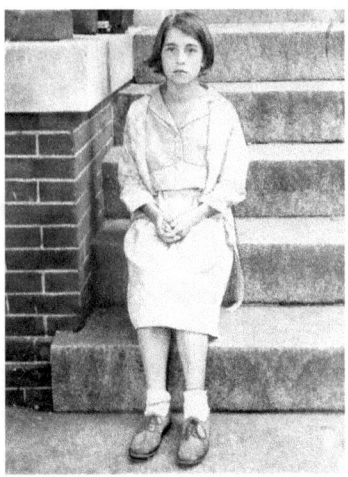

Lena Persiana, the twelve-year-old child "slave" in Camden in 1932.

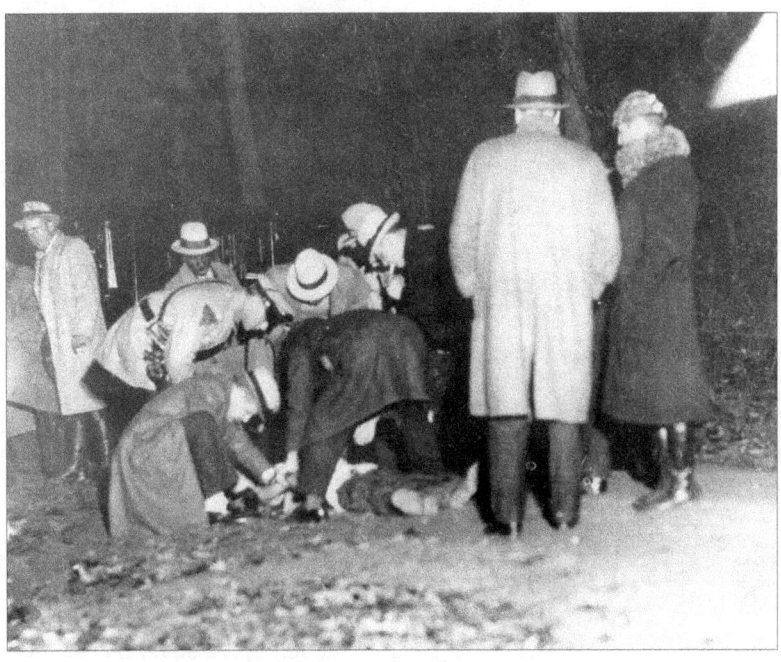

Police officers inspecting the body of one of the foiled "Petting Party" robbers shortly after the encounter. On the right is Trooper Austin, still dressed in a woman's hat and fur collared coat.

Horace Roberts Sr., who thought there was a link between the killing of Bradway Brown and the deaths of his son, Horace Roberts Jr. and his fiancée Ruth Wilson.

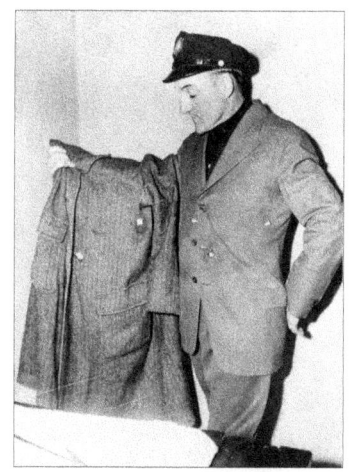

A police officer wears the coat and holds the overcoat Bradway Brown was wearing the night he was shot. Marks show the bullet holes.

Bradway Brown's coffin leaves his mother's home in Moorestown on its way for burial.

Bradway Brown's widow leaves the courtroom.

The jury inspects the garage where the Bradway Brown shooting took place.

Arthur Szewczak escorted into court by Burlington County detectives.

Solomon Lutz, who rented his car to the Bradway Brown killers, but was cleared of any criminal charges.

Beatrice La Falcia, the philosopher killer, in a Newark police station.

The Elizabeth Carteret Hotel, where Mendel Gassel and Max Greenberg met their ends.

"Waxey Gordon" Wexler, who left the hotel before his colleagues met their ends.

A search party seeking Charles Carslake, who disappeared in the Pinelands.

The Pfeiffer family, in happier times, before the pharmacy riot.

Congressman Charles Eaton looks at the site of the bomb planted in his car.

Sheldon Clark and family, with Audrey blanked out.

The death car in which Millard Edouard met his end.

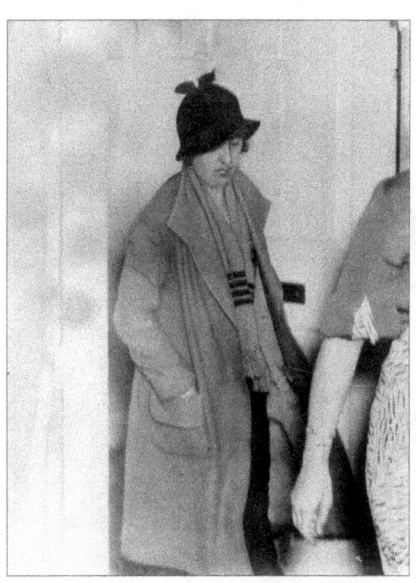

Ella May Edouard in her garb of "a big sweater and a pair of men's trousers, with an overcoat over that" in custody for questioning after her husband's death.

Millard Edouard, the multiple marriage con man.

Penns Grove National Bank, scene of the 1934 robbery.

This photo, taken at the time of the bank robbery arrest, shows, from left to right, Detective Benjamin Simon, John Farley, Charles Kent, Harry Greenberg, Rose Greenberg and Detective Clifford Del Rossi.

The getaway car used for the Penns Grove payroll robbery surrounded by the local deer hunter posse that discovered it in the Pinelands.

Detectives display the guns and robbery loot from the Penns Grove robbery.

The Schwartz liquor store in Carteret in 1934.

Vernon Shelters in a Newark Police station.

Eleanor Coleman.

German immigrants (right to left) Richard Rost, a 40-year-old Hoboken, New Jersey, stamp dealer, his 30-year-old wife Hildegarde and 41-year-old stationary engineer Paul Herman of Union City at police headquarters.

Edward Metelski (l), and Paul Semenkewitz in Newark Police Headquarters in a photo taken shortly after their arrest. The police claimed that they resisted arrest, and hence got "mussed up."

Emma Heisler being questioned at Camden Police Headquarters, shortly before she jumped out the window.

Camden City Hall in the 1930s. Heisler jumped out of a fifth floor window.

The *Morro Castle* from Asbury Park's Convention Hall in September, 1934.

William Scott (l), a gardener, and Robert Mantzinger a 22-year old plumber of Glen Cove, the trespassers on the *Morro Castle*.

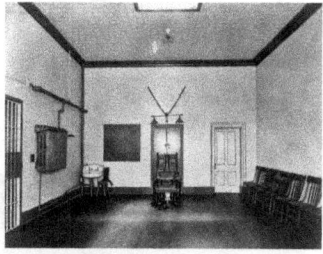

The New Jersey electric chair, "Old Smokey" photographed prior to the Hauptmann execution.

Edgar H. Crockett seated in Woodbridge police headquarters with Detective Sergeant George Keating.

The "Pompton Lakes Gang" cabin after the raid.

The Crempa home in Scotch Plains.

Camelia Crempa.

Mr. Crempa being carried into his first court appearance after the shooting.

Mr. Crempa and his daughter Camelia in a subsequent court appearance.

A Newark policeman investigates the scene of the Palace Chop House shootings.

Father Cornelius McInerney, who baptized and gave the last rites of the Catholic Church to the "Dutchman" talks with reporters as he leaves Newark City Hospital.

Ellis Parker, the famous Burlington County detective.

Paul Wendel (r) and his attorney after his return to Trenton.

Ellis Parker Jr. and his wife, during the Parker trial for kidnapping Wendel.

The car Gladys MacKnight and Donald Wightman drove around in after killing her mother, complete with tennis racket intended for the game they never got to play.

Gladys and Donald being arraigned at Jersey City police headquarters.

Elizabeth Fuery, waiting to testify at the MacKnight and Wightman murder trial.

Joe Fay, president of the Hoisting Engineers' Union.

Samuel Rosoff (center with glasses) with his attorney, Jonah Goldstein, to his right.

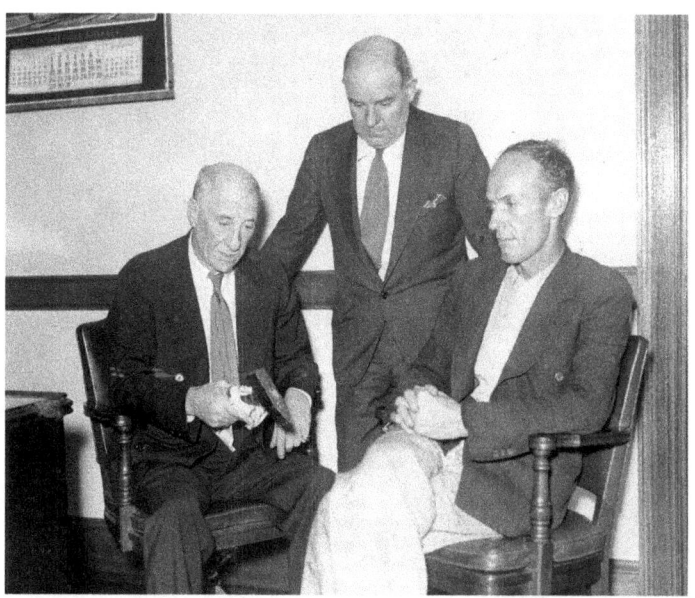

Lloyd Pusey, seated on the right, Linden Police Chief Hickey standing and Union County Prosecutor Abe David seated on the left, holding the hammer Pusey used on his wife.

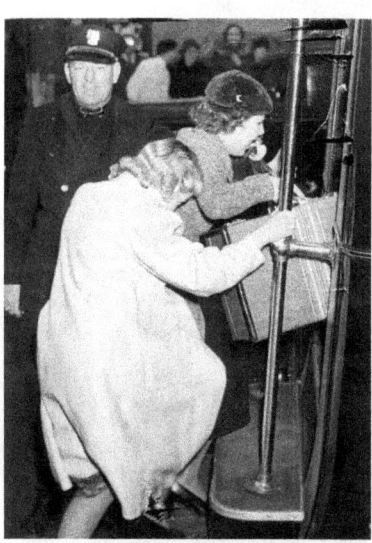

Two alleged prostitutes boarding a patrol wagon that will take them from the Camden federal court back to the Camden County Jail following their indictments.

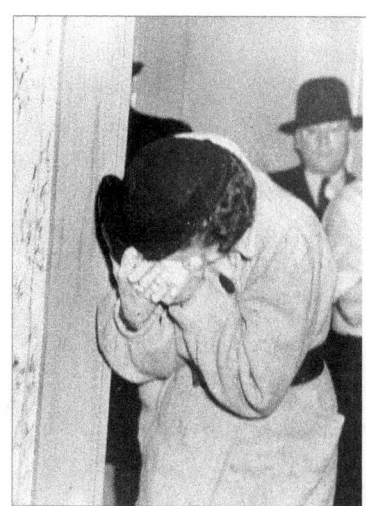

Peggy Stein leaves the courtroom in November, 1937, after testifying in the trial of her foster mother, charged with transporting her from Philadelphia to Atlantic City for the purpose of prostitution.

Hobo con man James Pride and his family in Nutley.

Margaret Drennan under arrest at the Woodbidge police station.

Margaret Drennan confers with her attorney during her trial.

The jury that determined Margaret Drennan's fate.

A happy Margaret Drennan leaves the courtroom free after her acquittal.

Ethel Sohl (l) and Genevieve Owens in custody after their capture.

Ethel Sohl after her capture.

Ethel Sohl entering court.

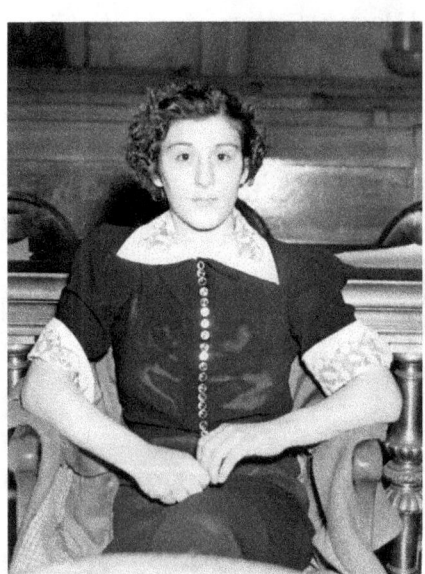
Genevieve Owens in court.

Genevieve Owens' mother (center) escorted from the court room after the guilty verdict was returned.

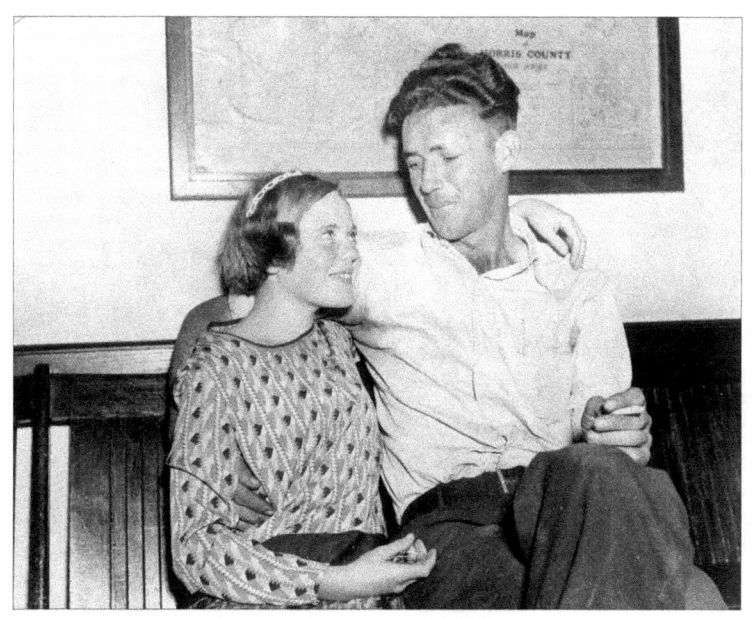

Theodore Flatt and his 12-year-old wife Helen in the Netcong police station.

Myrtle Flatt, 19 years old at the time of this photo, had married Flatt when she was 13.

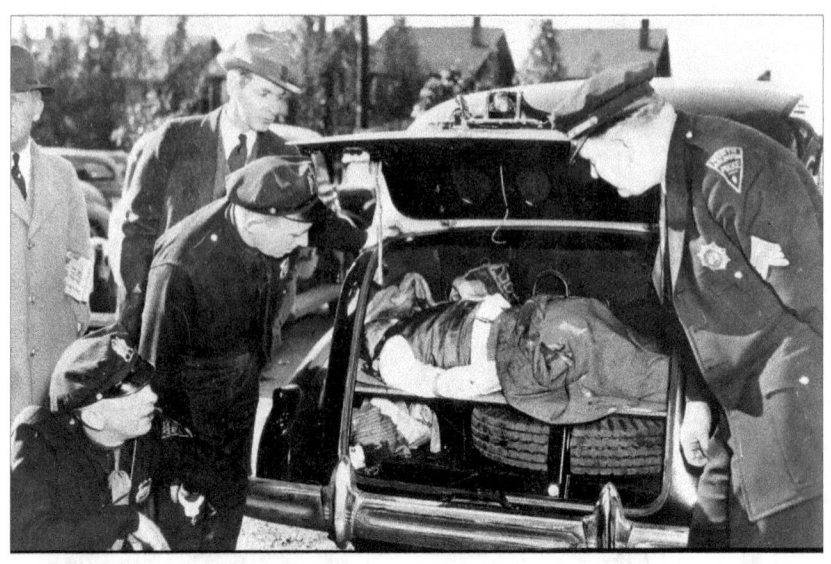

Doctor Littlefield's body discovered by North Arlington police in the trunk of his car.

Doctor Littlefield.

Paul Dwyer in custody in the North Arlington police station.

Mrs. Littlefield.

Barbara Carroll.

Francis Carroll (center) on his way into court.

New Jersey Congressman Edward Aloysius Kenney.

The arc of Congressman Kenney's swift descent to death.

Congressman Kenney's widow Elizabeth gazes at his photo during her failed campaign to replace him in the House of Representatives.

Gaston B. Means (center) and his attorneys at the trial for the Lindbergh swindle.

Joe DiBlasio, chain gang fugitive and hero.

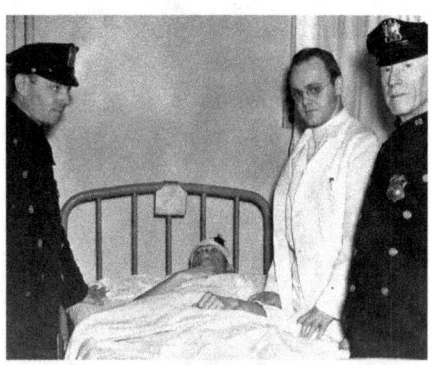

John Kern, one of the "newspaper bandit" brothers, in a heavily guarded hospital bed.

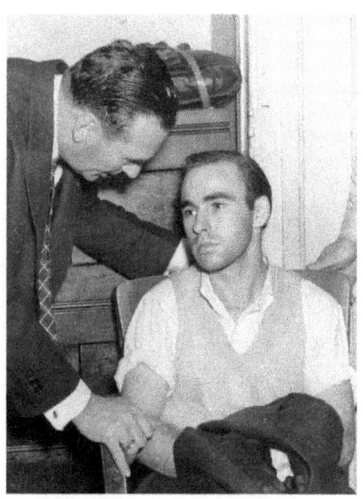

Frank Cheeseman being interrogated by an Asbury Park detective after his arrest.

Ann Clark at Cheeseman's trial for having murdered her mother.

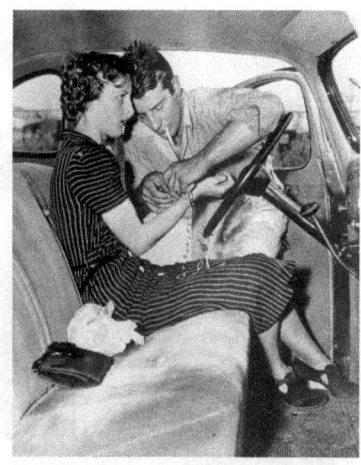

Gene Tortariello chaining Wilma Leaycroft to the steering wheel of his car.

Tortariello and the "electric umbrella."

Tortariello jumps into the Shrewsbury River.

Samuel Rushmore, the eccentric inventor.

Frank Hague Jr. being sworn in as a "lay judge" on the New Jersey Court of Errors and Appeals.

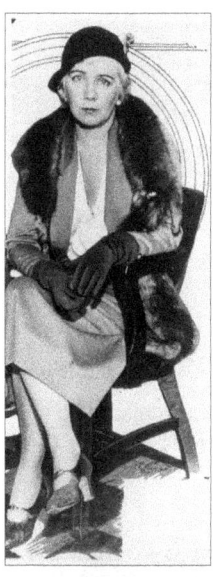

Hazel Rushmore in divorce court.

Samuel Crispino, alleged member of the Philadelphia murder ring that killed Arena.

Anna Arena (l), whose husband never returned from his boat ride off Sea Isle City and Rose Davis, also suspected of having her husband murdered, in court during the Rodia trial.

Mary Jobes Webb saying goodbye to her doll.

Wanda Dworecki.

Peter Shewchuck and Iron Mike Dworecki in custody.

Joe Rocco, aka Joe Rock, a material witness at the trial.

Florence and Nucky at the Miss America Contest in 1939.

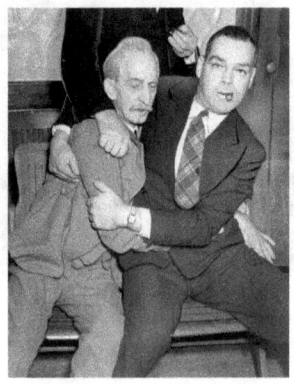

John Butler subdued by Councilman Paul Finkel.

The Asbury Park Post Office in a photo taken the day after the 1940 robbery.

Lieutenant Colonel
Leo P. Gaffney.

Bund members (l) separated from
protesting veterans in Union City.

Left to right, August Klapprott, Bund Attorney Wilbur Keegan and
national Bund leader, Camden-born Gerhard Wilhelm Kunze.

Nicholas Casale confers with
Representative Hartley in 1929.

Nicholas Casale on the
steps of the Capitol in 1939.

Michael Tenerelli, aka "Mickey Blair."

Samuel "Cappy" Hoffman.

Woodburn Miller at the time of his first arrest in 1940.

Jean Bush.

Carl Emil Ludwig Krepper.

Eugene Davis, Nutley's "Bobby sox cop."

Daniel Molnar in custody - Woodbridge.

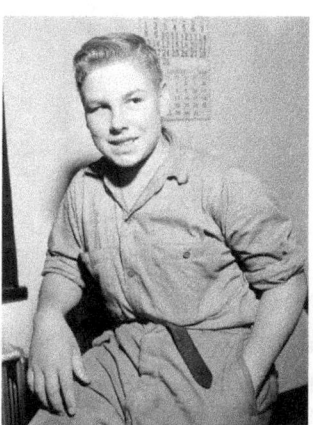

Buel Leberman in the Elizabeth police headquarters.

New York State Police brought their bloodhounds to the search for Bernard Doak.

Bernard Doak in custody at the Somerville State Police Headquarters. His captor, Trooper Louis Masin, is on the left.

The first helicopter used in a fugitive chase takes to the air in New Jersey.

Alice Paul. (*Library of Congress*)

Captain Thomas J. Rowe.

Captain Rowe's widow (l) and his daughter, Dorothy Scott, at the trial of Ann Powers.

Ann Powers being escorted out of the courtroom after pleading guilty to manslaughter.

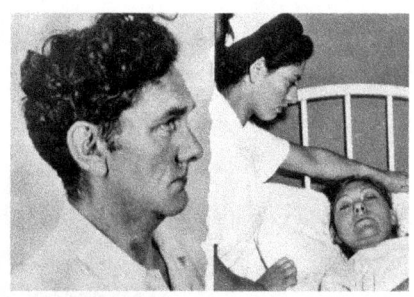

Thomas and Marie Morris after the harpoon incident.

The scene of Howard Unruh's rampage in Camden.

The siege of Unruh's apartment.

The arrest of Unruh.

Unruh in custody at Camden
police headquarters.

Willie Moretti's funeral procession.

Suzanne Fulinello.

Billy Loes.

End of Gallery

CHAPTER 12

1934- The Strange Case of "Millard Edouard"

In the early morning of January 27, 1934, Howard Ginther heard pounding on his door and then a woman screaming that her husband, who she had married thirteen days before, had shot himself. Ginther, a farmer near Florence, New Jersey, let the "hysterical bride" in, and then called the state police and the Burlington County prosecutor's office. Within a short time, two state troopers and Burlington county chief of detectives Ellis Parker arrived and began to question Ella May Edouard. Parker later recalled that Ella May "was somewhere in her forties, pretty good looking, but dressed in the queerest outfit you ever saw – a big sweater and a pair of men's trousers, with an overcoat over that."

Mrs. Edouard told the police that her husband, a Frenchman named Millard Edouard, had been driving and that she had dozed off and was awakened by a gunshot to see him draped over the steering wheel of their parked car. Parker checked out the automobile, where he found the late Mr. Edouard slumped over the steering wheel with entry and exit bullet holes in his head and a .25 caliber automatic pistol on the floor. The county medical examiner arrived and he and Parker went through the dead man's pockets, finding "many odd papers," including letters written in "some language none of us could recognize—it turned out to be

Serbian." There were also business cards and clippings and a photo of the dead man with his arm around "a chubby woman...not his wife," with the name "Millard Stephan" scrawled on the back.

Mrs. Edouard, "one of the kind that are anxious to talk," according to Parker, found a ready listener in the renowned detective. She said she and her husband had recently married in California and were on a honeymoon trip to New York City, where he had stashed $110,000 in cash in several bank safe deposit boxes. He told her that he could not access the money because he was not a United States citizen, but that she, as his wife, could, and that he would get her power of attorney to do so once they reached New York. As the couple got closer to their destination, she recalled, he seemed to become increasingly nervous and depressed.

One of the troopers told Parker he thought it was an open and shut case – Ella May had murdered her husband, and her story "was as full of holes as Swiss cheese." Parker said he wasn't so sure and wanted to investigate further. Mrs. Edouard was remanded to the Burlington county jail as a "material witness" while law enforcement figured the case out.

The chief of detectives met with the county prosecutor and the two troopers. Parker reflected on the angle of the wound, the position of Edouard's body and his hat and the statements of his wife. He then began considering the other physical evidence, including the fact that although Edouard claimed to be French, the letters in his pocket were not in that language, the photograph of him with another woman which indicated he had used another name, and a card from the "Midnight Follies" nightclub in Tijuana, Mexico. One of the troopers opined that the dead man was "a man that's nutty over women." Parker, however, concluded that he was a con man who specialized in scamming women, that there was no money in New York, that he was probably wanted elsewhere, and that he panicked at being caught and shot himself.

Parker was proved correct. The subsequent investigation revealed that Edouard's real name was Milan Fillipe. He had actually married seven American women around the country in succession, claiming in each case that he had money in safe deposit boxes in New York and then "living on them until their money was exhausted." Ella May had apparently unintentionally called his bluff.

There was more, however, and Parker told a reporter a year later that "it was as queer a story as you ever heard. He was a Turk, had been detained in Chicago to be deported, but escaped. He was allegedly "badly wanted by the French police for espionage and murder. He knew if he were picked up they'd send him back and guillotine him. A fellow told me afterward that the Mohammedans believe that if your head is cut off you have to go through all eternity without it. So, when he saw he was due to be caught anyway, he shot himself nice and neat, in order to be able to go to hell with his head on."

The Penn's Grove Bank Heist

On February 2, 1934, bandits intercepted two employees of the Penns Grove National Bank and Trust Company in Penns Grove, New Jersey, on the front steps of the institution and robbed them of a $130,000 (over $2,000,000 today) Dupont Company payroll they were transferring from the post office to the bank. In the immediate aftermath of the robbery, several people said they saw nationally known Depression era criminal "Pretty Boy Floyd" driving past Trenton in the last week and concluded that he must have staged the robbery.

There were several eyewitnesses to the crime, including hardware store clerk Carl Luger. When asked why he did not jump in his nearby car and follow the bandits, Luger responded "Not me. I looked in their car and they had too many guns on their laps. I was not armed." The car the thieves used, with a Pennsylvania inspection sticker and license plates stolen in Camden several days before, was later found on snow-covered Forked Hickory Road by a local citizen posse armed with their hunting shotguns, and a manhunt was launched across New Jersey, Pennsylvania and Delaware for the robbers.

The following day Camden police detectives Clifford Del Rossi and Benjamin Simon, checking on a car with Ohio license plates a motorcycle patrolman was suspicious about, arrested four people leaving a city rooming house. Those captured included forty-five-year-old Charles Kent of Camden, thirty-seven-year-old John Farley of New York City and twenty-nine-year old Harry Greenberg and his thirty-one-year-old wife Rose of Philadelphia, along with two suitcases containing $36,340 of the robbery loot. Kent allegedly offered arresting officers "$3,000 not to open the suitcase" and later offered them "$5,000 not to fingerprint him."

None of the suspects would confess, so the Camden police brought the two bank employees up from Penns Grove. Farley was quickly identified by witnesses as the driver of the getaway car. Kent was subsequently connected with the crime after tracing the Ohio license plates and fingerprints on the abandoned car. Ohio authorities identified him as Carroll Johnson. Johnson was previously a resident of Canton, Ohio, and had served prison terms in Ohio and Michigan for robbery. He was currently wanted in Michigan as the ringleader of a gang wanted for bank robbery and murder, as well as for a bank robbery in Louisville, Kentucky. He and Farley, whose real name was John Fodale and who was actually from Detroit, were transferred to the Salem County jail, where the sheriff ordered extra guards posted due to a rumor that prominent gangster John Dillinger was going to raid the jail to free the prisoners. The Greenbergs were released on bail.

Johnson and Fodale were formally charged with the robbery and, although police believed two other men were involved in the actual crime and had escaped with a share of the loot, prosecutors concluded that the Greenbergs "were not directly connected with the holdup" and they were not charged. Following indictments, Johnson, described by one reporter as a "gray-haired bandit chief who looks like a prosperous business man" avoided trial by pleading guilty but testified that Fodale did not participate in the robbery. He also claimed that he had paid Detective Simon $500 to "fix the case," and that Camden police stole over $22,000 of the loot. Neither judge nor jury believed any of his claims and Fodale, who did go to trial, was convicted. Both men were sentenced to fourteen to fifteen years in prison.

In August, 1934, another $16,000 of the Penn's Grove bank loot was discovered in Ohio in the car of E. E. Martin, "a roadhouse proprietor" arrested for murder. The money, "in a copper box, soldered shut," was identified via serial numbers supplied by Sergeant W. P. Kelly of the Penns Grove police department. The remainder of the money was never recovered, but was no doubt spent somewhere in Depression-wracked America.

The Disappearing Schwartzes

It was 1934, and liquor was legal once again, so entrepreneurial thirty-year-old Edward Schwartz and his cousin, twenty-eight-year-old Sigmund Schwartz, opened a liquor store at 78 Washington Avenue in Carteret, New Jersey. On April 5, the Schwartzes, who had most likely been in the alcohol business before it became legal again, and probably made some enemies along the way, received a telephone order for delivery of a case of liquor. They left the store with the liquor at 9:00 PM, and were never seen again. Edward's bloodstained car was subsequently discovered in "a lonely section of town." Local law enforcement immediately suspected that the cousins had been murdered. There was a large pond near where the Schwartz automobile was discovered, and police drained it in the belief that their bodies might be found there, but to no avail. Law enforcement also checked the nearby Rahway River, doing a bit of dredging, and found nothing.

The search for the bodies went on for some time. In June, hikers in some nearby woods told police they thought they had found two graves which might contain the remains of the Schwartzes. Police checked the site and declared that the purported gravesites were actually "storage places for rabbit food." In September, Edward's father, Isadore, a banker and former school commissioner in Carteret, told the press that he had located a "go between" to "negotiate for the return of the bodies" of his son and nephew, but nothing came from that effort either.

There would be one more recovery initiative. Several years later Isadore received an anonymous letter declaring that the cousins were still alive and that the writer would deliver them for a $40,000 ransom, which Isadore was instructed to leave in a garage adjacent to Rahway Reformatory. There was a reason for the ransom deposit location. The writer, one Andrew W. Daneko, who had no idea what had happened to the Schwartzes, was actually an inmate at Rahway, serving a ten-year sentence for an armed robbery of the Newark Compressed Steel Company in 1930. Daneko was lucky. He had shot Louis Brenner, the company's treasurer, during the robbery, but Brenner lived until 1931 before dying of his wounds. Since he died over a year after the crime, the perpetrator could not be charged with murder according to the law. Daneko was also a trustee who had a fair degree of freedom of movement on and around the prison grounds.

Isadore and the authorities knew the story was, to be kind, unlikely, and probably an attempt at a swindle, but played along with Daneko, advising him that the money had indeed been left as he directed. He was arrested on his way to the garage to retrieve it and was tried and convicted of extortion in Newark in 1938. The bodies of the Schwartzes were never recovered and the case remains unsolved to this day. Their store still stands. And it is still a liquor store, now known as State Liquors.

Gimme' Shelters

On June 13, 1934, Vernon D. Shelters, an auto salesman at the Newark Packard Company, appeared at Presbyterian Hospital in the city with the body of Eleanor Coleman of Orange, a stenographer for the same employer, propped up beside him in the front seat. Eleanor was dead. She had a broken neck, fractured skull and broken ribs. Shelters told hospital personnel that he and Eleanor had been out driving in Morris County and that "she alighted from the car following a visit to a roadhouse in Rockaway Township and didn't return. He said that he went to look for her after a while "and found her lying in the road." Shelters stated that there were no other cars on the road at the time.

Born in Spotswood, New Jersey, in 1892, Shelters had worked for the Packard Company for some time. In 1917 he was service manager for a Packard dealership in Buffalo, New York. At the time of Coleman's death Shelters was married with three children, and lived at 96 Dayton Street, across from Weequahic Park in Newark.

A subsequent news story reported that police were "puzzled" by the case, but not for long, as they arrested Shelters the following day. Dr. Carmine Berardinelli, the Essex County assistant medical examiner, examined the body and posited that he thought Coleman had been "run over by an automobile." There were no tire marks on her body, however. The police took Shelters back to the scene of the incident, and then inspected his car, finding what appeared to be "human hairs on the running board." They surmised that he backed the car into her and that was the cause of her death. He was charged with manslaughter and arraigned in Morristown.

Shelters' case was postponed a number of times, but in March, 1935, Eleanor Coleman's father Thomas filed a civil lawsuit alleging that his daughter had paid him ten dollars a week for room and board, and that because of her death he no longer had that income. Coleman also sued the Packard Company of Newark. The company admitted that Shelters was driving a company car at the time of Coleman's death, but maintained he was not doing so on company business. A Morristown jury dismissed both civil suits in March, 1935, citing "no cause." Shelters' manslaughter trial was delayed, but appears to have been dropped, as was a petition to renew the civil suit. By 1942, while maintaining his Newark address, he was working for the Federal government at Camp Evans, in Wall

Township, a substation of Fort Monmouth involved in communications and radar research. Shelters died in 1961 and is buried in New Brunswick's Evergreen Cemetery.

Wife for Sale. Cheap.

The headline read "Philatelist charged with sale of wife." Well, sort of. German immigrants Richard Rost, a forty-year-old Hoboken, New Jersey, stamp dealer, his thirty-year-old wife Hildegarde and forty-one-year-old stationary engineer Paul Herman of Union City were arrested on August 17, 1934, charged with "conspiracy to violate the State Moral Code" and held on $5,000 bail, which they were unable to meet, and so all three were held in the Hudson County jail.

According to police, Rost and Herman had signed a contract, witnessed by a Hoboken notary, to transfer the woman from one to the other for $700, and Hildegarde moved in with Herman, who Rost suspected was having an affair with his wife, after the agreement was signed. While they were in the police station Mrs. Rost reportedly yelled "you sold me so I hate you" at her husband.

The deal might have passed unnoticed, but Rost had apparently demanded that his wife move back in with him a few weeks after he made the deal, and when she rejected his proposal, he accused her of stealing $175 worth of his stamps, then brought his complaint to the police. Neighbors reportedly told Detective Lieutenant William Christie, who was investigating the case, that Rost was "... a terrible man. He sold his wife," and the whole story unraveled. Hildegarde told Christie that "she had been traded like chattel, and sobbed."

Rost denied that he had sold his wife, maintaining that the cash that changed hands was reimbursement for money he had paid a private detective to investigate his wife's affair with Herman. Meanwhile, perhaps ironically, the press opined that the trio had "conspired to shock, grossly and scandalously, the moral sense of the community, undermining one of the State of New Jersey's most cherished moral statutes."

Journalists and editors immediately saw great popular entertainment value in the story, and it made newspapers across the country. It also entered philatelist folklore in a somewhat garbled version, in which Rost sold his wife to get the money to buy a rare stamp, no doubt spurred by colorful reports like this: "It was not that Richard Rost loved his wife less, it was that he loved his postage stamp collection more." Apparently the case was eventually settled, and the Rosts did not reconcile, as the 1940 census lists Paul and Hildegarde Herman as married and living in Guttenberg, New Jersey.

A Wild Ride Ends in Newark

It was a story right out of the Bonnie and Clyde era, without Bonnie. Edward Metelski was born in Newark, New Jersey in 1908, where he established a "long list of arrests for misdemeanors" in his youth. When he was twelve years old Metelski was a resident of a youth correction home. A decade later, in 1930, he was an inmate of Rahway Reformatory, and by 1935, having left his native state for the south, he was serving time on a chain gang at Caledonian State Prison Farm in North Carolina for a bungled "safe robbery."

Metelski escaped from the North Carolina chain gang in August, 1934, and fled north to Philadelphia, where he teamed up with local thug Albert "Whitey" Morton. The pair robbed the Palm Garden Café in Philadelphia on November 9, although the loot wasn't significant —eighty-five dollars and five bottles of whiskey. The bandits took off across New Jersey after the robbery. When the duo reached Rahway, suspicious New Jersey state trooper Warren Yenser tried to pull them over, but a shotgun blast from the car killed Yenser. The trooper's death ignited an immediate massive manhunt. The bandits' car was discovered in the port section of Elizabeth and Metelski was captured at the city's train station. Morton made it back to Philadelphia, where he committed suicide.

Although he claimed Morton was the actual trigger man, Metelski was charged with Yenser's murder and held for trial in the Middlesex County Jail in New Brunswick. On December 14, however, Metelski, brandishing a revolver, escaped from the jail with another prisoner, Paul Semenkewitz, who was awaiting trial on robbery charges. Initially, authorities stated that the handgun used in the escape had apparently been smuggled into the jail by Metelski's cousin, Mary Truchanociz. Questioned by detectives as to whether she actually gave him the gun, Truchanociz was noncommittal, but then blurted out "I would give him a machine gun." It turned out that the gun had actually been smuggled in by another woman, Teresa Czicolic, an old friend of Metelski from

Newark, better known as "Terry Chiclet," who was employed as "a dancer in obscure New Jersey gin mills." She was promptly arrested.

On December 16, the two escapees showed up in Dunellen, where they robbed Semenkewitz's former employer Edward Clark, proprietor of the Clark Gable Inn on Route 29 (today's Route 28) of some clothing and five dollars and then ran into a nearby woodlot. The area was soon swarming with state troopers on the ground as a plane flew overhead, hoping to "spot the prisoners' hideout." The search proved fruitless as Metelski and Semenkewitz slipped away, stealing a car in the process.

Law enforcement officials, suspecting that the fugitives were heading for Newark, based on Terry Chiclet's connection to that city, assembled a 200 man police task force to apprehend them. Detectives discovered that "a beautiful redhead," who turned out to be Chiclet, had recently rented an apartment "for her husband and herself," in downtown Newark, and then flooded the area with officers. A team of six detectives spotted Metelski near the corner of West Kinney and Halsey Streets on December 18. He was cornered in an alley and captured. Semenkewitz was arrested after a brief struggle in a nearby restaurant. A photo of the badly battered escapees was taken shortly afterwards. The police claimed that they resisted arrest, and hence, unavoidably, got "mussed up."

Metelski went on trial for murder in New Brunswick in January 1936. Although he claimed that he was innocent because Morton fired the fatal shot, Metelski was found guilty and sentenced to die in the electric chair on February 17. The execution date was deferred as he appealed the sentence, but the state's highest court, the Court of Errors and Appeals, upheld the conviction and sentence in May. A second appeal, to the Court of Pardons, failed as well. Terry Chiclet, who had represented herself as Metelski's wife, was sentenced to five years in prison for her part in the escape, and Paul Semenkewitz had fifteen to twenty years added to his original sentence.

On August 4, 1936, Edward Metelski sat down in "Old Smokey," in the Trenton State Prison. He looked at the twenty witnesses, who included Irwin Yenser, State Trooper Warren Yenser's brother, arrayed on a bench along the wall to his left and said: "you people are watching an innocent man being murdered. I hope God will forgive me for all of the things I have done wrong." And then executioner Robert Elliott pulled the switch and Metelski, as the *Asbury Park Press*, which had a special interest in the case since Trooper Yenser was born in nearby Ocean

Grove, and described every detail of the execution in graphic detail, put it, "rubbed out his debt to society."

Murder in a "Disorderly House" in Camden

The details were garbled, but apparently three men were in the process of robbing "fifteen inmates, patrons and domestics" in the "alleged disorderly house" located at 243 Sycamore Street in South Camden, New Jersey and run by Mrs. Emma Heisler on September 2, 1934, when Camden detective William T. Feitz intervened. As Feitz turned to call in his partner, Detective Joseph Leonhardt, who was in a car parked outside the brothel, for assistance, he was shot four times in the back, dying shortly afterward. Feitz was the first Camden police officer ever killed in the line of duty since the department was created in 1869. The bandits fled out the back door.

When police reinforcements arrived at the scene shortly afterward, they questioned those in the house and arrested Mrs. Heisler as a material witness. Heisler was brought to police headquarters on the fifth floor of City Hall, where she was interrogated "almost without letup" for 48 hours by Camden detectives, who believed she knew the identity of the man who had killed Detective Feitz.

Camden mayor Roy R. Stewart stopped by the Detective Bureau to question Emma Heisler in person on September 4. Several hours later, during a break in the questioning, and shortly after a photograph of the interrogation was taken, Heisler, who the police thought was ready to identify the killer, stood up, rushed towards an open window and "without a moment's hesitation" jumped out. She landed on an "open parked car, the legs smashing the windshield," and was rushed to a hospital, where she was declared dead.

Although their principal witness was now deceased, the police rounded up possible suspects to no avail. At one point, they focused on Mickey Blair, whose real name was Michael Tenerelli. Blair, a well-known featherweight boxer, was also a shady local character who had been involved in a number of dubious enterprises in both Camden and Atlantic City. When Blair heard the cops were looking for him he surrendered. He admitted that he knew Heisler and had approached her about borrowing money to "buy flowers for his brother in law's funeral" the day before the murder. He stated that he was nowhere near the brothel when Feitz was killed, however, and was at "a roadhouse in Berlin [NJ]" at the time of the incident.

The investigation continued and eventually led to Charles Zied, who was arrested across the river in Philadelphia, identified by several witnesses as one of the three robbers, subsequently tried and convicted of Feitz's murder and electrocuted in Trenton on June 2, 1936. Zied's accomplices, Martin Farrell and Frank Wiley, were later captured and tried and executed for another killing in Pennsylvania. The incident led to a campaign to investigate the significant brothel business in Camden. Michael Tenerelli/ Mickey Blair would later open his own brothel in Atlantic City and meet an unhappy end in 1941.

Ghosts Aboard the *Morro Castle*

On September 8, 1934, the SS *Morro Castle*, a cruise ship bound from Havana to New York, caught fire off the New Jersey coast. The ship's controls burned out off Sea Girt, where it dropped anchor and chaos ensued as lifeboat launches failed and people jumped into the ocean. Later that day, a Coast Guard cutter began to tow the burned-out vessel north, but the towline snapped near Asbury Park and the *Morro Castle* drifted into the beach by Convention Hall, where it became a tourist attraction in Mayor Clarence Hetrick's fiefdom until towed away in March, 1935.

Enter now two goofy characters from "Lawn Guy Land," William Scott, a gardener, and Robert Mantzinger, a twenty-two-year-old plumber, of Glen Cove, who, in a prefiguration of "Jersey Shore," decided to visit Asbury Park to see the wreck. On arrival, according to their later story, each dared the other to board the shipwreck. They swam to the *Morro Castle*'s stern and then used the dangling broken tow ropes to climb up onto the deck.

In the days following the crash landing of the *Morro Castle*, Asbury Park police and fire department personal had a telephone line strung from Convention Hall to the ship, for communication with those who boarded on official business. That did not include, needless to say, Scott and Mantzinger, who were roaming around looking for and picking up souvenirs, including "a pair of handcuffs, a cigarette lighter and several other items, all without value."

How the dauntless duo were discovered is unclear. One story related that a fireman and two reporters on watch at Convention Hall called the wreck as a joke at 3:00 AM on September 11 and one of the dynamic duo picked up the phone and answered, and "the three had visions of ghosts aboard the liner." Another version has it that Asbury Park city fireman (thanks to Mayor Hetrick the city had a professional fire department) Carl Agreen, who was on night duty at Convention Hall, heard the phone ring as one of the trespassers, unaware that Agreen was on duty, called as a prank. No matter the actual sequence of events, the two were ordered ashore, where they were taken into custody by Asbury Park police officers Thomas Wilson and Lee Napier at 4:40 AM.

Later that day the Long Islanders appeared before Police Magistrate William E. Andrew, tentatively charged with looting the vessel. When neither Ward Line officials or Coast Guard officers appeared to formalize the charges, however, Andrew released Scott and Mantzinger with "a severe reprimand" and went on to say that "any further incidents similar to this would be dealt with severely, probably resulting in a jail term for the next offender."

CHAPTER 13

1935-"Old Smokey"

The New Jersey electric chair at Trenton State Prison is an iconic, if gruesome, state artifact. The development of this method of execution, deemed more humane than hanging, began in the late 1880s, and there was a New Jersey connection, involving experiments electrocuting animals, conducted at Thomas Edison's West Orange laboratory, in 1886 and 1889, with Edison himself present. It seems Edison was promoting the use of rival George Westinghouse's alternating current (AC) rather than his own direct current (DC), apparently to persuade people that the competing electricity delivery method was dangerous.

The actual use of the electric chair as an execution device in America dates from 1890, when the first one was utilized in New York state to execute Joseph Chappleau, who had beat his neighbor to death. It replaced hanging as a means of implementing the death penalty in New Jersey in 1906. The Jersey chair was built by Carl Adams, who owned an electrical contracting company in Trenton.

Leather straps were used to secure the prisoner in the chair and then a metal cap was placed on his head and electrodes attached to his right leg. The executioner pulled two switches in succession, coursing charges of 2,400 and 1,200 volts through the condemned man's body for thirty seconds each time. The first charge was intended to make the subject lose consciousness and become "brain dead," and the second one to destroy internal organs. Doctors then checked the prisoner for a pulse and, if he still had one, the executioner applied a third dose of 600 volts to finish the job.

The first man to meet his end in the New Jersey electric chair was Saverio DiGiovanni, who had been convicted of killing Joseph Sansone in Somerville and was executed on December 11, 1907. The last person to die in the chair was Ralph Hudson, convicted of stabbing his wife to death in Atlantic City on December 27, 1960, who was executed on January 22, 1963. A total of 160 men, including DiGiovanni and Hudson, died in the state's electric chair, also known as "Old Smokey," during those years. No women were ever executed in the New Jersey electric chair.

A photo, captioned "the room of death" dates from February, 1935, and was intended to show the public where perhaps the most famous temporary occupant of "Old Smokey," Bruno Richard Hauptmannn, who was on trial at the time for the Lindbergh baby kidnapping and murder, would draw his last breath should he be convicted. He was and did.

Although long retired, "Old Smokey" still exists, and is on public view in the New Jersey State Police Museum at 110 River Road in West Trenton, New Jersey.

A Murder in Woodbridge

You could say it all started in Asbury Park. That was where Edgar H. Crockett, a salesman who resided there as well as in Astoria, Queens, New York, met Dorothy Pettite, of Neptune, in 1933, and where they became "intimate friends." Crockett and Pettite had a falling out and he left for Florida, but came back to New Jersey and his Asbury Park residence, at 410 Third Avenue, and tried to resume the relationship. On May 9, 1935, the fifty-six-year-old Crockett took thirty-six-year-old Dorothy and her friend and roommate Dorothy Heller to Sam's Bar and Grill on New Brunswick Avenue in the Fords section of Woodbridge, where the trio "drank considerable liquor."

As the evening wore on, Pettite began to flirt with a young man named Oscar Madberg and when Madberg left the room Crockett angrily drew a Colt Model 1911 .45 caliber automatic pistol and shot her in the head, killing her instantly. He tried to shoot himself as well, but his gun jammed. Crockett was subdued by bar patrons and when police arrived he told them that Pettite had "broke up my home and ruined my business," without supplying specifics. Dorothy Heller was held as a material witness, although she claimed she had fallen asleep by the time of the shooting.

In custody at Woodbridge Police Headquarters, Crockett, allegedly a former New York City police officer who had served in the army from 1902 to 1920, rising from the rank of private to captain, told police "I was madly in love with her. I killed her out of jealousy." He was also described as "formerly in the music business in New York" and as the owner of a paint store in Asbury Park.

Dorothy Pettite's body was brought to Coroner Edward H. Finn's Woodbridge morgue, but, after three days no one had claimed her remains, although "several hundred curious persons viewed the body." Crockett subsequently pleaded guilty to second degree murder and, on July 26, 1935, was sentenced to eight to ten years in prison. The 1940 census does not list him as a prisoner, so he must have been released early. A draft card for 1941 reveals that Crockett was at that time a resident of the Soldiers' Home in Washington DC. He died there on November 4, 1955 and was buried in the U.S. Soldiers' and Airmen's Home National Cemetery.

In 1993, Nancy and Sam Nokes of Metuchen, who had purchased Sam's Bar and Grill seven years earlier, had North Brunswick paranormal investigator and air conditioner salesman Alfred Rauber check out some "strange goings on" at the tavern. Odd sounds, plates flying off shelves and brief apparent appearances of hazy figures who then disappeared were reported by both staff and tenants living in an apartment above the bar. In the end, Nokes came to the conclusion that "the disturbances are the work of the ghost of Edgar H. Crockett." He may still be there, knocking around at nights.

The "Pompton Lakes Gang"

It was June, 1935, in the depths of the Depression, and daily news of bank robberies and desperados, which, while reflecting the prevailing economic conditions, also provided average folks with cheap diversionary entertainment. It was in this environment that Paterson, New Jersey, police chief John Murphy received information from an undisclosed source that a bandit gang was hiding out in a bungalow along the Passaic River in Mountain View.

New Jersey State Police and New York City detectives staged

a raid on the cabin, bagging eight men and a woman they dubbed the "Pompton Lakes Gang," all of whom had been suspected or tried in murder cases in New York or New Jersey at one time or another, but never convicted. They were John Hughes, Edward Gaffney, James "Ding Dong" Bell, Joseph Carthy, Arthur "Scarface" Gaynor, Frank Fox, Louis D. Balner, and George Maiwald and his wife Edna, who lived next door and had rented the cabin to the gang. Hughes and Gaffney were suspected of being involved in a $427,500 armored car robbery in Brooklyn in August 1934, a crime described at the time as "the biggest holdup in American crime history."

The raiders reported that they had confiscated "enough nitroglycerine to blow up the state house in Trenton," along with "an arsenal which Included 9 revolvers, a rifle, a riot gun, 80 rounds of ammunition, a tear gas kit, stolen automobile licenses and a 'magneto jumper' used in stealing cars." One car parked nearby bore Monmouth county license plates stolen from a car in Keyport the previous January. The State Police denied published rumors that the gang was plotting to kidnap boxer Joe Louis, who was training nearby for a forthcoming title fight.

In the end, the whole incident seems to have become much ado about nothing. The arrested men were arraigned on the rather tenuous generic charge of being "enemies of the State," to which "Ding Dong" Bell entered a collective plea of not guilty. The law that Ding Dong pleaded innocent to was problematic. In the early 1930s several states passed "Enemy of the State" legislation, which sounds, on surface, to be more in line with a law in a Fascist or Communist country. Despite the ominous title, violation was merely a disorderly person offense.

New Jersey's "Public Enemy Act" passed in 1933, stated that "proof of recent reputation for engaging in illegal occupation...shall be prima facie evidence of being engaged in an illegal occupation." The law was clarified in 1934 by providing that "any person who...shall be proven...to have consorted with known...criminals, and/or ...shall have been...arrested [and] charged with crime on more than two separate occasions previous to such apprehension, whether convicted or not of such charges shall be... adjudged a disorderly person." Proving that would be difficult and the constitutionality of such a law is questionable as well.

The aim was, apparently, to create an offense to charge members of organized crime with in lieu of actual evidence of a crime, and the law could be violated, according to one account, by someone having "an evil reputation" or "consorting with thieves or criminals." The New York Supreme Court ruled on one case that the validity of the charge and/or conviction depended on "what proof is necessary to establish the facts on which the presumption is raised." Four out of five New York cases were dismissed. Similar laws were deemed unconstitutional in other states.

By the end of the year, the armored car robbery was still unsolved, despite a series of arrests of known gangsters around the country, none of whom could be tied to the crime, as suspects. The story of the Pompton Lakes gang quietly faded away.

Thanks are due to my law student son John for the legal information on the "Enemy of the State" laws.

The Battle of Crempa Farm

Polish born John Crempa, a farmer who lived at 112 Terrill Road in Scotch Plains, New Jersey, had a longstanding beef with the Public Service Company. Crempa, a pre-World War I United States army veteran, claimed that the company owed him money because its power lines crossed his land, but was unwilling to take the company's modest initial offer, demanding $100,000 (almost two million dollars in today's money). A court had agreed that $800 was a reasonable fee, but Crempa rejected the decision and, in response, aided by his son John, "short circuited the transmission line that crossed his tract, throwing several communities into darkness time and time again."

The dispute continued for the better part of a year, and despite an attempt to broker a compromise by New Jersey State Senator Charles E. Loizeux, who told Crempa the situation might well end badly, the stubborn farmer upped his demands to $150,000. On September 26, 1935, eight deputies from the Union County Sheriff's Office came to the Crempa home with arrest warrants for John for contempt of court and malicious mischief due to his destruction of Public Service property, and for his wife Sophie for assault for allegedly threatening a deputy who previously tried to serve the warrants with a handgun.

The officers banged on the door and fired a tear gas shell through a window into the Crempa home, driving out the Crempas and their nineteen-year-old daughter Camelia. What happened next was unclear. There was gunfire, everyone agreed on that. John claimed he tried to fire his Colt .45 automatic pistol but it jammed. He was either shot and dropped the gun or dropped the gun and was shot, with buckshot hitting him in the knee and the hand. Camelia picked it up and fired it into the air. Mrs. Crempa, riddled with buckshot, was dead. The deputies claimed all three Crempas came out firing, but only the one handgun was found.

Union County prosecutor Abe David ordered the arrest of Deputy Remley, as he was the only officer armed with a shotgun, and Mrs. Crempa died from shotgun wounds. Remley was released on bail, which was posted following a collection by his fellow deputies, pending a future trial. Crempa told a clergyman who visited him in the hospital that he thought the initial knock on the door was his attorney, and then the tear gas shell smashed through the window an instant later. He said he thought the deputies "wanted me to die. They treated me like a dog." The deputies brought Crempa and his daughter to the county jail before sending him to Elizabeth General Hospital.

On October 6, A rally of over 800 Polish-Americans, attended by Camelia Crempa, was held in support of Crempa at the Jersey City Polish Community Hall. The gathering adopted a resolution "demanding a searching investigation into the shooting and asked the support of all Polish organizations." The investigation dragged on into the new year.

On July 11, 1936, Judge Edward A. McGrath, claiming that "no public purpose can be served" by pursuing the charges from both sides resulting from the "Crempa farm battle," subsequently "nolle prossed" all the charges against individuals on both sides in the case, including Deputy Remley. The Crempas, previously convicted on contempt of court charges, had that charge dismissed as well, so long as they did not engage in similar conduct in the future.

In January, 1937, a newspaper reported that John Crempa had gone "missing." Actually, however, he had moved to New York to work six months earlier. The home at the center of the deadly controversy stood abandoned and Camelia and her brother John were living with relatives. Presumably the Public Service lines still stood. Crempa passed away in 1946, and was buried in Hillside Cemetery in Scotch Plains alongside Sophie.

Death Comes for the Dutchman

Arthur Simon Flegenheimer was born in the Bronx, New York, in 1902 to Jewish immigrant parents. Flegenheimer became a significant figure in a generation of Jewish gangsters who came of age in time for the "noble experiment" of Prohibition to provide them with profitable employment. In the 1920s, many poor young immigrants and children of immigrants, living in a society that was often hostile and denied them opportunity, turned to bootlegging and used their native talent and intelligence to rapidly evolve from petty thieves to wealthy men.

Flegenheimer adopted the moniker of "Dutch Shultz," reputedly in tribute to an earlier successful gang leader in his neighborhood, and, through astuteness and ruthlessness, became a major bootlegger. Following the end of Prohibition, Shultz, like many of his cohorts and rivals in the organized crime game, branched out into the lucrative illegal lottery "numbers racket," and also became a significant figure in labor racketeering and other nefarious businesses.

By the 1930s, law enforcement, which had difficulty proving cases against known mobsters, had discovered that tax evasion lawsuits were an effective tool, and federal authorities proceeded to try Shultz two times for tax evasion in New York City. He was found not guilty on both occasions. Harassed by New York authorities, who were planning state court suits against him, Shultz moved his headquarters across the Hudson to New Jersey, establishing an office in a back room in the Palace Chop House on East Park Place in Newark.

Shultz had always been a publicity hound. "The Dutchman" gave interviews to the press, had his picture in the papers often and was a well-known metropolitan area character. This troubled the more secretive leaders of the organized crime community, who did not want to draw undue attention to their activities. Charles "Lucky" Luciano, for one, was disturbed by Shultz's alleged threat to have New York Attorney General Thomas Dewey, who was prosecuting him on state charges, killed, which Luciano believed would prove his organization's undoing as it would result in a massive crackdown on gang activities. A decision was made by Luciano and his top associates – the Dutchman must go.

On October 23, 1935, Schultz was meeting with three of his henchmen, Bernard "Lulu" Rosenkranz, Otto "Abbadabba" Berman and Abe Landau, in the back room of the Palace Chop House. Around 10:00 PM, two men, Mendy Weiss, carrying a shotgun, and Charley "The Bug" Workman, with a pistol in his hand, barged through the front door of the Palace and rushed by a terrified bartender, heading for the rear of the restaurant. They entered the back room and gunned down

Shultz's associates, but he was not there. Workman kicked in the door of an adjacent men's room, saw Shultz at the urinal and shot him in the stomach. Both men then fled the Chop House. Landau staggered to his feet and followed Workman out the door, firing a few shots at him with his .45 automatic pistol, before he fell into a garbage can.

Police and ambulances arrived at the scene shortly after the shooting, which newspapers described as "part of a hoodlum war." One officer found Shultz sitting in a chair holding his side – he had left the men's room – and asked him "You're Shultz. Are you shot?" The Dutchman responded: "Yes and it's damn painful." The press was full of wild speculation, linking the murders to the death of Brooklyn thug "Pretty Louie" Amberg, who was killed with a hatchet and then roasted in a burning car the day before. They also noted that an adding machine tape found on the table and apparently used to total up the wages of crime, had "a long row of figures" ending with $827,253.54 (more than fourteen million dollars in today's money).

Ambulances brought all four men, who were still alive, if barely, to Newark City Hospital. His three underlings died there shortly afterward, but Shultz lingered into the next day, babbling incoherent phrases that were taken down by a police stenographer. Shultz's ramblings reportedly later inspired avant-garde "stream of consciousness" writers like William S. Burroughs.

Dutch Shultz died in Newark City Hospital on October 24. Surprisingly to some, one of the last people to see him alive was a Catholic priest. Shultz was in the process of converting to Catholicism at the time he was shot, and Father Cornelius McInerney was called to the hospital to a baptize "the Dutchman" and give him the last rites of the Catholic Church.

It was not until 1941 that police uncovered the identities of the shooters in the Palace Chop House slayings. Workman, arrested in Brooklyn, was extradited to New Jersey, tried in Newark and sentenced to life in prison for the murders. Weiss was executed at Sing Sing Prison in New York for the murder of another mobster, Joseph Rosen, the same year.

CHAPTER 14

1936- Downfall of a Detective

Ellis Parker, the nationally known Burlington County detective chief who was instrumental in solving many of the crimes described in this work, became interested in the Lindbergh baby kidnapping in 1932. His initial investigative contact was Paul Wendel, a pharmacist and attorney he had known for some time. Wendel had argued a case before the New Jersey Court of Chancery in 1919, and had forged documents to support his client. His deception was uncovered and he was tried and convicted of perjury, sentenced to nine months in the Mercer County Workhouse and lost his law license as a result. In 1924, Wendel, who was then working as a real estate agent, received a pardon, based on letters of support from among others, Ellis Parker, who knew his father, a prominent minister. Wendel received his law license back the following year, and the two developed a friendship of sorts.

In the immediate aftermath of the Lindbergh kidnapping, Wendel contacted Parker, suggesting that he could help with the investigation and indicating he had contacts with criminals in Chicago and New York who might provide information on the location of the child and perhaps arrange his return. Parker, who was apparently miffed that he had not been assigned to find the kidnappers and had a longstanding feud with New Jersey State Police superintendent Herbert Norman Schwartzkopf, accepted the offer, no doubt hoping he could uncover evidence of State Police incompetence in the investigation. After allegedly following a series of improbable leads, including the possible involvement of Al Capone in the crime, however, Wendel turned up nothing, but appears to have conned Parker out of some expense money.

As time went by, and the Lindbergh baby's body was discovered, Wendel assured Parker that the baby was not the Lindbergh child and Parker began to think that perhaps Wendel had somehow been involved in the crime himself. He recalled that Wendel, a narcissist whose sense of grandiosity was apparent to anyone who knew him, had once declared that if he had $50,000 he would become great – and the ransom was $50,000.

The arrest, trial and conviction of Bruno Richard Hauptmann in the case did not dissuade Parker from his opinion that others were involved, including possibly Wendel. This, along with his desire to show up the State Police, led him to eagerly accept a request to reinvestigate the case from Governor Harold Hoffman, who had visited Hauptmann in his death row cell and was not convinced of his guilt either. Hoffman gave Hauptmann a 30-day reprieve while Parker worked on the case.

Following Hoffman's request, Parker, with his son Ellis Jr. in charge of the actual operations, hired some dubious characters to kidnap Wendel, who was then living in New York to avoid prosecution on several New Jersey bad check charges. Parker's men forced Wendel into a car on February 14, 1936, and took him to a house in Brooklyn where they confined him in a cellar, knocked him around and demanded he confess that he had kidnapped the Lindbergh baby. Ellis Parker Jr. apparently appeared and told Wendel he would take him back to New Jersey if he signed a confession, which he did.

Once back in Trenton, via Mount Holly, Wendel denied a connection to the kidnapping and said his confession was forced through "torture." He displayed bruises from the beatings he had received, and it was apparent that he had no real connection with any of the physical evidence in the case. A grand jury refused to consider the charges, and Attorney General David Wilentz, who had personally prosecuted Hauptmann, referred to the Wendel affair as "the most vile fraud ever perpetrated on New Jersey."

Ironically, although Governor Hoffman refused to extradite the Parkers to New York to face trial in the Wendel affair, Federal kidnapping charges were brought against the detective and his son under the new Federal Lindbergh Law. They were convicted. Ellis Parker was sentenced to six years in Lewisburg prison and died there after six months, and his son served three years.

Ellis Parker Jr. was pardoned by President Harry Truman in 1947. Paul Wendel went on to a long career in the field of alternative medicine. He became an associate of Dr. Benedict Lust, a German born founder of The American Naturopathy Society. In 1944 he claimed he was a "Doctor of Metaphysics," but was arrested in Kings County New York in 1946 and spent six months in jail for practicing medicine without a license. Wendel self-published a number of books on various dubious medical procedures, and gained some of the fame he so desperately wanted from adherents of the fringe medical community before dying in 1956.

Axed for Being "Old Fashioned..."

Gladys MacKnight, a seventeen-year-old Bayonne girl, was smitten with eighteen-year-old Donald Wightman. The couple were in the living room at MacKnight's home at 826 Avenue A in Bayonne on July 31, 1936, and Gladys was, as usual, complaining to Donald about her "old fashioned" mother Helen. When Gladys asked the older woman to make the couple an early dinner so they could go play tennis, Helen refused, telling her to "get it herself." What happened next is unclear, but an argument ensued and all three ended up in the kitchen, where Mrs. MacKnight was struck six times in the head with an axe and killed by either Gladys or Donald. Gladys later claimed that her mother had attacked them with a knife. Mrs. Elizabeth Fuery, a neighbor who heard Helen screaming as she was axed, called up from the yard and asked what was going on, and Gladys said "Nothing. Mother just cut her finger." It was the first recorded murder of a president of the Bayonne Women's Club.

The two young people locked up the house, took Gladys' father's car from the garage, and drove away. When Mr. MacKnight, Works Superintendent of the General Cable Company in Bayonne, arrived home later and found his wife dead and his car gone, he called police. The culprits drove aimlessly around New Jersey and were arrested four hours later in Jersey City. At Jersey City police headquarters Donald initially confessed to the crime, but then claimed Gladys had wielded the axe. She initially denied it, but then confessed that she used the axe while Wightman held her mother's arms.

Under questioning, both Gladys and Donald admitted that they had previously discussed killing Helen, but only "jokingly." One detective recalled that Gladys "...was the coolest thing I ever saw. All the time she talked she sat with one leg thrown over the arm of the chair. She smoked one cigarette after another." A reporter described her as "unmoved, even by the recital of her own confession that she killed her mother with a hatchet." He went on to characterize her as a young woman who was "lithe and graceful like a cat," and who "maintained her indifferent bravado...as the state tightened the case it believes will send her and her choir singing sweetheart to the electric chair." Well, not quite.

At the trial, Gladys recanted her confession and again claimed Donald was the actual murderer. Her father testified that his wife was a "sick woman" with suicidal tendencies, and that when he discovered her body she did have a knife in her hand and that he initially thought she had killed herself. Two doctors who had treated Mrs. MacKnight over a period of years testified that she was "a hypochondriac," with "distinct neurotic symptoms." In the end, both defendants were convicted of second degree murder on May 28, 1937 and given the maximum sentence, thirty years in prison.

A newspaper speculated that Gladys would be forty-six years old on her release from prison, and although she had escaped the electric chair, "she loses the freedom so highly prized by youth...no more tennis matches, no college life, as she had planned -- and certainly not matrimony. Well, again, not quite.

On November 22, 1943 Gladys MacKnight was paroled from the Clinton Reformatory for Women after serving six and a half years of her sentence. A newspaper declared that she "will have atoned for a crime which sent her neurotic 47-year-old mother to her grave." A court spokesman described her as "an accidental offender." She left prison "with a record as a model prisoner." Wightman remained incarcerated. And no, Gladys did not go on to have a singing career with the Pips.

CHAPTER 15

1937-Joe Fay and the "Big Six"

According to one account, at a February 5, 1937 meeting gone awry between union leader Norman Redwood and subway contractor Samuel Rosoff in Rosoff's New York office, Rosoff jumped up from his desk, physically shoved Redwood and yelled "I will kill you stone dead." When Redwood scoffed at the threat, Rosoff retorted "I have two guns and if I don't use them, I will get the men who will use them." As Redwood left, Rosoff, a Russian immigrant described as a "dark, plump little man," concluded with "There is no man who ever pulled a strike on me and got away with it, and remember, Redwood, if you do anything like that you will be a dead man, and you can tell the police if you want to."

Norman Redwood was the business agent of Local 102 of the Affiliated International Hod Carriers, Builders and Common Laborers of America Union, and a strike by Local 102 would cost Rosoff a considerable amount of money. Redwood also had a confrontation with Joseph Fay of Newark, business agent and president of the International Brotherhood of Operating Engineers' union, who he angrily accused of strikebreaking and colluding with Rosoff. Fay and Rosoff, who were without doubt in cahoots, subsequently discussed their Redwood problem but what was said in that meeting has remained unreported.

On February 19, as Redwood parked his car in front of his Teaneck, New Jersey, home and reached for a package of strawberries he had bought for his wife, a car pulled up alongside him and he was shot four times in the head. A doctor pronounced him dead at the scene. Several days after the murder an unidentified man appeared at the Redwood house and told Mrs. Redwood that her husband had been killed by the orders of "Joe Fay and the Big Six. Joe Fay, the Big Six and Sam Rosoff were in a hall on 14th Street waiting for the news to tell them that Norman was done away with."

Bergen County prosecutor John J. Breslin, allotted a special $25,000 fund for the case, was determined to find and prosecute the perpetrators, who he believed, although they might not have been the actual trigger pullers, were indeed Rosoff and Fay. The prosecutor attempted to get Rosoff extradited from New York, but failed due to a lack of conclusive evidence, however. Breslin had no luck in finding the actual killer either, rumored to be Lou "Luger Mike" Saraga, an associate of the late Dutch Shultz. There was some retribution, however, as a ship owned by Rosoff docked on the Hudson River burned to the waterline days after Redwood was killed, and the police concluded it was a case of arson. That case, as well as the Redwood murder, remains unsolved.

Samuel Rosoff reappeared in the press almost two decades later, in May, 1956, when his daughter in law Joan sued him and his wife, who she said had falsely portrayed her husband, their son Stephen, as "a fine husband for any girl…thoughtful, considerate, unselfish…of fine character and reputation." Instead, according to Joan, the younger Rosoff "physically attacked me, inflicted personal injuries on me for which a physician was consulted, and in my presence demolished a plate glass window in a hotel in Atlantic City and smashed and climbed through a transom over the door of a hotel bedroom." Apparently, the apple did not fall far.

A "Psalm Singing Hillbilly" in Linden

Around 1930 Lloyd Pusey migrated from his birthplace in Pokomoke City, Maryland, to Oakland, New Jersey, where he labored on a farm and supplemented his income by working as a "tavern singer" in local speakeasies and later legal saloons. Five years later, after the death of his wife Winnie, Pusey moved to California, where he apparently found Jesus, became a self-ordained evangelist and met and married another street corner preacher, Mary Cannon. In the summer of 1937 the Puseys decided to return to New Jersey to spread the word and drove across the country in their "battered old automobile," earning travel money by "conducting revivals in automobile camps," where Mary would preach and Lloyd, who had left his two teenaged sons in Los Angeles with friends, performed backup as "a one man base choir."

Unfortunately, the couple also began to quarrel as they drove east, and in Arizona Mrs. Pusey actually wrote a letter claiming that if she was found dead, her husband had murdered her, and stuffed it in her luggage. The source of the dispute was apparently Mary's disclosure to Lloyd that she had been married four times before, which enraged him.

When they reached Linden, New Jersey, on the night of August 27, 1937, he "attempted to caress her," but Mary resisted his advances, and he grabbed a hammer from the floor of the car and hit her several times. He then drove to a gas station on Mopsick Avenue and filled up his gas tank. When an attendant heard a groan from the car he called police, who found Pusey parked on nearby Winans Avenue, with his now dead wife, a bloody Bible on her body, in the seat beside him.

Pusey, described by the press as a "raw boned evangelist," surrendered without a struggle and was taken to the Linden police station, where he signed a confession, saying "I did it, that's all." Although initially claiming Mary had threatened and attacked him and he decided to "get my licks in first" and so he had acted in self-defense, Pusey quickly dropped that justification and gave as an excuse for the murder the fact that Mary had not revealed her previous marriages, telling police, according to one source, that "we jest argued and argued all across the country. She orter told me she was married before. It got me sore." He did concede a possible otherworldly rationale, however, telling Linden Police Chief Frank Hickey that "the devil tried to rip our marriage apart," apparently successfully. A background check revealed that Pusey had been arrested for panhandling and passing bad checks during his travels.

In September, the Union County prosecutor had "two state alienists" [psychiatrists] interview Pusey to establish whether or not he was insane. They concluded that he was indeed sane for legal purposes and in November the forty-four-year-old "Psalm singing hillbilly," as one journalist characterized him, entered a guilty plea to a second-degree murder charge and was sentenced to a fifteen to twenty-year term in Trenton State Prison.

It appears that Pusey did not spend a long time in prison, as he was living in Nutley, New Jersey, in 1942. He died on August 31, 1953.

J. Edgar Strikes Atlantic City

In the late 19th century, cities and towns across America had either a legal red light district or an area where, for a modest fee, the police ignored brothels, often referred to in rural areas as "women's boarding houses" or "WBH" for short. In the early twentieth century, however, Progressives concerned with the exploitation of women, and Conservatives, alarmed with the increasing number of young women entering the workplace and socializing outside of a controlled environment, found common cause as the media began to sensationalize "white slavery."

Exploiting America's periodic anti-immigrant hysteria, newspapers alleged a nationwide conspiracy of "foreign" men out to seduce innocent young country girls who had come to urban areas seeking work, often entrapping them at urban ice cream parlors into lives of prostitution. The result was the "White-Slave Traffic Act" better known as the Mann Act after its author, Illinois Congressman James Mann. The law, passed in 1910, made it a federal offense to transport a woman or girl across state lines for the purpose of prostitution, "debauchery" or a vaguely defined "immoral purpose."

In the 1930s J. Edgar Hoover, always on the lookout for publicity, launched an operation against "white slavery rings." Hoover could not have picked a better central location for his public relations bust than Nucky Johnson's Atlantic City, New Jersey. Johnson had turned the city by the sea from a seasonal vacation spot for Philadelphians into a national resort during the Prohibition era. Celebrities from all over the country flocked to Atlantic City, as did conventioneers and people looking for all kinds of entertainment, legitimate and otherwise, in what became a year-round playground.

The Depression had hit the city hard, as entertainment was the first thing people cut back on in those dire financial days. Although businesses and banks closed, however, gambling and prostitution was still profitable, if less so than during the halcyon days of the "Roaring Twenties." Hoover did not make the decision to raid Atlantic City on his own, however, as the Treasury Department was interested in Nucky's income and his apparent tax evasion. A significant portion of that income was derived from brothel protection money.

On August 29, 1937, the FBI staged raids in New Jersey, Philadelphia and Delaware, rounding up people who were supplying sex workers to

Atlantic City's numerous brothels. Well over 100 people were arrested for dubious alleged Mann Act violations, including two men who drove a prostitute from New York to Atlantic City and Louis and Agnes Stein, charged with transporting their adopted daughter Peggy Stein from Philadelphia to Atlantic City for the purpose of engaging in prostitution.

A raid at a brothel at 15 North Illinois Avenue in Atlantic City netted a number of prostitutes, two women "procurers," or madams, and two African-American women who worked as maids, and led to the arrest of two doctors who were charged with "making periodic examinations of the inmates of the raided disorderly houses." Most of those arrested, however, were not the "foreign" men allegedly loitering in ice cream parlors, but "women and girls," and did not seem to be enslaved. The prostitutes were held as material witnesses, not felons.

Indictments, guilty pleas and trials following the big raid continued through the end of the year. Testimony from George Whitlock, an Atlantic City municipal jitney inspector, revealed "a direct link between politics and organized vice." Whitlock admitted that he had been directed to "make weekly collections from disorderly houses in Atlantic City and had turned the money over to Ray E. Born, under-sheriff of Atlantic County, a political lieutenant of Enoch L. Johnson, County Treasurer and Republican Leader." Every city employee in Atlantic City obtained his job through Nucky Johnson. In the end, sixty-five people were indicted following Hoover's big raid. Although Walter Winchell wrote that: "White slave raids in Atlantic City will result in the indictment of the town's No. 1 spender," presumably Johnson, he escaped untouched. The madams were charged with income tax evasion, but none would rat out Nucky.

Johnson, whose name comes up with some regularity in this book, was, of course, the inspiration for the characater "Nucky Thompson" in the HBO series *Boardwalk Empire*. While the real Nucky did not shoot anyone, or participate directly in violent crimes (and there were many more shootouts in the series than there ever had been in the City by the Sea), many of the series' story lines were based on actual incidents and characters. The technical accuracy of *Boardwalk Empire*, from clothing to cars, to slang, to firearms, was incredibly precise.

A Hobo Con Man in Nutley

On June 18, 1937, James Pride rolled his "dilapidated automobile" absent license plates, into a vacant lot in Nutley, New Jersey and announced "to anyone who wanted to argue the point" that the car was home to him, his wife Zelma and their four-month old daughter Dorothy. He explained to a curious journalist that "a man's Home was his castle," and that his particular castle was the back seat of the car.

When the local folks came over to see their bizarre new neighbor, Pride told them that he had a connection to a famous person – Jack Dempsey used to pick strawberries at his father in law's farm in Orem, Utah, which may well have been true. He proudly proclaimed that his only assets were the car, which he bought for thirty-five dollars, a bottle of milk, which had turned sour, and fifteen cents in cash. He added that "that was all right. He'd get along somehow." He added that "all I want is to be left alone. I don't want any charity."

Of course, despite his protestations, he had expended considerable effort in drawing attention to his situation. The locals called the Nutley police, who came to the scene and told Pride that the local "overseer of the poor" would take care of the family "until he got on his feet." Pride responded that he was already on his feet and that he just wanted a temporary job so he could buy "some gasoline and food and license plates and then we'll move on."

The Nutley cops were befuddled. There seemed to be no town code prohibiting a person from living in a car, so they called in John Forrester, the town's "overseer of the poor," despite Pride's protestations. Forrester told him: "We'll fix you up. We'll get you on relief." Pride's response was "nothing doing." He said he wanted to stay in the lot in his car until he got a job.

Pride provided Forrester with his back story: "He explained how he and his wife had hoboed their way across the country from Utah, where he met her in 1935 when he was a strawberry picker – like Jack Dempsey -- on her father's farm." Pride said he had been working as a laborer on the construction of the New York World's Fair but had lost that job a few days before appearing in Nutley. He claimed he had called up Jack Dempsey for a recommendation on buying a car, but when Jack did not get back to him, he bought the jalopy he was currently living in and started to head back to Utah, stopping in Nutley on the way.

Pride, who apparently liked publicity, told a reporter that "some people thought we should go on WPA relief but I don't believe in such things. We can take care of ourselves—we always have. You oughta see this lady hop freights."

Forrester was nonplussed. He consulted with other town officials and then told Pride he had a room for the family and wished they would take it, since "it looked bad for Nutley for them to be living in the back seat of a car." Pride accepted, implying that he was doing Forester a favor, but he also asked for a temporary job to buy gas to head back to Utah. There is no record of that, but it is likely the town fathers agreed, as Pride soon disappeared from Nutley, basically having conned the town into giving him lodging and money to leave the place. It is not unlikely that he repeated his performance art a number of times on the way west.

Margaret Gets Her Revenge

Margaret Drennan met twenty-five-year-old Jack Lyons one day in the summer of 1937, when the twenty-year-old Iselin secretarial student was walking home from school. Lyon subsequently took her for rides in his car, and then, according to Margaret, sexually assaulted her. Drennan later recalled that Jack then told her he was married with two children and that if she told anyone about what had happened, he would kill her. She found herself pregnant a short while later. Oh, and his name was not Jack Lyons. It was Paul Reeves.

Margaret encountered Reeves on the street in Iselin after discovering she was expecting his child, and told him she had to talk to him about something important. He told her to come to his home on Oak Tree Road on the evening of September 7, as his wife would be out. Before leaving her own home, Margaret stuck her father's .32 caliber automatic pistol in her purse, and arrived at Reeves' house about 8:30.

Although Reeves' wife was at a Rahway movie theater, his two children were asleep in a nearby room. What happened next, as is often the case in these situations, is unclear, but neighbors heard several shots fired and five witnesses saw a "woman in red" stumble out of the Reeves residence, fall, get up and hurry off. Fred Siebert, who lived next door, pursued the "woman in red," caught up with her and asked her who she was. She answered "John Drennan's daughter," and then ran away. Siebert went into a pharmacy and called the police. When police entered the house, they found Reeves nude and dead on the floor. He had been shot twice, in the leg and abdomen.

When Margaret got home she told her mother "something terrible has happened down near the movies." Her father walked down Oak Tree

Road to the theater, where he discovered that Reeves had been killed, and then returned home, where Margaret confessed to him that she had shot Reeves. That night the Woodbridge police arrived and arrested her. She was subsequently arraigned and indicted for murder.

On the witness stand during what the press dubbed the "New Brunswick honor murder" trial, Margaret gave her side of the story, saying she had brought the pistol with her because she was afraid Reeves would assault her again. She testified that when she entered the house she found him sitting nude on a couch and that he had advanced on her and grabbed her and that they wrestled until she broke free, drew the gun from her purse and, as he lunged at her again, shot him. She spent three hours on the stand and never changed her story, even under aggressive cross examination. After Margaret's testimony Reeves' widow, Myra, cried out "Tell me the truth, Margaret! You killed the father of my children. Please tell me the truth." Margaret threw up her hands then covered her face and sobbed.

A doctor testified that when he examined Drennan following her arrest she was severely bruised. After a deliberation of four and a half hours, Margaret Drennan was acquitted by the jury on October 22, 1937. At the announcement of the verdict, the courtroom erupted "in wild applause" and "spectators shrieked and cheered."

Back at home in Iselin, Margaret told a reporter that she was "planning a new clean future for herself and her unborn child." Although "husky railroad brakeman" Thomas McGovern wanted to marry her, she declared that she would "never marry in view of her experience." In 1940 she was living at the same Sonora Avenue address as in 1937, along with her parents, brothers and sisters and Robert, the son of the man she had shot.

Bunny and Chip Go on a Rampage

Two Newark girls, twenty-year-old Ethel "Bunny" Strouse Sohl and seventeen-year-old Genevieve "Chip" Owens, formed a "fast friendship" after meeting at the Essex County House of Detention, where Sohl had been held after her husband was found guilty of forgery and Owens, whose family said she was involved in "neighborhood escapades" was sentenced for vagrancy.

Once freed, both young women moved into the Owens family's

crowded apartment, and began a crime spree. After stealing a car and robbing two Bergen County gasoline stations, they flagged down a bus in Belleville on December 21, 1937. While Owens waited behind the steering wheel of the getaway car, Sohl entered the bus and robbed the driver, William Barhorst, a Totowa resident, of his coin-carrier. Barhorst resisted, and as he grabbed the sawed off .22 caliber rifle Sohl was brandishing, it went off, killing him. Both women then fled and left the stolen car in a vacant lot, $2.10 richer from their crime. They were arrested soon afterward and went on trial in Newark in January, 1938.

Owens' defense was based on the claim that she was led astray by the older woman, and her mother asserted that Genevieve's "interest in the 'gun molls' of gangster movies" was responsible for her daughter's delinquency. Sohl, daughter of a Newark police officer, who was described as having "a mannish appearance with her close-cropped bob and severe dress" claimed that "the narcotic cigarettes she smoked made wrong things seem right," and her attorney contended that she was a victim of "Marijuana Madness," Her temporary insanity plea was supported by the testimony of her parents. Another witness, who had lived in a house where Sohl once worked as a maid, testified that although "Bunny" stole some money from her, she did not "run around with boys." No doubt.

Sohl herself testified that she "took to a life of crime from smoking marijuana cigarettes" which she started to remedy pain caused by an automobile accident. Doctor James C. Munch of Temple University was called on as an expert witness to bolster Sohl's story of drug madness. Munch testified that he had tested the effects of marijuana on "100 Mexicans," and then smoked a joint himself, and "dreamed that I had lived in an ink bottle for 200 years. Then I climbed to the neck of the bottle and wrote a book. Then I flew out of the bottle and flew around the world twice. Then I awakened." Both defenses failed, the young women were found guilty and on February 16 were sentenced to life in prison. Since a life sentence allowed possible parole after fifteen years, both were subsequently sentenced to a consecutive twelve-year term for the gas station robberies in Bergen County.

On June 16, 1940 Ethel Sohl, along with two other women, escaped from the State Reformatory for Women in Clinton "through a second story window by tying sheets together and securing one end to a radiator." She and her accomplices were recaptured on Jugtown Mountain, a few miles from the prison, after several days on the loose. Owens escaped on

August 25, 1943, using the same method, after being denied parole, and was recaptured two days later in a Manhattan movie theater.

Sohl was paroled on July 14, 1959. Prison authorities said at the time that she had "become a leader among the more than 300 inmates" and that they "regretted to see her go." Sohl said on her release that her prison life had been "full" and went to work at a nearby dairy farm. She died on May 31, 2001, in Stockton, New Jersey.

Bigamy in the Boondocks

So they arrested Theodore "Bud" Flatt Jr. and brought him down to Netcong police headquarters in September, 1937, along with his wife Helen. If Helen looked a little young to some, it was because she was. Helen was twelve. They did not arrest Flatt for being a sexual predator or a pedophile, but for bigamy, as he was already married to Myrtle Ward, who was thirteen at the time of their nuptials six years before. What, you say, Married? Yup. Today in New Jersey, the earliest age at which you may marry is sixteen, and you need parental permission until you are eighteen. That was not the case in 1937, though.

Flatt, described by a reporter as a "lanky mountain boy" was taken from Netcong to the Warren County Jail in Belvidere, where he was held without bail. The "backwoods youth" maintained that he thought he was divorced from Myrtle, conceding "although I never saw no papers nor nothing." Flatt's second nuptial was performed by a justice of the peace in Hackettstown and was "attended by Helen's stepfather, Joseph Koezeno and her mother," who said Helen was fifteen years old. Flatt stated that he married Helen because she and her mother told him she was going to have a baby but "by gosh she really ain't."

Helen, the child bride, maintained that she had "loved Bud a long time. I asked him to marry me. We were very happy, but they had to spoil it." The investigation that resulted in Flatt's arrest began when Helen failed to show up for school, but she said she was done with school, and that she had "put away her dolls for good" because "I'm a married woman and got a right to have my husband."

Flatt pleaded guilty on September 28, 1937, and the "strapping 27-year-old laborer" was sentenced to seven to ten years in state prison and fined $1,000 for bigamy. The sentencing judge, noting that Flatt was already on parole from Rahway Reformatory after serving time for robbery, stated that "there is nothing that I can think of that may be said on behalf of this defendant." Afterward Flatt told a reporter that he did not mind going back to jail so much, but he was "a mite ashamed that it was for such a little thing like getting married."

So, what was the law in New Jersey at the time? To get the answer I called on my crack staff legal scholar, son John. And this is what he came up with: "NJ had a sexual assault statute concerning minors that was passed in 1887. Prior to that, there appears to have been a common-law rule established in Cliver v. State, an 1883 NJ Supreme Court case that established a precedent that a sexual act with a child under ten was assault regardless of the child's willingness."

Farrell v. State was an 1892 prosecution under the 1887 statute. According to that, it was a "high misdemeanor" (a third-degree crime, in modern parlance) to "carnally abuse a woman under the age of sixteen years, with or without her consent" when the perpetrator was over sixteen."

"Age of consent for women to marry at common law was twelve. The source for this is 55 C.J.S. Marriage § 14, John J. Dvorske. Generally speaking, sexual assault and rape laws did not protect married women on a broad scale until the 1980s. New Jersey was likely governed by common law in this matter because he was prosecuted for bigamy—not sexual assault. Flatt protected himself from the 1887 statute by marrying the twelve-year-old with her parents' permission - but then got tripped up for bigamy because he was already married to Myrtle."

Murdered in Maine, Found in North Arlington

"Hey guys, check this out!" One can imagine a North Arlington, New Jersey, policeman saying that to his fellow officers on October 18, 1937, when he and fellow officers discovered the body of South Paris, Maine, Doctor James G. Littlefield, who had been murdered, in the trunk of his car. Littlefield had been stuffed in the trunk and driven to New Jersey by eighteen-year-old Paul "Buddy" Dwyer, who North Arlington police noticed sleeping in the car and awakened for questioning. After a brief search, the cops not only found the doctor in the trunk, but his murdered wife Lydia in the rear seat, covered by a blanket.

Dwyer confessed to the murders, saying that while checking him out in his home bathroom for possible venereal disease, the doctor made a crack about Dwyer's former girlfriend Barbara Carroll being pregnant.

According to Dwyer, the comment enraged him and he punched the doctor and then bashed him on the head with a hammer, killing him. He then stuffed the body in the trunk of Littlefield's car, drove to the doctor's home and told his wife that her husband had hit a couple of pedestrians with his car and ran off by train to Boston. This unlikely story was allegedly accepted by Mrs. Littlefield, since the doctor was, according to Dwyer, addicted to morphine with a tendency to bizarre behavior. Dwyer said that he drove Mrs. Littlefield around for several days, supposedly looking for her husband, and then, when she became suspicious and began to ask questions, strangled her, tossed her in the back seat and headed south.

Dwyer was interrogated by detectives, signed a detailed confession in the North Arlington police station, and was returned to Maine, where police had found some blood on the bathroom floor and Doctor Littlefield's false teeth under Dwyer's bathtub. He was tried and convicted for the doctor's murder and sentenced to life in prison. A few months later, however, while still admitting he was present during the murders of the Littlefields, Dwyer accused Francis Carroll, a deputy sheriff and the father of his former girlfriend, with actually committing them, claiming that the doctor was planning to expose Carroll for committing incest, or, as the newspapers explained, "improper conduct," with his daughter. Dwyer further claimed that Carroll had threatened to kill him and his widowed mother if he did not confess to the crime himself.

Carroll was arrested, indicted and brought to trial in South Paris, Maine, in August, 1938, for the murder of Doctor Littlefield. Carroll's defense attorney said that the case posed "many perplexing and confusing angles," and that, as far as he was concerned, was "a case the like of which has not been seen in the annals of crime in America." Although Dwyer's testimony was the main evidence against Carroll, Hazel Talbot, a "surprise witness," testified that she saw Carroll lurking near Doctor Littlefield's home on the night of the murder. The deputy was convicted and sentenced to life in prison at hard labor, but still maintained his innocence. Neither man was tried for the death of Mrs. Littlefield.

Both men remained in prison until September 1950, when a judge reviewing Carroll's conviction declared that "The case seethes with inadmissible evidence, hearsay, opinion," and ordered him released. Dwyer, who had unsuccessfully petitioned for a pardon in 1941 and 1949 (Carroll was denied a pardon in 1949 as well.), was released on parole the following month. Carroll got a job making furniture and died in 1956. Dwyer got a job in a restaurant in Norway, Maine, married and died sometime in the 1990s. Who actually committed the murders, Dwyer or Carroll, remains a mystery.

CHAPTER 16

1938-The Congressman Goes Out the Window

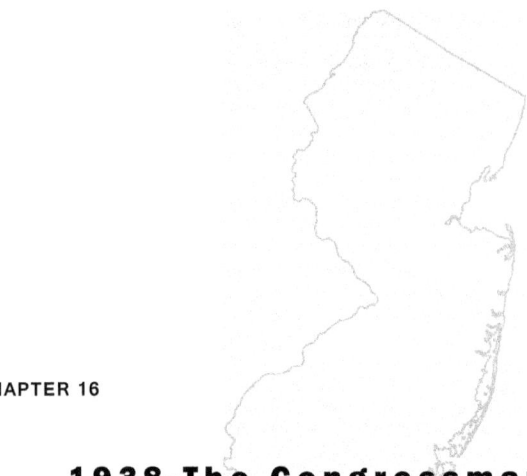

Oops went the congressman! In 1938 Congressman Edward Aloysius Kenney was a man on the rise. Born in Massachusetts in 1884, Kenney graduated from NYU law school in 1908. He established a law practice in Manhattan and then moved to Cliffside Park, New Jersey, opened an office in Hackensack and got involved in New Jersey politics, serving as a legal advisor to the New Jersey draft board during World War I.

The ambitious Kenney ran unsuccessfully for mayor of Cliffside Park as an independent, then as a Republican and then as a Democrat. Rejoining the Republicans, he was appointed to several local positions and to the party's county committee in 1925.

New Jersey gained two congressional seats following the 1930 census and Kenney saw a chance for higher office. The new Ninth District consisted of southern Bergen County and portions of Hudson County. When feuding Republican factions led to chaos in the party's nomination process Kenney contacted Hudson County boss Frank Hague and offered to run as a Democrat. Hague, who was feuding with the Bergen County Democratic Chairman, helped Kenney secure the nomination.

The election of 1932 was a good year for Democrats, who rode the coattails of the Franklin D. Roosevelt landslide, and Kenney was elected with a comfortable margin. He was re-elected twice.

Every year, the New Jersey Chamber of Commerce sponsors a train ride from New Jersey to Washington DC for public officials, businessmen and lobbyists, culminating with meetings with the state's senators and congressmen and a dinner party. In January, 1938 Congressman Kenney was selected to give the keynote speech at the dinner, which was apparently a pretty lively affair, with abundant access to cocktails.

Kenney had a very good time at the dinner, and retired to a bedroom in the Carlton Hotel where the event had been held. At some point during the early morning hours, later estimated at around 6:00 AM, he was pitched out the sixth-floor window in his underwear, hitting the ground and dying instantly. Hotel employees found Kenney's body at 8 AM.

So, what, or who, killed the congressman? Was it suicide, murder or an accident? The initial conclusion was that Kenney's death was accidental. His room had "French windows," which ran to only eighteen inches above the floor. A newspaper reported that: "Police surmised that Kenney, groping in the darkness of the winter morning, mistook the windows for a closet or bathroom door and stumbled into space." The Washington DC coroner ruled that his death was accidental and that there was no need for an inquest.

Kenney's widow Elizabeth, no doubt with the encouragement of Frank Hague, decided to run to succeed him. Her campaign manager Mary Hicks suggested to the press that the Congressman may have been murdered by members of organized crime, due to his efforts to sponsor a national lottery that would threaten the numbers racket. She claimed that there were signs of a struggle and that money and a ring were missing from the hotel room. Nothing came of her assertion, however, which was unsubstantiated by any other evidence or testimony, and Mrs. Kenney lost the election.

The Greatest Con Man

Gaston B. Means, like many of the bizarre characters of early twentieth century America, passed through Atlantic City a number of times and was a bit player in several New Jersey crime stories, from the Lindbergh kidnapping to the bootlegger murders at the Elizabeth Carteret Hotel to his semi-fictional role as a character in the Atlantic City based *Boardwalk Empire* HBO series.

Born in 1879 in North Carolina, the grandnephew of Confederate

General Rufus Barringer, Means moved to New York City to work as a salesman in 1902 and then joined William J. Burns' detective agency. In 1914 he was hired by the German government to investigate British activities in America. Burns was hired by the British to investigate German plots, and both men apparently swapped fabricated intelligence information to feed to their employers for a tidy sum. Every case uncovered seemed to require additional investigation—at $100 ($2,400 in today's currency) per day.

After America entered World War I, squelching the German business, Means managed to win the confidence of wealthy Manhattan widow Maude King, and became her business manager, a role in which he moved large sums of her money into his own accounts. In 1917 he brought Maude down to North Carolina and took her target shooting. Means returned from the shoot with Maude's dead body, explaining that she had accidentally shot herself, although a local farmer, Charles Dry, testified that he heard two shots and thought he saw someone shooting another person at a distance of 150 yards from his house. Indicted for murder, Means was acquitted after a fifteen-minute deliberation, the jury apparently annoyed at the "fancy New York lawyers" the prosecution called in for aid.

Subsequently prosecuted for forging a will that left all of King's money to him, Means made a deal with the judge to drop the charges if he delivered a secret trunk he said was full of correspondence from German spies. He handed over the trunk, which turned out to be empty, but he was a free man.

In 1921, Means was hired as a Bureau of Investigation agent by the agency's new director and his old friend William J. Burns. He quickly went to work in Washington "fixing" things for bootleggers, selling government documents and handling bribes for President Warren Harding's administration officials, but was eventually indicted, prosecuted and sentenced to two years in prison. While incarcerated, Means hired a ghostwriter to author a book in his name claiming that Warren Harding had been murdered by his wife, then cheated the writer out of her share of the royalties.

Released from prison, Means swindled some wealthy New Yorkers into paying him to investigate a non-existent Soviet threat to the United States. His final act was the Lindbergh kidnapping scam, where he bilked a wealthy Washington woman out of $100,000, claiming the baby was alive and in Mexico. Means claimed he had delivered the money to a New Jersey bootlegger, who was conveniently dead. He was convicted of fraud, sentenced to fifteen years in federal prison and died in Leavenworth Penitentiary in 1938.

The Governor Gives DiBlasio a Break

It was January, 1938, and Joe DiBlasio was in trouble, although he no doubt thought it long behind him, left in a Monmouth County farm field more than two decades in the past. The charge against DiBlasio reported in the paper was unclear, noting he was "arrested in New York City on a gun charge after befriending a woman." The details went unsaid. Once the New York cops had Joe in custody, however, they discovered there was an outstanding warrant for him as an "escaped convict" from New Jersey—dating from 1914. Back then DiBlasio had been working on a "Monmouth County prison road gang" when he absconded. What he had done that ended him up on the road gang was unknown, as the records, including the original warrant, had been destroyed in a fire in Freehold many years before – and Joe wasn't saying – nor was his attorney.

DiBlasio's story following his escape was an interesting one. In 1917 he had joined the army, serving in the 82nd Division's 326th Infantry Regiment and participating in the St. Mihiel and Meuse Argonne offensives in France during World War I. He claimed that the gun he was charged with possessing was actually an inert war trophy he had picked up on the battlefield in 1918. While he could have been released on bail for the gun charge, the New Jersey warrant assured that he would remain incarcerated until the matter was cleared up one way or another, as he refused to agree to extradition.

The case dragged on until it came to the direct attention of New Jersey Governor A. Harry Moore in March. Moore interviewed DiBlasio's World War I commanding officer, who attested that his army behavior had been impeccable and that he had "never been guilty of a breach of discipline during his term of service." Moore declared that he would go directly to the state's Court of Errors and Appeals and arrange for a pardon, saying "A fellow who has served his country as Di Blasio has done deserves a break."

The "Newspaper Bandits

They called them the "newspaper bandits." In their Depression-era New Jersey crime spree, during which they robbed more than fifty grocery stores, twenty-year-old John Kern and his twenty-seven-year-old sibling Henry "shielded their faces with newspapers in one hand and held a gun in the other." The brothers, children of Austrian immigrants, lived at 615 Jefferson Street in Elizabeth, but targeted grocery stores in Essex, Bergen and Passaic counties, where they led law enforcement officers "on a merry chase" for eighteen months. Ironically Henry declared his occupation as "grocery clerk" in the 1930 census.

The chase ended abruptly and not so merrily on February 5, 1938. Based on an anonymous phone tip, police officers Samuel Gatti and John Koehler spotted the Kerns, who were sitting in their car on a Paterson street in front of a store they were probably planning to rob. On noticing the officers approach in their "radio car," one brother shot at them though his own windshield, and both attempted to flee on foot. Gatti and Koehler jumped out of their patrol car, "ducking wildly aimed bullets" and "shot and clubbed their way through the barrage" to capture the bandits.

The aftermath of the melee left John Kern with four bullets in him and Henry with a fractured skull. The battered brothers were brought to Paterson General Hospital, where, according to Paterson police chief John Murphy, they "confessed to the series of stickups." Some thought that John would not survive his wounds, but he did. In succeeding days Paterson city officials, including the police and fire commissioners, led by Mayor Bernard L. Stafford, lavished praise on Gatti and Koehler for their courage and efficiency.

It didn't take long to get the case moving in the justice system, where the newspaper bandits "pleaded no defense to 15 indictments – 13 charging robbery and two charging assault with intent to kill." On February 19, 1939, Common Pleas Judge Robert H. Davidson sentenced the Kern brothers to "75 to 100 years each in state prison." Davidson told them "you boys had murder in your hearts and you deserve no consideration. Society must be protected from people like you."

A survey of the Trenton State Prison prisoner population in the 1940 census failed to turn up either brother, but John appeared to be an inmate in the State Mental Hospital in Ewing Township.

Failed Elopement Turns into Murder in Asbury Park

Frank Cheeseman bought a "defective, antiquated pistol" from Neptune, New Jersey, ASPCA agent Forrest Brenner, ostensibly to shoot rats with. On August 6, 1938, however, he stuck the .32 caliber revolver in his pocket and went over to Ann Clark's house to demand that she elope with him to Elkton, Maryland. Cheeseman and Clark had known each other for four years, but Ann had, according to one source, "recently obtained a position at Fitkin Hospital, Neptune [and] acquired a new outlook on life and decided she was not ready to get married." Added to that, her mother, Elizabeth Yetman, apparently detested Cheeseman.

When Cheeseman arrived at Clark's home at 162 Ridge Avenue in Asbury Park, he ran upstairs to her bedroom and ordered her to "get your clothes, kid, we're going." When she refused, he pulled the gun and threatened to commit suicide. Clark's sister and stepfather were out of the house, but her mother was home and responded to Clark's screams for help. A struggle ensued, a shot rang out, and the mortally wounded Mrs. Yetman staggered out the door and "pitched down a flight of stairs." Cheeseman ran out of the house, but returned and surrendered to police who had arrived on the scene.

Frank Cheeseman was indicted for first degree murder, but was offered a deal – plead guilty to second degree murder and accept a twenty- to thirty-year sentence. He decided, however, to take his chances on a trial. It appeared that defense attorney Alvin Newman was going to have his client plead not guilty due to temporary insanity, but then he took a different tack, claiming that the shooting was accidental, as Mrs. Yetman had got in the way of Cheeseman's gun as he was attempting to kill himself. The case went to trial in Freehold in October, 1938.

Assistant Prosecutor Edwin F. Juska called twenty witnesses, including Ann, her stepfather and the arresting officers. Ann declared that she had never actually dated Cheeseman and Juska produced a confession in which Cheeseman admitted culpability. In conclusion, he told the jury they should "send Cheeseman to the electric chair for deliberately murdering Mrs. Yetman, who was 'cowering, cringing and backing away from him.'"

Newman called Cheeseman's friend Thomas McLaughlin to the stand to testify that he had seen Ann and Cheeseman together a number of times and that Cheeseman bought a sterling silver engagement ring for Ann at an Asbury Park boardwalk shop in 1937, arguing that his client's despondency over the ending of the relationship was the ultimate cause of Mrs. Yetman's death. The jury, after deliberating for three hours and nineteen minutes, delivered a verdict of not guilty, and Cheeseman was freed.

In the aftermath, an outraged prosecutor charged Cheeseman with carrying a concealed weapon and threatening suicide, and he was rearrested, indicted, convicted, and spent several months in prison. After his release, he returned to Neptune, where some unhappy local citizens set a cross afire on his lawn, leading the editorial staff of the *Asbury Park Press*, recalling local Ku Klux Klan activity in the previous decade, to state, referring to the burning cross, "we don't want any more of them."

Frank Cheeseman later married and had two children. Everything was not well, however, and in May, 1942, his wife Theresa brought domestic violence charges against him. The couple apparently reconciled, but separated in 1948, after which Cheeseman broke into the house where his wife and her new boyfriend were living and charged them with adultery in a case that was dismissed. In 1949 he was arrested for failure to pay child support and sentenced to probation, but subsequently disappeared from the news.

A Depression Era Publicity Hound

Over the 350 or so years of New Jersey history, its citizens have witnessed more than their share of hucksters, poseurs, con men and grandiose self-promoters. One such who never quite made the big leagues was Gene Tortariello. Beginning in the late 1930s, Tortariello, a Neptune resident, was involved in a series of hoaxes apparently designed solely to get his name in the newspapers.

In September, 1938, Tortariello chained Wilma Leaycroft, an "attractive and docile young woman of 18," who he claimed was his fiancée, to the steering wheel of his car while he worked as a welder in a Linden plant, returning to unshackle her for lunch and a walk and then re-chaining her. Appalled onlookers called the police, who, on investigating the situation, released Wilma but said the girl would not file charges and seemed happy with her situation. The story, along with a photo of Tortariello chaining Leaycroft to the steering wheel, made newspapers across the country, and included Tortariello's claim that he shackled her because "you can't trust women these days." Perceptive Linden police Chief Frank Hickey told reporters that "it looks like a publicity stunt...but it doesn't make sense." It was indeed a hoax, and Wilma later announced that she had decided not to marry Tortariello, described in one newspaper as a "veteran prankster and self publicist."

It wasn't the first time Tortariello made the news. In 1937 he had "tested" an "anti-drowning pill" in the ocean off Asbury Park. When the boat monitoring his test began to sink, he and his associates had to be rescued by lifeguards, who advised him to never return to Asbury Park. On another occasion, he announced to the newspapers that he was going to fly a plane nonstop from New Jersey to Rome, although there is no evidence he ever had a pilot's license.

In June, 1939, Tortariello jumped off the Highlands/Sandy Hook Bridge into the Shrewsbury River to demonstrate an "electric umbrella" claimed by its alleged inventor, Mayer Abrams of Asbury Park, as an improvement on the parachute. The jump was judged "a dismal failure" as Tortariello plunged directly into the water, but he made news again.

Tortariello's next exploit, and apparently his last, occurred in April, 1941, when he "got himself wedged in a hole in a stone breakwater" in Sea Bright, and it took "fifty firemen, State policemen and first-aid crew members" to extricate him. Tortariello claimed he slipped and fell into the hole, but local police concluded he had crawled in. He was arrested on charges of "disorderly conduct and creating a disturbance," and Justice of the Peace Walter J. Sweeney ordered him to see a psychiatrist. Tortariello did make the *New York Times*, though -- and then disappeared from New Jersey history.

CHAPTER 17

1938-Wealthy Wacko Runs Amuck in Plainfield

"Hellzapoppin on the Hill Today," was the headline in the *Plainfield Courier-News* on March, 7, 1939. Long known as an eccentric, Samuel Rushmore, a sixty-seven-year-old Plainfield, New Jersey, entrepreneur who had made a fortune inventing and producing automobile starters, hydraulic systems and headlights, hung out a banner proclaiming "Liberty is Dead," then ordered trees chopped down and bushes torn up and set fire to several cars on his estate at 777 Belvidere Avenue.

What was the reason for Rushmore's public tantrum? He said it was a protest against Jersey City mayor and political boss Frank Hague. Rushmore told a reporter that he wanted to leave the state "because Hague is the law," paraphrasing the mayor's famous comment referring to himself, and adding that: "The state of New Jersey is not safe for life or property, the courts give us no protection and I intend to cut all strings." He said that although he considered leveling his spacious home before leaving New Jersey, he was also giving thought to "converting it into a maternity hospital open to all creeds and races, including Negroes."

Unsurprisingly, Frank Hague actually had nothing to do with inciting the eccentric Rushmore's wrath – although the Jersey City boss' son might have had a vague connection with the outburst. The immediate cause of the inventor's ire was apparently that the New Jersey Court of Errors and

Appeals (to which Frank Hague Jr. had been appointed as a "lay judge,"), the state's highest court, had upheld the New Jersey Chancery Court's decision to dismiss Rushmore's lawsuit against his ex-wife Hazel and her attorney, who he had charged with conspiracy – to do what, was not clear. A newspaper reported that Rushmore, "whose marital troubles have intrigued his neighbors for years," had fought Hazel's divorce case and the alimony awarded and wanted revenge, although there is no record that he contested her accusation that he had spanked her with a hairbrush.

In the end Rushmore did not leave New Jersey and did not destroy his home, but he kept up taunting Hague, although it is unlikely "duh mare" was unduly concerned, for some time, subsequently buying a coffin and having it hoisted onto his roof and planting a sign saying "Liberty is Dead. Heil Hague" on his lawn and putting a garbage can on his porch with a sign above it reading "Hague is the Law. Dump Law Books Here."

The 10,000-square foot Rushmore mansion, with its six bedrooms and six baths but minus its anti-Hague signs, still stands on a 2.59-acre lot, and was offered for sale for $1,150,000 in 2014.

The "Insurance Murder Ring"

Taking a few liberties with details, it seems that when he was arrested and questioned in May, 1939, seven years after the incident, Samuel Crispino basically said: "Hey, we wuz fishin' and I turns around to bait my hook, and I hears a splash and when I looks back he ain't there no more." At least that was Crispino's story and he was sticking to it, for a while at least. The splash he mentioned resulted in the death of Joseph Arena, who went to sleep with the fishes off a boat out of Sea Isle City, New Jersey in 1932.

In the first months of 1939, Philadelphia was abuzz with stories of an "insurance-murder ring" uncovered in the city. The criminals involved contracted with persons who were the insurance beneficiaries of their victims, usually, it seemed, a spouse, and killed their victims with arsenic, gaining the newspaper name tag of the "arsenic syndicate" The gang was revealed when Mrs. Millie Giacobbe confessed that she had contracted with the ring to murder her husband and split the insurance money with them. The ring's work spread beyond Philadelphia, and included a number of New Jersey clients

It turned out that there was another Philadelphia gang involved in the same business. A tad more sophisticated, they used a variety of methods to slay their victims, including poisoning them with hard-to-detect antimony. Police interviewing members of that mob came to the conclusion that Crispino, in 1939 a hat maker in Reading, Pennsylvania, along with his fishing partner for the day, Dominick Rodia, had tossed Arena overboard in fulfillment of an insurance scam agreement that involved Rodia's wife Anna in what came to be called in the media the "three men in a boat murder." Mrs. Rodia collected $3,128, which she presumably split with Crispino and Rodia.

Since the murder took place in New Jersey, it would be tried there, and state law enforcement officials, including Cape May County assistant prosecutor Herbert Campbell, came to Philadelphia to interview Crispino, Rodia and Mrs. Arena. Rodia confessed to killing Arena and was extradited to New Jersey.

Once he came to trial, Rodia testified that the Philadelphia police beat a confession out of him and that he was innocent. The prosecutor called Crispino, Mrs. Arena and Morris Bolber, the alleged ringleader of the insurance murder gang who had already been convicted of a poisoning murder, as witnesses against Rodia. The prosecutor told a reporter that he had not indicted the other three for murder because they "could not be tried 'under New Jersey law.'" When the puzzled journalist pressed him as to why, "he did not explain." The highlight of the trial was apparently the reaction of Anna Arena when Bolber testified that she had said to him "my husband is no good. I should do something about it," and she stood up in court and yelled "that's a lie," then ran out into the hallway and collapsed. The jury failed to convict Rodia, and everyone went back to Philadelphia, presumably to resume business as usual.

A Child Bride in the Pinelands

We had a story of a 1930s child bride in the boondocks of the New Jersey north country a while back, and so now it is the turn of the Pinelands. In the summer of 1939, Murrell Webb was a sturdy twenty-seven-year-old laborer on a farm on Elbow Lane, near Mount Holly, New Jersey. Since he was making $12 a week, and getting on in years, Webb apparently thought it was about time he got hitched.

Webb found a potential bride in Mary Jobes, a fourteen-year-old 8th grade student in Burlington. Unbeknownst to Mary's parents, the pair took off for Maryland to get married and returned in a day. Mary rejoined her twelve brothers and sisters at home for a bit, then announced she was going to a movie. She did not return. Her mother, also named Mary Jobes, heard she had moved in with Webb and his mother Mamie in their tenant farm dwelling, and went over to demand that her daughter come home. She left in a huff, claiming that Webb had assaulted her by hitting her with what he said was a marriage license. Mrs. Jobes claimed that he "so violently waved a marriage license under her nose that it struck her and she fell" Webb was arrested and lodged in the Burlington County Jail.

Things became even more confused when Murrell and Mary, perhaps not the brightest lights in the Pinelands, said, respectively, that they were married in Havre de Grace and Elkton, causing local authorities to question whether or not they were actually married at all. The certificate that Webb allegedly hit his mother in law with was produced, however, and was actually issued at Belair, Maryland on August 3, 1939. The fact that Mary gave her age as 18 was duly noted, but apparently did not become an issue. At some time during the saga Mary posed for a photograph, symbolically saying goodbye to her doll.

Webb made his $300 bail, and immediately went to the Jobes house, where Mary had returned after his arrest, and told her mother "Mrs. Jobes, Mary is my lawful bride and I have a right to take her home." Mrs. Jobes answered that if he left Mary with her she would drop the charges against him. Webb went home, milked the cows on the farm, and then returned, more determined than ever. When she saw him drive up, Mary "bid goodbye to her parents, ran out to her husband, and said: 'I love you. Let's go.'" And off they went. The charges against Murrell Webb were apparently dropped, although this might have been due to the fact that his mother in law was hit by a car and killed in October, 1939.

Perhaps surprisingly to some, Murrell and Mary's marriage endured. Mary died in 1974 and Murrell in 1976. They are buried side by side in the Odd Fellows Cemetery in Pemberton.

The Minister Hires a Murderer

In 1939 there was a minister in Camden named Walter Dworecki. Dworecki, pastor of the Polish Baptist Church, was nicknamed "Iron Mike" because of the severity of his fire and brimstone sermons. Iron

Mike made public war on sin, but in his own life, as is often the case, things were different.

Dworecki had three children, one of them an eighteen-year-old girl named Wanda. Wanda apparently did not share Iron Mike's sense of sin, and was characterized as "of wayward disposition, apparently oversexed and frequently in male company of doubtful morality."

Iron Mike sought a solution to this problem, and he hit on one that could not only end his embarrassment, but, coincidentally, make him a buck. He took out two $1,000 insurance policies on Wanda, each with a double indemnity clause should she die of an accident, and then contracted with two local thugs, John Popola and Joe Rocco, aka "Joe Rock," to kill her for a $1,000 fee. Although murder was a new idea for Iron Mike, he was an old hand at insurance fraud, as he "had once been charged with lucrative arson by a fire insurance company." Dworecki's hired hoodlums muffed the job, however, and Wanda escaped from their car, naked but unharmed, and apparently unaware of her father's complicity in the attempt on her life.

The preacher did not give up, however. He had taken in a twenty-year-old unemployed "carnival roustabout" named Peter Shewchuck as a boarder, and Shewchuck got to know Wanda quite well, apparently in the Biblical manner. Seeking a bargain after the previous fiasco, Dworecki promised the young ne'er do well $100, payable on receipt of the insurance money, to kill his daughter. The down payment of fifty cents, however, would be all that Shewchuck would ever collect.

On August 8, 1939, while Iron Mike was conducting a tent revival across the Delaware River in Pennsylvania, providing him with a plausible alibi, Shewchuck picked Wanda up at the intersection of Haddon and Kaighn Avenues in Camden and drove her to a secluded lover's lane location in South Camden, where he strangled her and then beat her with a rock. After the body of "dull, unbeautiful," as one news outlet called her, Wanda, was discovered the following morning, witnesses advised the Camden police that she was last seen alive with Shewchuck, who was soon in police custody.

Shewchuck quickly implicated Iron Mike, who was also arrested. Both men were taken in Camden Police Headquarters, where they signed confessions, but the minister later recanted. Dworecki was found guilty by a jury, however, and sentenced to death. He was electrocuted at Trenton State Prison on March 28, 1940, making the record books as the first clergyman executed in New Jersey history. Shewchuck, tried separately, was sentenced to life in prison, and left the court on May 3, 1940, "gleefully proclaiming he 'got a break.'"

"Nucky Gets Engaged"

In September, 1939, Enoch L. "Nucky" Johnson, Republican political boss of Atlantic City and Atlantic County, the south Jersey political equivalent of Hudson County Democrat boss Frank Hague, attended the Miss America contest. The ever-dapper fifty-six-year-old Nucky was accompanied by his current girlfriend, thirty-three-year-old showgirl and model Florence Osbeck. In November Osbeck announced her engagement to Johnson, declaring that their wedding would occur "sometime before Christmas." It would, however, not be that Christmas.

Unlike the more socially moral tea-totaling Hague, with whom he was acquainted and worked with on occasion, and whose extra revenue mostly (but not all) came from conventional political payoffs, Johnson went well beyond the usual avenues of political enrichment. For a cut of the action, he protected Atlantic City's illegal gambling, prostitution and, until the repeal of Prohibition, liquor businesses, and hobnobbed with organized crime figures of the day. Johnson's income has been estimated at $500,000 a year (about $7,000,000 in today's money) the year he hosted a national gangster convention with Al Capone, Lucky Luciano, Meyer Lansky, and other captains of illegal industry, including Newark's own Abner "Longie" Zwillman. The result was the founding of the first national crime syndicate.

The federal government, encouraged by the Hearst Newspapers (allegedly due to the fact that Nucky had won the affections of William Randolph Hearst's favorite Atlantic City escort lady) began to look into Johnson's finances in the 1930s. The decade brought hard times from other quarters for Johnson and his city. The economic crash of the Great Depression had hurt the tourist business, and the repeal of Prohibition had removed one of Atlantic City's main attractions for visitors. J. Edgar Hoover's prostitution raids did not help matters either.

Hearst's prodding bore fruit, and the FBI and IRS began a joint investigation in 1936. In May, 1939, Johnson was indicted for tax evasion on $125,000 in protection money he had skimmed from Atlantic City numbers racket operators. Nucky successfully delayed his court appearance for some time, and certainly did not look unduly apprehensive in a photo taken of him and Florence at the Miss America Contest in 1939. The case was finally adjudged in July, 1941, and Johnson was indeed found guilty, sentenced to ten years in prison and fined $20,000. On August 1, two weeks before beginning to serve his sentence at Lewisburg Penitentiary, he married Florence.

Johnson was released in 1945, after serving four years, and took a "pauper's oath" to avoid paying his fine. During his absence from the Atlantic City scene, Nucky's henchmen had reportedly quietly transferred much of his wealth to his bride. He returned to Atlantic City, where he lived quietly, honored as an elder statesman of the Atlantic County Republican party, until his death on December 9, 1968, at the age of eighty-five.

According to his obituary in the *New York Times*, Johnson once said: "We have whisky, wine, women, song and slot machines. I won't deny it and I won't apologize for it. If the majority of the people didn't want them they wouldn't be profitable and they would not exist. The fact that they do exist proves to me that the people want them." And he was right.

CHAPTER 18

1940-The Tax Collector Goes Berserk

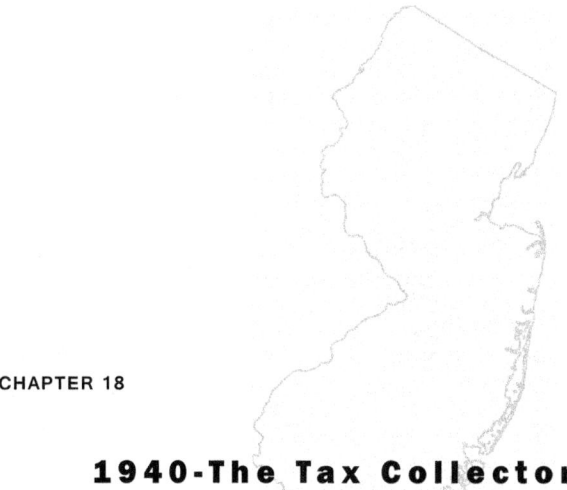

One would think they would have seen this coming, as people like John Butler tend to provide more than a few clues during their lives. If so, no one noticed, and Butler ended up as the tax collector of the town of Kenilworth, New Jersey. On New Year's Day, 1940, the day of the town council reorganization meeting, the seventy-two-year-old Butler stormed into the office of Borough Clerk August Stahl waving two revolvers and began shooting. In a matter of seconds, he had killed Stahl and moved on towards the council meeting room to finish the task he had set for himself, killing three council members. Police officer Andrew Ruscansky, who heard shooting from police headquarters one flight below, ran upstairs and tried to subdue Butler, but was shot in the struggle. The berserk tax collector was finally restrained by "husky councilman Paul Finkel," who held him in a headlock.

In the aftermath, Kenilworth Police chief George Conklin said that Butler had claimed that the town government was plotting against him and spreading rumors about him and that he intended to kill the three councilmen and Stahl in revenge. Stahl, a former mayor, apparently ran against Butler in a Republican primary contest for the treasurer's office in 1937, but lost the election. Over the next two years, the town council had passed legislation restricting the authority of Butler's office, much to his displeasure.

The English-born Butler had a long municipal career in Kenilworth, as both a Democrat and Republican, after moving to the borough with his wife and two children from Elizabeth in 1911. He was elected to the town council in 1914, and served as police commissioner and chief during World War I. Failing in a 1922 election for mayor, he succeeded in winning office as tax collector-treasurer in 1925, running unopposed and being re-elected for five successive terms as a Democrat and then a Republican.

Middlesex County Prosecutor Abe David had three physicians examine Butler the day after the shooting incident, and they reported that their assessment "indicated that the prisoner held on a murder charge was mentally ill" and "described Butler as a paranoic suffering from a persecution complex."

On January 25, 1940, Butler "was adjudged insane" by the Union County grand jury, and Judge Edward A. McGrath signed papers committing him to the state mental hospital in Ewing Township. Butler was listed as an inmate of the New Jersey State Hospital in the census of 1940. He reportedly worked at the hospital as a librarian and died there on April 20, 1945.

In 2013, Kenilworth Historian Walter E. Boright filled in Butler's back story in a comprehensive article in the *Cranford Chronicle*. Ironically, he reported that Officer Ruscansky's daughter, Joan Ruscansky Merrill, who was seven years old at the time of Butler's rampage, recalled that: "My father and Mr. Butler were friends before the shooting and remained so afterwards. Mr. Butler was always apologetic for having wounded our dad. In fact, until Mr. Butler passed away my father visited him every New Year's Day, the anniversary of the shooting. Dad brought Mr. Butler a box of cigars which he enjoyed."

The Asbury Park Post Office Heist

It was the biggest heist in the history of the New Jersey shore. On July 30, 1940. J. Clarence Barton Jr., an Asbury Park Bank and Trust Company messenger, and his guard, Joseph Sturm, were carrying two bags with $108,000 in cash ($1,837,018.29 in today's money) to the Asbury Park Post Office, for pickup and transport by the American Express Company to the Federal Reserve Bank in New York City. The bank employees double parked their car on Bangs Avenue in front of the Post Office and were proceeding into the building when Barton felt a gun muzzle in his back and the words "I'll take care of that." There were three bandits and they also took Sturm's gun and headed for their car. A subsequent newspaper account noted that: "The daring holdup in the heart of the business center here occurred in full view of many passers-by." Alfred Bennett was turning the corner into Bangs Avenue when he had to slam on his brakes to avoid hitting the three bandits as they raced across the street to their getaway car. "Later he realized that if he had scattered them he would have stopped the robbery, and possibly collected a reward."

The robbery took place so fast that "not even the guards were sure what had happened, except that they knew the money was gone and that the men who took it had escaped toward Allenhurst in a car bearing Pennsylvania license plates." The bandits' car turned left onto Main Street and sped north, almost hitting the automobile of Mrs. Alma Kaplan of Belmar in the process. Kaplan, like Bennet, was one of the few people who actually got a good look at the robbers. When the bandits reached First Avenue they made a sharp left, and crossed the tracks just in front of a passing freight train, which blocked immediate pursuit.

Two days later the getaway car was found abandoned in Somerville, during an investigation involving federal, state and county law enforcement. Colonel Mark O. Kimberling, Superintendent of the New Jersey State Police, announced that "tentative identification" of the robbers had been made from fingerprints and other evidence found in the car, which included "two empty money bags bearing the markings of the Asbury Park National Bank and Trust Company" and Joseph Sturm's handgun. Ward Kremer, Supervisor of the Asbury Park Police Department, said that he had turned over a "highly important clue" to the FBI, which had joined the investigation, but refused to say what it was. Bennett had stated that one robber wore sunglasses and gloves, and those objects were found in the vehicle as well, and they were probably the "clue."

The investigation stalled until October, 1940, when two men were arrested for robbing $700 from a crap game in Perth Amboy. While they were incarcerated in the Middlesex County Jail, their fingerprints were found to match those found in the getaway car. They were identified as Nicholas Cioffe of Orange and Benjamin Bondiego of Newark, but turned out to be Nicholas Cioffe and Alfred F. Duggan, the former from Orange, but the latter actually from Jersey City. The third member of the bandit trio was never found, and both Cioffe and Duggan proclaimed their innocence. They went to trial on federal bank robbery charges in Newark, but were acquitted on January 20, 1941 after a jury deliberation of five hours.

Monmouth County was quick to prefer state charges against Cioffe and Duggan, who were transferred to the Monmouth County Jail in Freehold. To avoid a case of double jeopardy, they were charged with and indicted for having "taken the money personally from a bank guard and messenger." Cioffe and Duggan were tried in Freehold in March, 1941. The result was a hung jury when one juror held out for acquittal when the other eleven held the defendants guilty.

Not about to give up, Monmouth County tried the alleged robbers again. Clarence Barton identified Cioffe as the gunman and passerby Lemuel G. Layman and Alfred Bennett concurred. Alma Kaplan testified that she recognized Duggan as he rode by in the getaway car. In their defense, Cioffe and Duggan offered alibis. Cioffe claimed that he was in Newark, working for his father in law, while Duggan said he was on the beach at Sea Bright with friends at the time of the robbery. Under cross examination, Cioffee admitted that he worked erratically around the state, making his living at "selling betting pads, dice and paraphernalia of this sort" as an associate of "Gyp" DeCarlo. Duggan, who had claimed he was renting a house in Navesink at the time, was found to have left that residence the day before the crime. The fact that Duggan had a criminal record as a drug dealer was also introduced by the prosecutor. Hoboken-born Angelo "Gyp" DeCarlo was a representative of the Genovese crime family in northern New Jersey, involved in numerous criminal activities. He was eventually sent to prison for a number of offenses but pardoned by President Richard Nixon when he developed a fatal illness. DeCarlo was portrayed as a character in the film "Jersey Boys."

Cioffe and Duggan were found guilty on May 4, 1941. On May 16, Judge John C. Giordano sentenced Duggan to twelve to fifteen years in prison and Cioffe to eight to ten years. He did not explain the disparity in sentencing. The two men appealed the decision on technical grounds, including the possibility of double jeopardy due to the federal trial in Newark but their appeal was denied by the New Jersey Supreme court. Cioffe's subsequent life is unknown, but after his release from prison, Duggan became a labor union organizer, and was murdered in a dispute in the 1950s. The Asbury Park Bank and Trust Company was reimbursed in full for its loss by the Federal Deposit Insurance Corporation, but who the third bandit was and what happened to the actual currency stolen that day, in the largest robbery in Monmouth County history, remain mysteries.

The Colonel was a Crook

Leo P. Gaffney, of Plainfield, New Jersey, seemed to have played the game right. By 1940 the World War I veteran had risen from the rank of lieutenant to lieutenant colonel in the New Jersey National Guard, where he served as an aide to New Jersey Governor A. Harry Moore. The rank and position reveal that Gaffney had political, as well as military, proficiency. In the civilian sphere, the former Prohibition Agent had become the president of Bankers Industrial Service, Inc., a Wall Street Investment firm. The Gaffneys lived large, and Leo's wife Ellen, a leading Middlesex County socialite, was a "patroness" of the Laurel League of Plainfield's Luncheon-Bridge Party at the Blue Hills Plantation in 1937.

But then there was an inquiry into "practices which the government alleges led to a $1,000,000 loss to investors." It turned out that Bankers Industrial Service, in which Gaffney and several other men had sold shares, had been, according to one investigator, "an empty shell." Gaffney and his fellow corporate officers were indicted by a federal grand jury in November 1940.

Gaffney, who used about "$200,000 ($3,354,457 in today's money) of the corporation's funds in the purchase of a fifty-seven-foot yacht and other luxuries," and his associates were found guilty of mail fraud, violation of the Securities Exchange Act of 1933 (aka Glass-Steagall Act), and conspiracy. Gaffney, "the principle figure in the swindle" was sentenced to three and a half years in prison.

New Jersey's Nazis

In retrospect, the week the Germans occupied the Sudetenland might not have been the best time to call a German-American Bund meeting, but call one they did, on the evening of October 2, 1938, in Union City, New Jersey—and better yet, the local Bundists invited national leader Fritz Kuhn to come and celebrate the occasion.

Several Czechoslovakian American associations were meeting earlier in the day at neighboring Gutenberg, and the Jackson War Veteran Democratic Club rented a hall across the street from the Bund venue, which adjoined City Hall Tavern, to provide protestors with a headquarters. Union City police asked local Bund leader August Klapprott to cancel, but he said he refused.

In the end, Kuhn arrived, fresh from a speech at Camp Nordland, the Bund vacation spot in Andover in Sussex County founded by Klapprott, where Kuhn had proclaimed Hitler the "master of all situations." More than 5,000 protesters waving signs condemning the Nazis and carrying a straw effigy of Hitler, which they burned, also came to town. The veterans attempted to break into the hall and physically eject Kuhn, but were halted by police. The police chief finally told the Bund boss to leave town, which he did, amidst a hail of bricks directed at his car. Kuhn was subsequently arrested and convicted in New York of embezzling the Bund's cash for his own purposes, but New Jersey would not see the last of Nazis.

In October, 1940, a sub-committee of the Special Committee to Investigate Un-American Activities, better known as the Dies Committee after its chairman, Congressman Martin Dies Jr., met in Newark, New Jersey, and subpoenaed leaders of the German-American Bund to testify. A news photographer took advantage of the occasion to take a photo of three seemingly amused Bund leaders, Klapprott, identified as the eastern organizer for the organization, Bund attorney, Wilbur Keegan, and Kuhn's successor as the Bund's National Bundesfuehrer, Camden-born Gerhard Wilhelm Kunze.

Klapprott and Kunze had been arrested, along with the Bund's National Treasurer, Mathias Koehler, in a Memorial Day 1940 raid by the Sussex County sheriff on Camp Nordland. They were freed on bail while a Sussex County grand jury considered charges against them for "uttering statements tending to incite racial hatred."

The Dies committee tried to connect Bund behavior with Communist Party activities, including possible shipyard sabotage, an accusation hotly denied by Klapprott and Kunze. Kunze described the Bund as "an American minority group" and claimed that he was a "German racially" but an "American politically." He did concede that he had "stickers bearing the slogan 'The Yanks are not coming'" which were associated with Communists, in his possession, although he said he did not recall how he acquired them. Kunze went on to say that the Bund members who attended the Ku Klux Klan meeting at Camp Nordland prior to the camp's closure did so on their own, not as official representatives of the Bund.

John C. Metcalfe, a former Bund member working as an investigator for the committee, testified that the Klan was seeking to join with the Bund in forming a "Nazi-Fascist movement" of "kameraden" in the country that would also include "the Italian black shirts, the Ukrainian brown shirts, the silver shirts, the gold shirts of Mexico and the Russian National League of America."

Meanwhile, in Sussex County, ten Bund members, including Klapprott and Kunze, were indicted on charges of "promoting hatred against members of the Jewish religion." One Bundist was quoted as having said at a meeting that the organization's members "are against all Jews and non-Aryans. The real fifth column in this country is Roosevelt and his Jewish bosses. You are the real Americans...our day is coming. We know who you are, all Jews, and we'll get rid of you."

The accused were convicted of violating New Jersey's recently passed "race hatred" law and fined. Kunze was arrested several times during 1941 in various areas of the country. In 1942, following American entry into World War II, he was convicted of spying for Germany and sentenced to federal prison, but fled to Mexico.

The Tiniest New Jersey Soldier

Nicholas Casale, of Newark, New Jersey, laid claim to being the smallest man to serve in combat in the United States army in World War I. When he registered for the draft in June of 1917, Casale, who had been born in Harrison in 1892, but then lived at 127 Ridge Street in Newark, was described as "short" and "slender." Drafted in April, 1918, he was assigned to and served for a year in Company C of the 148th Infantry Regiment.

In France, the 148th Infantry fought in the Meuse-Argonne and Ypres-Lys offensives for three straight months in late 1918 until the November 11 Armistice. On November 2, 1918, during the Ypres-Lys campaign, the regiment was the first allied unit to cross the Scheldt River in Belgium, suffering a large number of casualties from heavy machine gun and artillery fire. Successfully crossing the Scheldt inspired the regimental motto: "We'll do it." Following the Armistice, the 148th remained in Europe for several months before it returned to the United States and was demobilized in April, 1919.

Little Nicholas Casale from Newark was in the thick of all the fighting, even though they had to cut down his rifle stock so his finger could reach the trigger. He claimed that he "had a hard time in the service, because the rest of the army wouldn't take him seriously. Once he had to serve time in the guard house for throwing a brick at a six-foot sergeant who called him a Boy Scout." He told a newspaper reporter that "the humiliation was awful."

After the war, it appeared that Casale was apparently never meant to be there in the first place, because he was drafted even though he failed to meet the minimum height and weight physical standards set by the army, although those standards were not set until June, 1918. In November, 1929, Casale began a campaign to gain recognition and receive "a gold medal" from the federal government as an award for his unique status.

Casale secured the assistance of Representative Fred Hartley of Kearny, New Jersey, at that time the youngest United States Congressman, who provided him with "an affidavit from the U.S. Veterans Bureau" which certified his actual height and weight when drafted. The affidavit certified that he was four feet, ten inches tall and weighed 106 pounds (Casale maintained that he weighed only 104 pounds.), and the army's minimum draft height and weight standard, set in June, 1918, was five feet three inches and 113 pounds – it was amended downward that September to five feet and 110 pounds.

Although the Veterans' Bureau supplied him with the data he requested, the bureau refused his request to declare Casale "the smallest man" who had served overseas in the war, stating that it would "require months for clerks to scan the record of every man who served with the A.E.F."

In response, Casale initiated what would become a more than ten-year campaign to be officially recognized as the smallest man who had served in the American Expeditionary Force to France. When his story initially hit the newspapers, two other claimants to the title appeared, Braggio Romano of Lake Hopatcong, New Jersey, who claimed he had weighed 103 pounds and William Geyer, of Pittsburgh, Pennsylvania, who said his weight was a mere 96 pounds on induction. Neither of his competitors appear to have been shorter than Casale, however, nor did they produce the official paperwork he had obtained.

Representative Hartley continued to support Casale's claim and the tiny Newarker hired an attorney, John Massa, to assist him in his quest. In 1937 Casale picketed the Capitol building in Washington with a signboard stating his case. A New York newspaper conceded that while Casale "may be egotistical," he "may merely be seeking justice." After summarizing his case, the paper concluded that: "All this was obviously unfair, and Uncle Sam could afford to make amends. And there should be an end to snootiness among military men in the matter of size. The Japanese, who average about Casale's height and weight, are probably as effective soldiers as any in the world. The Japs know that a little man can pull a trigger or touch off a cannon as well as a giant. And has advantages. He is harder to hit, and he can usually think faster."

In 1939, New Jersey Senator Warren Barbour introduced a companion bill to Hartley's resolution and in May, 1940, Casale, at the time a timekeeper for the Newark Street Cleaning Department, appeared to plead his case before a subcommittee of the Senate Military Affairs Committee. Although one Senator asked him "didn't you ever measure yourself," the committee was sympathetic and, although Casale never got the gold medal he was seeking, the New Jerseyan was awarded an "official Congressional certificate of acknowledgement" attesting to his claim of being the tiniest American—and New Jersey—soldier in France in 1918 —and perhaps ever.

CHAPTER 19

1941-The Puppy Love Slaying

The Quicks were an old New Jersey family, with origins in New Netherland. Perhaps the most well-known member of the clan is eighteenth century Sussex County frontiersman Tom Quick, and his probably apocryphal revenge killing of one hundred Indians for a French and Indian War incident.

Unfortunately, a latter day Quick was a tad too quick on the trigger. In August 1941, Young Tunis Quick, a twenty-year-old Montclair resident and grocery delivery boy, became smitten with fourteen-year-old "village vamp" Rosemary Abbott. Quick, his cousin, seventeen-year-old Roslyn Romaine, and Rosemary and her friend Anna Herterick rode around in Tunis' car on a couple of occasions, during which Rosemary sort of indicated that she would become Tunis' "steady girl," but then reneged and started to pay attention to Roslyn, who welcomed it.

During a "necking party" in the Quick living room on August 13, Tunis, although paired up with Anna, kept staring at Roslyn and Rosemary passionately kissing on a couch a few feet away, then jumped up and ran to his room, returning with a sawed off .22 caliber rifle, which he pointed at Rosemary. As those present testified later, "it went off" and the bullet struck Rosemary, killing her, and then Tunis exclaimed "My God, I didn't know it was loaded!" Captain Timothy Fleming of the Montclair police, who subsequently interrogated Quick, later testified that he had confessed to him that he had loaded the gun in his room, but had not intended to fire it, explaining that it "had slipped in his perspiring hands" and fired when he grabbed at it. He added that he "figured that if I gave her a good scare, she would come back to me."

Tunis went on trial in Newark in what became known to reporters as "the puppy love slaying," although the prosecution did not call for the death penalty. He changed his story once again, reverting on the witness stand to his original claim that he did not know the gun was loaded. In the end, Quick was convicted of manslaughter and, although facing a potential term of ten years in state prison, was sentenced to eighteen months in the Essex County Jail.

The Montclair tragedy made national news, and was used as an example of "what's the matter with kids today." Lawrence Gould, a "well known consulting psychologist" opined that the case provided confirmation that "adolescence is the natural age for so-called 'criminal tendencies' to show themselves." He advised parents who wanted to avoid their children growing up to be like Tunis Quick to "instill a healthy sense of consequences" in their offspring early on, offering as an example: "A boy who has had to walk to school because he spent his pocket money too fast is less likely to feel he can get away with other thoughtless actions than he would if Mother slipped a dollar in his pocket when Dad wasn't looking." Gould concluded that young people were "human high explosive, and need to be handled skillfully and gently if we don't want them to blow themselves – and us too – sky high."

Journalist Lillian Vergara was blunter, advising that "oldsters whose idea of a 'kissing party' is an old-fashioned game of 'spin the bottle' or 'post office'" should be aware of societal norms changing for the worse right under their noses, and that the "nightmare" that occurred in the Quick living room was a warning bell they had better heed. Vergara claimed that for the past decade "psychologists and educators the country over" had spent "one half of their time shaking a collective head over the 'younger generation' and the other half warning its parents." She summed up the core of the problem as the fact that "the boys and girls of today are so seemingly precocious, so quick on the trigger with all the answers, so blatantly 'sophisticated' that they're quite able to take care of themselves and don't need any advice from grandma, thank you…they're amazing, to hear them talk."

It should be noted that those feckless boys and girls of 1941 are the people we refer to today as "the greatest generation." The more things change….

"Cappy done it"

Nineteen-year-old Mickey Blair and two of his friends celebrated the New Year in 1928 by getting in a brawl with the Camden cops. The judge, however, suspended their "drunk and disorderly" sentence saying "surely if you were sober this never would have happened." They may have got off easy because the 5' 5" tall Blair, whose real name was Michael Tenerelli, was a well-known up and coming featherweight boxer. It was probably not Tenerelli's first encounter with the law, and it would certainly not be his last. He was never convicted of anything he was charged with, however, including the armed robbery of an Atlantic City cigar store in 1932, an alleged threat to blow up a Pennsauken man's house in 1933 and his refusal to testify as a witness to the murder of a Camden police officer in a city tavern in 1934.

Tenerelli's boxing career effectively ended in 1931, but he fought and won one more fight as a welterweight in 1936. In the census of 1940, Tenerelli, then allegedly living in New York City, claimed he was employed as a "salesman," and his wife Jean declared she was a "saleslady." In reality, they owned the Pleasure Bay Inn, a "club" in Atlantic City. Tenerelli was apparently well acquainted with the City by the Sea's criminal element, including Samuel "Cappy" Hoffman, a "widely known Atlantic City night life character." Hoffman, who had served a prison term after being convicted of a drug offense in 1930, was characterized by one journalist as "a figure in the resort's gambling and night life" and described by another as the "overlord of Atlantic City's rackets"

At 2:00 A.M. On November 4, 1941, or so the story went, Tenerelli and his wife were leaving their "resort," also known as "Atlantic City's most notorious bawdy house" on Missouri Avenue. Tenerelli got into his automobile and suddenly a figure arose from behind the seat and shot him twice. Tenerelli got out of the car, staggered fifteen feet away, and collapsed. The gunman followed him, fired four more shots into his prostrate body and then ran to a getaway car.

Tenerelli was declared dead at the hospital and Mrs. Tenerelli identified Samuel Hoffman as the killer. The police went to Hoffman's home, arrested him and brought him to the police station, where Jean declared "that's the rat that killed Mickey." She said that her husband's last words, as she knelt by him, were "Cappy done it." Mazie Kelly, a "maid" at the Tenerellis' "resort" confirmed Jean's accusation.

Hoffman was subsequently indicted for the murder. But Jean Tenerelli later claimed she had been forced to identify Hoffman as the killer by Mayor Thomas T. Taggart and police officials, who threatened to take her child away if she did not cooperate with them. At the trial, she refused to identify Hoffman as the killer, and on February 15, 1942, Cappy was acquitted. In subsequent actions the Atlantic City mayor and police were "exonerated" for their handling of the case and Mrs. Tenerelli herself was indicted. On October 28, 1942, she was sentenced to five to nine years in prison "on charges of operating a disorderly house, permitting immoral relations with a girl under 18 years and false swearing." The Tenerelli murder remains unsolved.

The accused in the case, Samuel "Cappy" Hoffman, was born in Philadelphia in 1905. Although his father was a rabbi, Cappy had a more secular career in mind, and was arrested twenty-three times between 1923 and 1962. He became known as "the vice king of Atlantic City," and as an enforcer or "hatchet man" for political boss Nucky Johnson. In 1932 Hoffman, who, perhaps with a sense of irony, listed his occupation as "butcher," was sentenced to twelve years in prison for gambling and possession of narcotics, but was released on parole after four years and five months.

Over the subsequent years, Cappy expanded his criminal enterprises into labor racketeering and other illegal activities in both Atlantic City and Philadelphia. In 1950 he was subpoenaed by the Kefauver US Senate committee investigating racketeering, but refused to appear. Brought to trial over his refusal, he was convicted of contempt, but the Supreme Court later reversed his conviction.

In 1970, Hoffman was "awaiting an appearance before a Philadelphia grand jury investigating alleged corruption in housing and urban renewal projects" when he cheated the prosecution one last time, dying of cancer in a Philadelphia hospital.

CHAPTER 20

1943-Murder in the Pinelands

Woodburn Miller was the type of guy you wanted to stay away from. In 1940, when he was twenty, he kidnapped eighteen-year-old Beatrice de Camp, mother of a one-year-old child and wife of a soldier serving at Fort Dix, from her mother's home in Medford, New Jersey. Miller, described variously as a "woodsman" and a "cranberry bog worker," held de Camp at gunpoint at several different cabins in the Pine Barrens before New Jersey State Troopers freed her. Miller was sentenced to a year in Rahway prison for the abduction.

In the summer of 1942, Miller presented thirteen-year-old Jean Bush, of Four Mile, a small community in Woodland Township, with an engagement ring. Jean had another boyfriend, however, a sailor whose sister she had been visiting in Brooklyn a few weeks before. Bush did not turn down Miller's engagement offer, however, she later told her mother, because she was "afraid of hurting his feelings."

On August 31, Miller took Bush out for a ride, and when they did not return, her mother called the State Police, who found her lifeless body near an abandoned Pinelands cabin. She had been shot to death. Miller, covered with blood, was discovered in a nearby parked car. He claimed that "a soldier" had killed Bush and then wounded him with a shotgun and fled the scene. He said he knew the assailant was a soldier because he was "wearing soldier pants."

Miller was seriously injured, and was hospitalized while police began to investigate his story, which was considered shaky. He provided them with several versions of his relationship with Jean Bush, saying at one point that he "thought a lot of her" and on another occasion that he "wasn't in love with her," but admitted to having "intimate relations with her" shortly before she was killed. He also contradicted his initial statement as to the killer, claiming that he was a local cranberry picker. The man was questioned and quickly released and Miller was charged with Bush's murder on December 7, but escaped from the hospital and remained at large in the Pinelands until recaptured at his sister's house in Chatsworth on January 2, 1943.

Woodburn Miller went to trial in Mount Holly in March, 1943. The prosecutor charged that he had killed Bush and then shot himself. When his contradictory statements to police were brought up during the proceedings, Miller stated that he "didn't know what I was saying" because the police kept threatening him with the electric chair.

One prosecution witness, nineteen-year-old hospital orderly Arthur Frake of Mount Holly, testified that Miller had told him while in the hospital that "he was sorry he done it and shouldn't have done it," although without clarifying what "it" was. Unfortunately, Frake was "a resident of the state home for feebleminded males at Four Mile" and the defense challenged his competence. A more substantial witness was Mrs. Florence Franz, owner of a "Chatsworth tap room" who attested that Miller had told her, referring to Bush, "If I catch her cheating on me, I'll fix her." Miller was convicted of second degree murder on April 4, 1943 and sentenced to twenty-five to thirty years in prison.

CHAPTER 21

1945-A Nazi in Newark

Carl Emil Ludwig Krepper was born in 1884 and emigrated to America from his native Germany in 1909 as a theology student. Krepper had studied in the Kropp Lutheran seminary in his homeland, an institution designed to provide pastors for the German-American church. He transferred to the Lutheran Theological Seminary at Philadelphia for a year of final preparation, before being ordained and assigned to a Lutheran church in Pennsylvania or New Jersey. He filed citizenship papers in 1919 and was granted citizenship in 1922. During World War I a number of his fellow Kropp students in America were accused of attempting to undermine the war effort, but not Krepper, who registered for the draft, although he was not conscripted.

In 1923 Krepper was transferred from his parish in Philadelphia to become pastor of two Lutheran churches in Rahway and Carteret, New Jersey, and would spend the rest of his clergical career in the state. In 1932 he was appointed pastor of the First German St. John's Evangelical Lutheran Church in Newark. Krepper was active in church activities, but began, around this time, to take trips back to his native Germany, and became active in the German-American Business League (DAWA) an organization that campaigned against proposed boycotts of German goods and for boycotting Jewish owned businesses, as well as the Bund organization of Nazi sympathizers. In 1935 he took a two-year leave of absence and then resigned from his parish to make several long trips back and forth to Germany, where he met Walter Kappe, a German intelligence officer who recruited him to "do propaganda work for Germany in the United States and provide funds and haven for Bundists persecuted by Jews" in New Jersey.

He did far more than that. Leaving his wife behind in Germany, Krepper returned to America for a final time via Portugal on December 16, 1941 and was soon deeply involved in Operation *Pastorius*, as the American contact to provide safe houses and money for German saboteurs landed from submarines on Long Island and in Florida in June, 1942. No longer a pastor, Krepper was working as a bookkeeper for The Downtown Club in Newark and living in a rooming house at 68 James Street. The saboteurs tried to contact Krepper and failed, and before they could make another attempt, were captured.

The FBI caught on to Krepper, put him under surveillance and caught him in a sting operation in 1944. He was charged with a variety of espionage related crimes and housed in the Hudson County Jail in Jersey City until his trial in February, 1945. Convicted, Krepper was sentenced to twelve years in jail. Attempts to appeal his conviction were denied in 1947 and 1950, and after his release he faded into history. Carl Emil Ludwig Krepper died at a nursing home in Massachusetts in 1972 and his body was cremated. No one claimed his ashes.

The Bobby Sox Cop

In May of 1945, Nutley, New Jersey, apparently had a problem with "automobile Lotharios cruising through Nutley's streets molesting lone women and girls." The men involved were not molesting in the current sense of the word, but were apparently engaged in what is today called "catcalling."

The remedy to Nutley's problem? "Hey, rookie patrolman Davis, I got a job for you." The job was for Eugene Davis to dress up as a "bobby soxer – and a mighty attractive one at that" and send him out into the town's dark streets to "nab the wolves." The press reports noted that Davis was dressed in "a girl's coat, a bright yellow kerchief, dirty saddle shoes, red bobby sox and a purse containing an automatic pistol and a blackjack." They also noted, in case anyone was curious, that Davis was married, not so subtly hinting that he was not in drag because he wanted to be.

A newspaper advised that "sidewalk Lotharios accosting women" were "taking an awful chance" in Nutley, when they "give the old 'Hi babe' to the pert miss portrayed by Davis, who "strolls the streets at night in feminine finery." A report soon came in that "one wolf was clipped on the paw."

The paw belonged to Joseph De Rosa. When De Rosa tried to pick up the cop in drag, he ended up with "a sore jaw and a hundred dollar fine." And so, Nutley did its part in maintaining a civil society in America as the war in Europe came to an end.

A Runaway's Tale from Elizabeth

Back in the "good old days," things weren't always so good. When fourteen-year-old Buol Leberman was stopped by police in Elizabeth, New Jersey, on July 28, 1945, he told a tale of woeful wandering. According to Leberman, his father had died before he was born and his mother had married and abandoned him at their farm home in Minnesota two years before. He told police that he did not know where she had gone and had been "hunting her ever since," traveling to "all sections of the U. S. and into Canada and Mexico." During Leberman's search, a newspaper reported, "he had learned all the tricks of the hobo and, in true vagabond fashion, spent his winters in the south and his summers in the north, taking odd jobs where he could find them." Leberman said that he had been "heading west for the orange picking season when he was picked up" in Elizabeth.

There was a local outpouring of sympathy for the "14-year-old vagrant" when his story hit the newspapers, and a number of people in New Jersey offered to adopt him. He seemed amenable to that, telling the press that he was "convinced that he would never find his mother, adding, 'I don't care so much now. If she doesn't want me why should I care."

As is often the case, the truth of the matter was somewhat more complex. The 1940 census had Leberman living with his grandmother, Carley Coburn, his mother Susan and four-year-old brother Donald in Itaska, Minnesota. Buol's mother was found in a Grand Rapids Michigan hospital shortly after his appearance at the Elizabeth police station. A divorcee, not a widow, she said that she had not abandoned him, but had "placed him in a home in Duluth, Minnesota" and left for Texas to be with her second husband, an army sergeant, and so she had actually abandoned him in a sense. She characterized Buol as a troublesome child, and said that he had "run away from four homes in which she had placed him, including Father Flanagan's Boys Town, Omaha, Nebraska."

A War Worker Explodes in Carteret

On December 7, 1944, twenty-five-year-old Daniel Molnar went berserk in Carteret, New Jersey. Described as an "ex-serviceman" in press reports, Molnar, then working in a nearby defense plant, was quarreling with his estranged wife over custody of their three-year-old daughter Barbara Ann. Earlier that Pearl Harbor Day Molnar spent some time in the City Line Tavern in Carteret. According to a barmaid at that establishment, he spent the afternoon drinking whiskey with beer chasers and played "Hillbilly music and 'The Prisoner's Song,'" a depressing country classic first recorded in 1924 which remained popular for decades, on a jukebox before leaving the bar in an angry state of mind.

Arriving at the home of his father in law, Adam Roszanski, Molnar started ranting and opened fire, murdering Roszanski and then, when police arrived, shooting his way out of the building, using Barbara Ann as a shield. During his escape, he killed Deputy Police Chief Robert Shanley and Patrolman Walter Rusniak, and wounded two other officers responding to the incident. An innocent bystander, fourteen-year-old Alice Scott, who was sitting on a nearby porch, was also killed as Molnar sprayed bullets around the neighborhood. His escape was short lived, as that evening he appeared at Woodbridge Police Headquarters and surrendered.

On December 10, 1944, two "alienists" (psychiatrists) interrupted Molnar's pinochle game with other prisoners to examine him and come to a conclusion on his sanity. The psychiatrists reported that he was not really an "ex-serviceman," as journalists had reported initially, but had been classified as 4-F due to mental problems. Despite Molnar's draft status, after a "mental test" the doctors found him fit to stand trial. Middlesex county prosecutor John Lynch asked the grand jury to indict Molnar on four first degree murder charges. In the end, he was only charged and tried for the killing of his father in law.

The case went to trial in February, 1945 in New Brunswick. Dr. William Wilentz, the Middlesex County Medical Examiner, testified that he had interviewed the accused along with the "alienists" on several occasions and that Molnar had repeated each time that he had planned the killing of his father in law, and planned to also kill his wife prior to the incident. He intended to commit the murders on Christmas day, but was so enthusiastic about the task that he decided that he "could not wait until the holiday."

Molnar went to the Roszanski house armed with a .38 caliber revolver and a .22 caliber rifle. He had acquired the revolver in a trade with Louis Crosz, an Iselin bartender, swapping "two antiquated revolvers" for the more modern gun. Crosz ended up in jail himself, as he had been paroled from prison following an atrocious assault and battery conviction, and was charged with violation of that parole by possessing a handgun.

The county coroner testified that Molnar had killed the two police officers with the revolver and Roszanski and Alice Scott with the rifle. On February 17, Molnar was convicted and sentenced to death. His relatives appealed twice on his behalf, but the appeals failed, and Daniel Molnar, the first Carteret resident ever executed for murder, walked down death row to take a seat in "Old Smokey" on November 28, 1945. His last words were "I believe in God." Funeral services, private by law, were held the following day at the Gowen Funeral Home on Somerset Street in Carteret, and were conducted by Reverend Rev. Julius Szathmary, pastor of the Lutheran Reformed Church of Carteret. Molnar was buried in Clover Leaf Memorial Park in Woodbridge.

CHAPTER 22

1946-A Lower Case Bonnie and Clyde

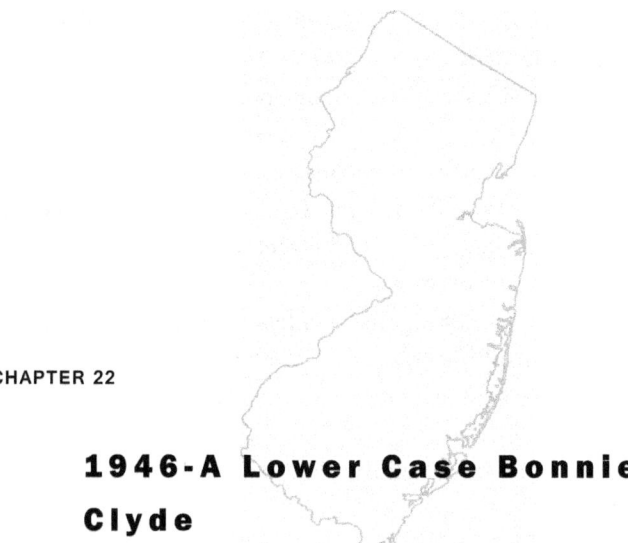

August Bernard Doak had a penchant for capturing cops. In 1940, while fleeing from robberies, he kidnapped a deputy sheriff and then a police officer in Ohio, but later released them and escaped. He was subsequently arrested, convicted and sentenced to prison for an armed robbery in Michigan. In 1945 the twenty-nine-year-old Doak escaped and headed south, committing a few robberies on the way. He ended up in Memphis, Tennessee, and, under the alias "Jimmy Blackwood" took a job as a handyman at the Convent of the Good Shepherd, described as a "correction home" for allegedly "wayward" girls, but in actuality a Catholic institution that allowed pregnant unmarried young women to give birth and put their child up for adoption away from prying eyes. "Jimmy" met 16-year-old Constance Clemente at the Good Shepherd. Constance had been "confined there with the consent of her mother" after she had "run off with a band of gypsys." In the summer of 1946, a day before she was scheduled to be released to her mother, Constance proceeded to run off with Doak, and they were married on the road.

The newlyweds took a wandering honeymoon crime tour through Georgia, Alabama and the Carolinas "leaving behind them a score of slick stickups." Constance wrote her mother that she was truly in love and "had found a good man with whom she could lead a normal life."

The couple decided to visit Mrs. Clemente in New York and headed north, crossing into New Jersey on August 1. New Jersey state trooper motorcycle patrolman Robert Kell saw them speed past him in Raritan Township and pursued. Hearing a siren and spotting the trooper, Doak, who was driving a stolen vehicle, accelerated, and then stopped suddenly, causing Kell to swerve and topple his car over. Doak jumped out of his car, gun in hand, disarmed the trooper and forced him into his car, where Constance held his own gun on him.

Motorists who had witnessed the incident quickly informed the police and a massive manhunt was soon underway with roadblocks throughout the area. Doak pulled into a country lane, ordered Kell out of the car and told him "I'm wanted and I can't have you on my hands." Fearing he was about to be shot, Kell kicked Doak in the groin and took off through the woods.

As the manhunt heated up, Doak abandoned his car and Constance near Hopewell. A call went out to the New York state police for bloodhounds, and they responded, along with officers to handle them. In the end the bloodhounds were not needed, as trooper Louis Masin spotted Doak trudging along a railroad track. Although armed with two handguns, the fugitive offered no resistance.

In perhaps the quickest court proceedings in New Jersey history, August Doak pleaded guilty and was sentenced to life in prison on August 7, 1946. The police "were puzzled by the girl. They did not know whether to treat her as a trigger-happy gang moll or a juvenile delinquent." In the end, she was sentenced to the women's reformatory in Clinton as a juvenile delinquent.

In April, 1952 there was a serious riot at the New Jersey state prison. The leader? August Bernard Doak. Doak served fifteen years of his sentence in New Jersey and then was released to Michigan authorities to finish out the term he was serving there when he escaped.

"Western Thugs" Cross the Delaware

In August, 1946, twenty-two-year-old Jack Smith and nineteen-year-old William B. Hinkle escaped from a California chain gang and headed east, stealing cars and committing "a score of holdups" along the way. When they hit Somerset County, Pennsylvania, in November, however, their luck gave out, at least temporarily. Arrested for auto theft by Somerset law enforcement, they were detained in the County Jail, but managed to "saw the bars and escape" and head for—where else? New Jersey.

So how did they get the saw to facilitate the jailbreak? Wilmer A. Kimmel helped them. The fourteen-year-old, six-foot-tall, 200 pound Kimmel was temporarily incarcerated by request of his father for "incorrigibility." Since Kimmel, who was apparently not very bright in addition to being incorrigible, was due to be released, the two "western thugs" told him that if he delivered hacksaw blades to them they would, in turn, give him "$1,000, an airplane trip to Hollywood and a job." Kimmel produced the blades, but, needless to say, was disappointed in the outcome, as he remained broke, unemployed and back in jail in Pennsylvania.

New Jersey authorities were advised that the escapees were most likely headed their way, and they were subsequently spotted in Camden. Hinkle was captured after a wild chase through and then out of the city, but Smith eluded the police and disappeared. The New Jersey State Police, who enlisted the aid of thirty shotgun armed deer hunters, launched a massive search, aided by the FBI. For the first time ever, the pursuit received air support from a helicopter.

Smith managed to make it to Merchantville, where the "nattily attired" fugitive was arrested by FBI agents as he walked down a local street. Both men were held in the Camden County jail until they were extradited back to Pennsylvania, where they were sentenced to twelve and-a-half to twenty-two years in prison.

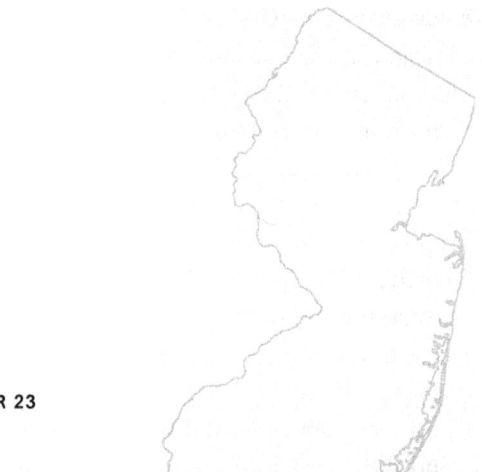

CHAPTER 23

1947-Alice Would Have Been Embarrassed

It seems to have all started with Alice Paul, or at least Alice provided an excuse for Louisa Strittmater's obsessions and actions. New Jersey native Alice Paul was one of the most significant suffragists in the country in the early twentieth century, and endured much in the struggle to gain women the right to vote and, once that was secured, fought throughout the rest of her life for gender equality.

In 1916, Paul was one of the founders of the National Woman's Party. More a lobbying group than an actual political party, once suffrage was achieved the organization moved on to advocate for an Equal Rights Amendment and other equality legislation. The National Woman's Party ceased to be a lobbying organization in 1997, and has transitioned into an educational association.

Louisa Strittmater, of Bloomfield, New Jersey, joined the Woman's Party in 1925 and volunteered one day a week in the party's New York office from 1939 to 1941. When Strittmater, who was born in 1896, died in 1944, her will left her $15,000 estate to the National Woman's Party. But there was much more. It turned out that Louisa really hated men. Scribbled notes in the margins of books and on scraps of paper found in her effects reflected her opinion that men "would revert to apes" and that they were "...that dirty breed of leeches and parasites—he inveterate enemies of women." Louisa was looking forward to the day "when science would enable women to bear children without the aid of men, and advocated, once women had acquired sufficient power, the killing off of all males at birth." Part of her estate was in gold coins she had buried in her basement, allegedly because she could not find a bank run by women to deposit them in.

Louisa had an axe to grind with others as well, and, although described as having an early loving relationship with her parents, who died in 1928, described her father in a 1934 note as "a corrupt, vicious and unintelligent savage, a typical specimen of the majority of his sex. Blast his wormstinking carcass and his whole damn breed." A decade later she wrote on a photograph of her mother the words "That moronic she devil that was my mother." Louisa was reportedly subject to fits of violence as well, allegedly killing a kitten and smashing objects in her house.

Strangely, Strittmater apparently ran her business of renting apartments very efficiently, was skilled in maintaining them, and had cordial and "reasonable" relations with her male attorney, as well as her bank, even though it was not run by women. Her will was contested by two male cousins who were not mentioned in the document and a female cousin who had been left $100. They appealed to the Probate Court, claiming Louisa was insane.

The only medical witness in the subsequent hearing was Strittmater's physician, Doctor Sarah D. Smalley, who was not a psychiatrist. Doctor Smalley opined that Louisia "suffered from paranoia of the Bleuler type of split personality. [schizophrenia]" The New Jersey Court of Errors and Appeals agreed, and, on May 15, 1947, set aside the will for "lack of testamentary capacity." Alice Paul, who was still alive (she lived until 1977) and who had numerous male and female friends throughout her life, was not available for comment.

Ironically, as my law student son John points out, "By getting the court to set aside the will, her estate instead was distributed through the NJ intestacy statute - which, most likely, meant that the two male cousins would get the bulk of it, and the female second cousin a smaller portion. She even got shafted by men after she died!"

CHAPTER 24

1948-The Redhead and the Cop

Newark, New Jersey, Police captain Thomas J. Rowe was caught in the act, so to speak, by his daughter Dorothy and her husband Andrew Scott, who encountered the fifty-five-year-old Rowe with thirty-nine-year-old waitress Ann Powers in his parked car. An outraged Dorothy told Rowe: "Daddy I am giving you two weeks to end this affair, to resume a normal life with mother and me and have the same kind of fun we used to have."

Whether or not he intended to do what Dorothy requested would never be known, as Rowe died on May 21, 1948, six days later. It happened after a nighttime "tour of Newark taverns" by Rowe and Powers that ended at 4:00 AM in his First Precinct office, where they both entered and closed the door. A short while later a shot rang out, and Detective Ramon Poquette ran to the office where, he later testified, he found Rowe on the floor and Powers kneeling beside him sobbing and saying "I did it." Rowe got up, staggered towards the door and collapsed, stating, according to Poquette, "the ____ ____ ____ ____; she did it." He was rushed to Newark City Hospital with a bullet wound in his stomach from his own revolver, which lay on the office floor, and died shortly afterward.

Powers later insisted that she was actually innocent and maintained that she had fallen asleep in a chair in the office and was awakened as Rowe shot himself, but the "tall redhead" was arrested and charged with second degree murder. A newspaper photo showed a stock image of

Rowe and a photo of Powers as she was escorted out of the First Precinct after her arrest. Powers went to trial in October, 1948, still claiming her innocence. After a week of testimony, however, she made a deal with prosecutors, pleading guilty to manslaughter, ending the trial. She was sentenced to nine to ten years in the Women's Reformatory in Clinton.

Interestingly, in 1937 Rowe was involved in a shooting incident with a twenty-two-year-old girl in his automobile. She said she had been offered a ride by Rowe and when she brushed against an automatic pistol in his pocket it fired and the bullet hit her in the thigh. Rowe was cleared of responsibility.

Harpoon Tommy

A lot of people are not aware that Newark, New Jersey, was a whaling port of sorts in the early nineteenth century. In 1838 the city on the Passaic provided anchorage for two whaling vessels. On July 20, 1948, that tradition was apparently revived, although it is doubtful that the participants were aware of the historical context or had ever heard of Ishmael. Thomas Morris, a forty-five-year-old machinist who worked in a factory in Kearny, was accused of harpooning his thirty-one-year-old "shapely blonde wife" Marie, the mother of his four children.

Marie told her side of the story to a journalist from her bed at Newark City Hospital, where her photo was taken. She claimed that her husband met her on the back stairs of their apartment house as she returned "home early today" and "lunged at her with the harpoon," causing severe stomach wounds.

Thomas Morris, unsurprisingly, told a different tale. He maintained that the couple had been at a party the previous evening and that Marie had "left with another man" and, while trying to sneak back into their apartment by climbing in the bathroom window, fell on the harpoon, which just happened to be stored directly underneath it, with its barbed point facing upward. Why Morris would store his five-foot-long homemade harpoon, which he claimed he had fashioned for fishing, under the bathroom window, went unexplained. The police did not buy his story, and he was charged with atrocious assault and battery.

CHAPTER 25

1949-Mass Murder in Camden

Howard Unruh was a loner, and the neighbors and local merchants in Camden, New Jersey, thought him more than a tad odd. Unruh picked up on that, and plotted "retaliation" against those he thought were plotting against him, making notes on who to kill, interspersed with religious jottings, in a notebook. The unemployed World War II veteran had dropped out of Temple University's Pharmacy School after a month, had not held a job for years, and was supported by his mother. Unruh stayed in his room most of the time, reading a Bible and going down to his improvised basement shooting range on occasion, where he practiced with a 9mm Luger he had purchased at a Philadelphia gun store.

Unruh took revenge on his purported detractors on September 6, 1949, when he awoke at 8:00 AM, dressed himself in "a light suit, a white shirt and a bow tie." loaded his Luger, stuffed extra cartridges in his pocket and began a shooting spree that earned him the dubious distinction of becoming the only true mass murderer in New Jersey history. The only persons to come close were Ernest Ingenito, another World War II veteran, who killed his wife and four members of her family in Franklin Township in November, 1950 and John List, who killed his mother, wife and three children in Westfield in November, 1971. While Unruh had served honorably and well, aside from his peculiar habit of writing down the details of every dead German he came across, Ingenito had been court martialed twice, served time in a military prison, and been dishonorably discharged. Interestingly, he also used a German Luger in his rampage.

Although Unruh's intended targets were neighbors and merchants he felt had disrespected him, and he did kill local storeowners with whom he had minor disputes, those unfortunate enough to cross his path, including the driver of a car who slowed down to see what was happening, also became victims. Before he ran out of ammunition and fled home as he heard approaching police cars, Unruh had killed thirteen people, including three children aged two, six and nine years old. He shot the six-year-old off a hobby horse barber chair. Sixty police officers besieged him in his apartment above a store at 3202 River Road, exchanging occasional shots with him, before he surrendered. During the siege, a reporter got through to him by telephone, and asked him why he was killing people. Unruh's response was "I don't know. I can't answer that yet. I'm too busy."

Once in custody, Unruh told officers that "the neighbors had been talking about me and making derogatory remarks about my character. I had been thinking about killing them for some time." The night before his rampage, he had apparently binge watched repeated showings of a double feature in a Philadelphia movie theater until 3:00 AM. The films he saw were reportedly "For You I Die" and "Fear in the Night," although another account cited them as "The Lady Gambles" and "I Cheated the Law." They may, or may not, have incited him to finally finish off his imaginary enemies.

Unruh was taken to Cooper Hospital for treatment of a minor wound incurred when he traded shots with police. He was eventually pronounced insane (a subsequent diagnosis unsurprisingly specified schizophrenia) and lived for the rest of his life in the Vroom building for the criminally insane at Trenton Psychiatric Hospital, where he spent "most of his time walking in a circle." He died there on October 19, 2009.

CHAPTER 26

1951-A "Mercy Killing" in Cliffside Park

Willie Moretti, born Guarino Moretti in Italy in 1894, moved with his family to New Jersey as a child. Willie got into trouble early. Arrested for robbery in New York City in 1913, he served less than a year in prison. By the early 1930s Moretti had moved up the crime ladder and was involved in running illegal gambling operations in New Jersey and New York as a close associate of Frank Costello and Newark gangster Abner "Longy" Zwillman. Criminal activity was good business for Moretti, who became very wealthy, with a large home in Bergen County's Hasbrouck Heights and a summer residence in the exclusive Monmouth County seaside town of Deal.

As his wealth grew, Moretti's influence in the entertainment industry did as well. One of his associates was a cousin of Frank Sinatra's first wife, and it was rumored that Moretti stuck a gun in Frank Dorsey's mouth to convince him to release Sinatra from a contract with the bandleader. Moretti was also friendly with Dean Martin, Jerry Lewis, and Milton Berle, all of whom, along with Sinatra, performed at his daughter's wedding.

In 1950 Moretti was one of a number of organized crime figures called before the United States Senate Special Committee to Investigate Crime in Interstate Commerce headed by Senator Estes Kefauver. The mobsters, with the notable exception of Moretti, declined to testify on the Fifth Amendment grounds of self-incrimination. Moretti, on the other hand, joked and talked a lot with the senators and counsels, saying at one time "Whaddya think, the Mafia hands out membership cards?" He might have enjoyed himself, but by the standards of the mob, he was entirely too talkative. Believing that Moretti was losing his mind due to advanced syphilis, and that this was endangering security, Mafia Boss Vito Genovese issued a contract to kill him. Genovese allegedly described it as a "mercy killing," reportedly saying "the lord have mercy on his soul, he's losing his mind."

On October 4, 1951, Moretti was having lunch with four other men at Joe's Elbow Room Restaurant in Cliffside Park, New Jersey. The group appeared to be having a pleasant conversation when shots rang out and the four left the restaurant in a hurry, having shot Moretti several times in the head "as a sign of respect." Following a funeral mass at Corpus Christi Catholic Church in Hasbrouck Heights, Moretti was buried at Saint Michael's Cemetery in South Hackensack. His funeral was attended by over 5,000 people, and his hearse was followed to the cemetery by forty flower cars, laden down with farewell blossoms contributed by "underworld celebrities" including Frank Costello, Albert Anastasia and Joe Adonis. Various aspects of Moretti's career reportedly inspired storylines in *The Godfather* and *The Sopranos*.

The Dad Who Wasn't

And we end on a lighter note. In 1952, Suzanne Fulinello, a twenty-year-old Newark, New Jersey, woman, found herself pregnant. At the end of October, two months before her due date, Fulinello filed a paternity suit in Newark's family court against twenty-two-year old Brooklyn Dodger pitcher Billy Loes. She claimed that "she was intimate with Loes several times last March in a Miami hotel while the Dodgers were in spring training." Based on Fulinello's testimony, Magistrate Harry Pine signed a warrant for Loes' arrest on paternity charges.

When informed of the suit filed against him by the "attractive brunette," Loes dismissed the allegation and told a reporter he "didn't even know her," casually adding "you know how broads are."

Dodger owner Walter O'Malley came to his player's defense, claiming that the charges were untrue, and casting doubt on Fulinello's veracity by noting that she had been jailed in Essex County for shoplifting and violating parole. He added that "too many reckless charges are made against ball players because they are in the public eye." Loes was actually the second Dodger pitcher in two years to be the subject of a paternity suit. The other was Hugh Casey, who was found culpable and subsequently shot himself.

Loes, who lived in Astoria, Queens, with his parents, "who he helps support on his $5,000 (about $45,000 in today's dollars) salary plus bonuses such as his share of World series money," could not legally be extradited from New York to New Jersey to face a paternity charge and was safe as long as he avoided the Garden State.

Things changed by the summer of 1956, however, when Fulinello, who had had a second out of wedlock child, was arrested and then convicted of assault with intent to rob a Newark real estate office. The city of Newark filed a civil suit against Loes, then pitching for the Baltimore Orioles, because the child Fulinello claimed he fathered was now a "public charge," unless paternity was proved. Loes agreed to come to Newark to resolve the issue after the baseball season and the case came to court in November, when he and Fulinello, who was brought to the hearing from prison, testified before a judge who concluded that the pitcher was indeed not the father of Fulinello's child. She returned to jail and he returned to baseball, later playing for the San Francisco Giants, and finished his eleven-year career in 1961 with an 80-63 won/lost record and an earned run average of 3.89.

Bibliographical Note

Bizarre New Jersey stories, particularly those involving murder and crime, have been covered before, in several books, which were invaluable in putting this work together, and often providing the initial idea for a story. They are included in the brief bibliography below. Most significant in the follow up and detailed coverage of these long forgotten tales, however, is the relatively recent availability of digitized information, particularly newspapers, but also court case and appeal summaries and genealogical information available on line, as well as the period original news photos available for sale as newspapers sell off their photo collections of a hundred years or so.

Books

Joynson, George. *Murders in Monmouth: Capital Crimes from the Jersey Shore's Past.* (Charleston, SC: The History Press, 2007).

King, John P. *Murder and Mayhem in the Highlands: Historic Crimes on the Jersey Shore.* (Charleston, SC: The History Press, 2008).

Logan, Andy. *The Man Who Robbed the Robber Barons: The Story of Colonel William d'Alton Mann, War Hero, Profiteer, Inventor and Blackmailer Extraordinary.* (New York: W. W. Norton and Company, 1965).

Mappen, Marc. *Jerseyana: The Underside of New Jersey History.* (New Brunswick, NJ: Rutgers University Press, 1992).

Martinelli, Patricia A. *True Crime: New Jersey, The State's Most Notorious*

Criminal Cases. (Mechanicsburg, PA: Stackpole, 2007).
Pratt, Fletcher. *The Cunning Mulatto and Other Cases of Ellis Parker, American Detective.* (New York: Smith and Haas, 1935).
Reisinger, John. Master Detective: *The Life and Crimes of Ellis Parker, America's Real-life Sherlock Holmes.* Glyphworks Publishing, 2012.
Tomlinson, Gerald. *Murdered in New Jersey (expanded edition)* (New Brunswick, NJ, Rutgers University Press, 2006).

Newspapers

Asbury Park Press
Bernardsville (NJ) News
Boston Journal
Brooklyn Daily Eagle
Bridgeport Connecticut Telegram
Bridgewater (NJ) Courier-News
Burlington (VT) Free Press
Camden (NJ) Courier Post
Cincinnati Enquirer
Danville, Pennsylvania Morning News
Decatur, Illinois Daily Review
Detroit Free Press
Franklin, Pennsylvania News-Herald
Gettysburg (PA) Times
Harrisburg Telegraph
Havre, Montana, Daily News
Hopewell (NJ) Herald
Indiana Herald
Maysville, Kentucky, Evening Bulletin
Monongahela Pennsylvania Daily Republican
Mount Carmel (PA) Item
Nashua, New Hampshire, Telegraph
Newark (NJ) Evening News
New Brunswick (NJ) Daily Times
New York Age
New York Evening World
New York Herald
New York Times

Olean, New York Times-Herald
Philadelphia Inquirer
Philadelphia Evening Public Ledger
Pittsburgh Press
Pottstown, Pennsylvania Mercury
Red Bank (NJ) Register
Scranton Republican
Shamokin, Pennsylvania News-Dispatch
Trenton (NJ) Evening Times
Wilkes-Barre Pennsylvania Record
Wilmington, Delaware Evening Journal
Wilmington, Delaware Morning News

# Index

148th Infantry Regiment, 151
15th New Jersey Infantry, 1
1st Michigan Cavalry, 1
7th Michigan Cavalry, 1
82nd Division's 326th Infantry Regiment, 133
A.B. Blaters (barge), 87
Abbott, Rosemary, 154
Abrams, Mayer, 137
Adams, Carl, 105
Adamski, Edward, 84-85
Adinolfi, Theodore (Harry King), 75-76
Adonis, Joe, 175
Agreen, Carl, 104
Alaska Sportsman Magazine, 79
Albany, NY, 62
Albright Radio and Electric, 19
Alderney Dairy Company, 45
alienists (psychiatrists), 6, 119, 163
Altoona, PA, 20
Ambassador Hotel (Atlantic City), 76
Amberg, "Pretty Louie," 112
American Expeditionary Forces (AEF), 152
American Express Company, 146
American Naturopathy Society, 115
Anastasia, Albert, 175
Anderson, Peggy, 34-35
Andrew, William E., 104
Ann May Spring Lake Hospital, 20
Anti-Saloon League, 55
Arena, Joseph, 139
Arnold, Dorothy, 62
Asbury Park National Bank and Trust Company, 146-148
Asbury Park Police Department, 147
Asbury Park Post Office, 146
Asbury Park Press, 43, 56, 101, 136
Astoria, NY, 106, 176
Atlanta, GA, 28
Atlantic City Beauty Pageant, 71

Atlantic City Board of Taxation, 72
Atlantic County Republican Party, 144
Atlantic Foto Service, 5
Austin, Stanley H., 82
Balner, Louis D., 108
Baltimore Orioles, 176
Baltimore, MD, 5, 8, 35, 48, 59, 63
Bankers Industrial Service, Inc., 149
Barbour, Warren, 153
Barhorst, William, 125
Bark, Samuel, 35-36
Barringer, Rufus, 132
Barton, J. Clarence Jr., 146, 148
Bayonne Women's Club, 115
Beach, Willis, 33-36
Bearmore, George, 20
Belair, MD, 141
Bell, Arthur Hornbui, 29, 31
Bell, James "Ding Dong," 108
Belmar Maloney Gas Works, 20
Bennett, Alfred, 147-148
Berardinelli, Carmine, 98
Bergen, Jack "Handsome Jack," 14-16
Bergen, Margaret, 16
Bergen, Mary (Gribben), 16
Berle, Milton, 174
Berman, Otto "Abbadabba," 111
Berry, Raymond, 44
Beverley National Cemetery (NJ), 80
Big Six, 117-118
bigamy, 37-38, 126-127
Bilby, John, 109, 127, 169
Biringer, Kathryn Crawford, 64
Birth of a Nation (movie), 30
Bishops' Law (prohibition), 3
Blair, Mickey, 102-103, 156
Blue Hills Plantation, 149
Blumenthal, Marcus "Jack Markham," 75-76
Boardwalk Empire (TV series), 78, 87, 121, 131

Boederman, Henry, 60
Boiardo, Ruggerio "Ritchie the Boot," 61-62
Bolber, Morris, 140
Bonaparte, Jerome, 5
Bondiego, Benjamin, 147
bootlegging, 13, 43, 52, 62, 75-78, 85-88, 111, 131-133
Bordentown New Jersey State Prison, 36
Boright, Walter E., 146
Born, Ray E., 121
Bowers, Nellie, 13
Brenner, Forrest, 135
Brenner, Louis, 97
Breslin, John J., 118
Bronx, NY, 110
Brooklyn Dodgers, 175-176
Brooklyn, NY, 27, 58, 60, 108, 112, 114, 158
brothels, 3, 65, 120-121
Brown, Bradway, 83-84
Brown, Margaret, 51
Brunen, "Honest John," 7-11
Brunen, Doris (Mohr), 8-12
Brunen, Dorothy, 8
Brunen, Ellis, 8
Brunen, Hazel, 8-10
Buffalo, NY, 98
Bull Moose Party, 55
Burke, Tessie, 72
Burns, Robert Elliot, 80
Burns, William J., 132
Burroughs, William S., 112
Bush, Jean, 158-159
The Butcher's Advocate, 4
Butler, John, 145-146
Byram, H.L., 86
Caledonian State Prison Farm, 100
Camp Dix, 13
Camp Evans, 98
Camp Merritt, 89
Camp Nordland, 31, 150
Campbell, Henry Colin, 48
Campbell, Herbert, 140
Campbell, Mildred (Mowry), 48-51
Campbell, Richard, 48-50
Campbell, Rosalie, 48
Canadian Royal Mounted Police, 26
Cannon, Mary, 118-119

INDEX

Canton, OH, 96
Capone, Al, 61, 114, 143
Carbo, Frankie, 86
Carroll, Barbara, 127
Carroll, Francis, 128-129
Carslake, Charles L., 87-88
Carthy, Joseph, 108
Casale, Nicholas, 151-153
Casey, Hugh, 176
Chamberlain, William, 28-29
Chappleau, Joseph, 105
Cheeseman, Frank, 135-136
Cheeseman, Theresa, 136
Chicago, IL, 45, 62-63, 74, 80, 91, 94, 113
Christie, William, 99
Cicero, Anthony, 52
Cicero, Dominic, 52
Cicero, Michael, 52
Cicero, Patrick "Patsy," 52
Cioffe, Nicholas, 147-148
Civil War, American, 1-2
Clark, Ann, 135
Clark, Audrey (Smith), 91-92
Clark, Priscilla, 26-28
Clark, Sheldon, 91-92
Clark, Sheldon Sr., 91
Clark, William J., 26-28
Clarke, Edward Y., 30
Clearwater, Gorum, 32
Clem, John, 2
Clemente, Constance, 165-166
Cleveland, OH, 37-40, 90
Cline, George, 14-16
Cline, Mary, 15
Cliver v. State, 127
Close, Henry C., 50
Clover Leaf Memorial Park (Woodbridge, NJ), 164
Coast Guard, United States, 4, 74, 103-104
Coburn, Carley, 162
Cohen, Herman, 77
Cold Spring Presbyterian Cemetery, 68
Coleman, Eleanor, 98
Coleman, Thomas, 98
Collier, Lewis, 54
Collier's Weekly, 2
Columbus Cemetery (NJ), 88
Coney Island, NY, 8
Conklin, George, 145
Conover, Elizabeth, 11

Convent of the Good Shepherd, 165
Cooper University Hospital, 173
Corbo, Paul, 77
Cornell University, 74
Corpus Christi Catholic Church, 175
Costello, Frank, 174-175
Coughlin, William, 73
Cowan, Joseph, 27-28
Crane, Wellington, 71
Cranford Chronicle, 146
Crawford, Demarest, 64
Crawford, Frank Jr., 64
Crawford, Louise, 64
Crempa, Camelia, 109-110
Crempa, John, 109-110
Crempa, Sophie, 109-110
Crispino, Samuel, 139-140
Crockett, Edgar H., 106-107
Crosz, Louis, 164
Cusick, William Michael, 76
Custer, George, 1
Czicolic, Teresa "Terry Chiclet," 100-101
Daneko, Andrew W., 97
Danner, Fred, 78
Dauphin County, PA, 67
David, Abe, 51, 110, 146
Davidson, Robert H., 134
Davis, Eugene, 161-162
Davis, Mabel, 45
de Camp, Beatrice, 158
de Conturbia, Anna St. Clair, 5
De Rosa, Joseph, 162
DeCarlo, Angelo "Gyp," 148
Del Rossi, Clifford, 95
Delaware River, 46, 142
Demick, Steve, 42-43
Dempsey, Jack, 122
Dewey, Thomas, 111
DiBlasio, Joe, 133
Dies, Martin Jr., 150
DiGiovanni, Saverio, 106
Dillinger, John, 96
Dillon, Amelia (Martin), 24
DiMaggio, Joe, 62
Doak, August Bernard "Jimmy Blackwood," 165-166
Dover, DE, 49

Drennan, John, 123
Drennan, Margaret, 123-124
Drennan, Robert, 124
Drinker, Cecil, 44
Drischman, George, 4
Drischman, Mary M., 4-6
Dry, Charles, 132
Duffy, Edith, 77
Duffy, Mickey, 76-78, 86
Duggan, Alfred F., 147-148
Duncan, James Edward, 79
Dupont Company, 95
Durant Automobile Plant, 69
Dvorske, John J., 127
Dworecki, Walter "Iron Mike," 141-142
Dworecki, Wanda, 142
Dwyer, Paul "Buddy," 127-129
Eastern State Penitentiary, 41
Eaton, Charles A., 90-91
Edison, Thomas, 105
Edouard, Ella May, 93-94
Edouard, Millard, 93-94
Egbert, Minnie (Wright), 22
Eiseman, Sigmund, 53
El Paso, TX, 29, 87
electric chair (Old Smokey), 24-25, 46, 71, 101, 105-106, 116, 135, 159
Elizabeth Carteret Hotel, 85-86, 131
Elizabeth General Hospital, 110
Elizabethport Banking Company, 87
Elkton, MD, 48, 67, 135
Elliott, Robert, 46, 71, 101
Elwell, Joseph B., 7
Emmo Manufacturing, 38
Essex County Courthouse, 24
Essex County House of Detention, 124
Essex County Jail, 26, 155
Evanenko, Nikita, 42-43
Evergreen Cemetery (New Brunswick, NJ), 99
Faggia, Amelia, 44
Fairview Cemetery (Middletown, NJ), 39
Farley, John, 95-96
Farrell v. State, 127

Farrell, Martin, 103
Father Flanagan's Boys Town, 163
Fay, Joseph, 117-118
Federal Bureau of Investigation (FBI), 120, 143, 147, 161, 167
Federal Deposit Insurance Corporation, 148
Federal Reserve Bank, 146
Feitz, William T., 102-103
Feldman, James, 85
Fillipe, Milan, 94
Finkel, Paul, 145
Finkelstein, Theodora, 60
Finn, Edward H., 107
First German St. John's Evangelical Lutheran Church, 160
Fitkin-Paul Morgan Memorial Hospital, 135
Flatt, Helen (Koezeno), 126
Flatt, Myrtle (Ward), 126-127
Flatt, Theodore "Bud" Jr., 126-127
Flegenheimer, Arthur Simon "Dutch Shultz," 110-112, 188
Fleming, Lillian, 54
Fleming, Timothy, 154
Fodale, John, 96
Forman, Dick, 20
Forrester, John, 122-123
Fort Dix, 158
Fox Films (20th Century Fox), 14
Fox, Arthur, 47
Fox, Frank, 108
Frake, Arthur, 159
Franklin, Ben, 8
Franz, Florence, 159
Frazer, Charlotte, 19
Frazer, Hilda, 70
Frazer, Mabel, 19
Frazer, William, 69-71
French and Indian War, 154
Fryer, Grace, 44
Fuery, Elizabeth, 115
Fulinello, Suzanne, 175-176
Fury, Thomas, 87
Gaffney, Edward, 108
Gaffney, Ellen, 149
Gaffney, Leo P., 149
Galent, Joseph, 90
gambling, 3, 8, 65, 75, 79-80, 120, 143, 156-157, 174

Gannon, Howard, 12-13
Gardner's Basin, 3
Gassel, Mendel, 85-86
Gatti, Samuel, 134
Gaynor, Arthur "Scarface," 108
General Cable Company, 115
Genovese, Vito, 175
George, Harold, 58, 60
German American Bund (Federation), 31, 149-150, 160
German American Business League (DAWA), 160
Gerry, Elbridge, 5
gerrymandering, 5
Gettysburg, battle of, 1-2
Geyer, William, 152
Giacobbe, Millie, 139
Giampietro, Victor, 45-46
Giberson, Ivy (Richmond), 12-14, 36
Giberson, William, 12-14
Gilbert, William S., 16-18
Ginther, Howard, 93
Giordano, John C., 148
The Girl in the Red Velvet Swing (movie), 66
Glass-Steagall Act, 149
The Godfather (movie), 175
Godfrey, Carleton, 6
gold shirts of Mexico, 151
Golding, George E. "Hard Boiled," 62-63
Gough, Fred, 20
Gould, Lawrence, 155
Gowen Funeral Home (Carteret, NJ), 164
Great Depression, 31, 57, 75, 84, 107, 120, 143
Greater Chicago Magazine, 80
Green, Betty, 74-76
Green, Clarence, 75
Greenberg, Harry, 95-96
Greenberg, Joseph "Max," 86
Greenberg, Rose, 95-96
Greenville, PA, 48
Greenwood Cemetery (NJ), 27
Griswold, Alice Gerry, 4-6
Grossman, Sammy, 77
Gump, Frederick, 66
Hagerstown, MD, 72
Hague, Frank, 130-131, 138, 143

Hague, Frank Jr., 139
Hall, Frances, 35
Hallock, Edward, 22
Hapgood, Norman, 2
Harding, Warren G., 87, 132
Harlem, NY, 74
Harris, Robert H., 15
Harrisburg, PA, 59
Hartley, Fred, 152
Harvard University, 44, 64-65
Hassell, Max, 85, 87
Hauptmann, Bruno Richard, 106, 114
Havana, Cuba, 62, 103
Hearst Newspapers, 35, 143
Hearst, William Randolph, 143
Heisler, Emma, 102
SS *Helen*, 73
Heller, Dorothy, 106-107
Hempstead, NY, 74
Hensler Brewery, 62-63
Hensler, Joseph, 63
Herman, Hildegarde, 100
Herman, Paul, 99-100
Herterick, Anna, 154
Hetrick, Clarence, 55-57, 103-104
Hickey, Frank, 119, 136
Hicks, Mary, 131
Hillside Cemetery (Scotch Plains, NJ), 91, 110
Hinkle, A. Cameron, 35-36
Hinkle, William B., 166-167
Hobbs, Harry, 28
Hodkinson, Albert, 77
Hoffman, Gov. Harold, 114
Hoffman, Samuel "Cappy," 156-157
Hollinshead, Ralph K., 47
Hoover, J. Edgar, 120-121, 143
Hopewell Herald, 90
Hossek, Eric, 82
Hotel Vendig (Manhattan, NY), 75
Howland, Cook, 20
Hubbard, Caleb, 20
Hubbard, William, 20-21
Hudson County Jail, 161
Hudson River, 74, 118
Hudson, Ralph, 106
Hughes, John, 108
Huntington's Chorea, 25

INDEX

I am a Fugitive from a Georgia Chain Gang, R. Burns, 80
Ingenito, Ernest, 172
Ingersol, Robert A., 6
International Brotherhood of Operating Engineers' Union, 117
Iona Lake Hotel, 45
Irwin, TN, 28
Italian black shirts, 151
Jackson War Veteran Democratic Club, 149
Jaeske, Elizabeth (Brunen), 9
Jayne, William, 14
Jensen, Ira, 70
Jersey Boys, 148
Jersey City Polish Community Hall, 110
Jobes, Mary, 141
Johnson, Carroll, 96
Johnson, Enoch "Nucky," 3, 31, 55, 57, 65, 120-121, 143-144, 157
Jolley Trolley Casino, 62
Jugtown Mountain, 125
Juska, Edwin F., 135
Kamelia Klan, 27
Kaplan, Alma, 147-148
Kappe, Walter, 161
Katzenstein Brothers, 4
Kean, Sen. Hamilton F., 14
Keegan, Wilbur, 150
Kefauver Committee, 157, 174
Kell, Robert, 166
Keller, Alice, 60
Kelly, Mazie, 156
Kelly, W.P., 96
Kelsey, J.E., 9
Kenney, Edward Aloysius, 130-131
Kenney, Elizabeth, 131
Kent, Caroline, 26
Kent, Charles, 95-96
Kermis, Charles, 85
Kern, Henry, 134
Kern, John, 134
Kessler, Charles M., 57
Ketchikan, AK, 79
Kilmer, Val, 80
Kimberling, Mark O., 147
Kimmel, Wilmer A., 167
King, Maude, 132
Klapprott, August, 149-151
Knapp, Phillip Knox, 74
Koehler, John, 134

Koehler, Mathias, 150
Koezeno, Joseph, 126
Kremer, Ward, 147
Krepper, Carl Emil Ludwig, 160-161
Ku Klux Klan, 26-31, 55, 136, 150
Kugler, Arthur, 52
Kugler, George, 52-54
Kugler, Margaret, 52-54
Kugler, Marjorie, 52-53
Kugler, Raymond, 52-54
Kuhn, Fritz, 149-150
Kunze, Gerhard Wilhelm, 150-151
La Falcia, Beatrice, 85
La Falcia, Victor, 85
Lackawanna, NY, 45
Lake, Herschel, 67
Lake, Mary, 68
Lakehurst Naval Air Station, 88
Landau, Abe, 111-112
Lansky, Meyer, 143
Las Vegas, NV, 62
Laurel League of Plainfield's Luncheon-Bridge Party, 149
Layman, Lemuel G., 148
Layton, Leslie, 40
Leaycroft, Wilma, 136-137
Leberman, Buol, 162-163
Leberman, Susan, 162
Lee, George B., 45-46
Leonhardt, Joseph, 102
Letford, Mrs. W.F., 11
Lewis, Jerry, 174
Lewistown, PA, 19-20
Lilliendahl, A. William, 33, 35-36
Lilliendahl, Alfred, 33-34, 37
Lilliendahl, Margaret, 33-37
Lincoln, NE, 17
Lindbergh kidnapping, 87, 106, 113, 131-132
Lindbergh Law, 114
List, John, 172
Littlefield, James G., 127-128
Littlefield, Lydia, 127-128
Loeb, Charles, 73
Loes, Billy, 175-176
Logan, Andy, 3
Loizeux, Charles E., 109
London, Aaron, 57-58
London, Flossie, 57-58
London, James, 57-58

Loudenslager, Henry D., 91
Louis, Joe, 108
Louisville, KY, 96
Luciano, Charles "Lucky," 61, 111, 143
Luger, Carl, 95
Lust, Benedict, 115
Lutheran Reformed Church of Carteret, 164
Lutheran Theological Seminary, 160
Lutz, Solomon, 84-85
Lynch, John, 163
Lyons, Jack, 123
Mackay, William B., 16
MacKnight, Gladys, 115-116
MacKnight, Helen, 115-116
Madberg, Oscar, 106
Madden, Lloyd, 70
Madison Square Garden, 66
Maiwald, Edna, 108
Maiwald, George, 108
Malanga, Louis, 45-46
Malfatto, Ophelia "Vivian Lee," 77
Maloney, Martin, 20, 21
The Man Who Robbed the Robber Barons, A. Logan, 3
Manhattan, NY, 1-2, 65, 75, 126, 130
Mann Act, 29, 120-121
Mann Boudoir Car, 1
Mann, James, 120
Mann, Sophie, 2
Mann, William d'Alton, 1-3
Mantzinger, Robert, 103-104
Marshall Plan European Recovery Program- (ERP), 91
Martin, Annie, 25
Martin, Dean, 174
Martin, E.E., 96
Martin, Frank, 23-25
Martin, Frank Jr., 23
Martin, Helen, 23
Martin, Martha, 23-25
Martin, Otto, 58
Marx Brothers, 56
Masin, Louis, 166
Massa, John, 152
Master Butchers Association, 4

Mathis, Tom, 14
Matteawan State Hospital for the Criminally Insane, 66
McBrien, James "Jersey Kid," 45-46
McCarter, Robert H., 36
McClyment, Mary, 66-68
McClyment, Myrtle, 68
McCroy, Claude, 73
McDermott, Harold A., 43
McGovern, Thomas, 124
McGrath, Edward A., 110, 146
McInerney, Father Cornelius, 112
McKenna, Lura, 72
McKeown, Walter S., 10
McLaughlin, Thomas, 135
Means, Gaston B., 87, 131-133
Meisterknecht, Herbert O., 37-40
Meisterknecht, Sophie (Schreiber), 37-38
Meisterknecht, Susan, 38-39
Memphis, TN, 165
Mercer County Workhouse, 113
Merriam-Webster's Dictionary of Law, 35
Merrill, Joan (Ruscansky), 146
Metcalfe, John C., 150
Metelski, Edward, 100-101
Meyer, Peter, 21
Miami, FL, 66
Mighty Doris and Colonel Francis Ferari Combined Shows, 8
Milford, PA, 29
Miller, Charlie, 6
Miller, Woodburn, 158-159
Mineola, NY, 74
Miss America Pageant, 71, 144
Mitchel Air Force Base, 74
Mobile, AL, 1
Mohr, Bessie, 10
Mohr, Harry, 9-11
Moller, Wilfred, 73
Molnar, Barbara Ann, 163
Molnar, Daniel, 163-164
Monmouth County Jail, 54, 148
Montauk Point, NY, 3
Montgomery, Douglas, 31

Montgomery, John L., 53
Montgomery, Madeline (Clearwater), 31-32
Moore, Gov. A. Harry, 71, 80, 133, 149
Moretti, Guarino "Willie," 174-175
Morris, Marie, 171
Morris, Thomas, 171
SS *Morro Castle*, 57, 103
Morton, Albert "Whitey," 100-101
Mount Carmel, PA, 8
Mount Moriah Cemetery (Philadelphia), 77
Munch, James C., 125
Muni, Paul, 80
Murphy, John, 107, 134
Mustoe, William S., 40
Napier, Lee, 104
Nash, Charlotte Isabel, 71-73
Nashville, TN, 28
National Education Association, 56
National Woman's Party, 168
Nesbitt, Evelyn, 65
New Jersey
  Absecon, 57-58
  Alloway, 54
  Andover, 150
  Asbury Park, 43, 55-57, 86, 103-104, 106-107, 135, 137, 146
  Atlantic City, 3-6, 14, 31, 55-57, 65-66, 72-73, 75-77, 86, 102-103, 106, 118, 120-121, 131, 143-144, 156-157
  Atlantic County, 4, 34-35, 57, 121, 143
  Basking Ridge, 22
  Bayonne, 115
  Belleville, 125
  Belmar, 20-21, 52-53, 147
  Belvidere, 126
  Bergen County, 118, 125, 130, 134, 174
  Berlin, 103
  Bloomfield, 23, 31, 168
  Bound Brook, 31
  Bridgeboro, 87
  Burlington, 140
  Burlington County, 7-9, 12, 42, 88, 93-94, 113, 141

  Camden, 9-10, 42, 66, 68, 73, 78, 80-82, 95-96, 102-103, 141-142, 150, 156, 167, 172
  Cape May, 68
  Carteret, 85-86, 96-97, 160, 163-164
  Chatsworth, 87-88, 159
  Cinnaminson, 83
  Clementon, 82
  Cliffside Park, 130, 174-175
  Clinton, 14
  Cranford, 49
  Cresskill, 89-90
  Darby, 59
  Deal, 174
  Dunellen, 101
  East Orange, 64
  Edgewater, 15-16
  Egg Harbor, 79
  Elizabeth, 25-26, 37, 49, 59-60, 71, 76, 100, 134, 146, 162
  Essex County, 24, 26, 37, 46, 98, 134, 175
  Ewing Township, 25, 134, 146
  Florence, 93
  Fort Lee, 14
  Franklin Township, 172
  Freehold, 42-43, 54, 133, 135, 148
  Glassboro, 52
  Glendola, 53
  Gloucester County, 45, 92
  Gloucester Township, 67
  Guttenberg, 100
  Hackensack, 16, 130, 175
  Hammonton, 33
  Harrison, 151
  Hasbrouck Heights, 174-175
  Highlands, 37-38
  Hillside, 26-28
  Hoboken, 99
  Hopewell, 90, 166
  Hudson County, 31, 99, 130, 143
  Irvington, 12, 19-20, 25, 28
  Iselin, 70, 123-124, 164
  Jersey City, 30, 115, 138, 147, 161
  Kearny, 152, 171
  Kenilworth, 49, 145-146
  Keyport, 39, 108

INDEX

Lackawanna, 19
Lake Hopatcong, 152
Lakehurst, 12-14, 36
Lakewood, 39
Linden, 59, 119, 136
Livingston, 62
Maplewood, 19
Medford, 158
Mercer County, 26
Merchantville, 167
Metuchen, 107
Middlesex County, 100, 146-147, 149, 163
Middletown, 39
Monmouth, 29, 39-40, 45, 53, 56, 99, 108, 133, 148
Montclair, 50, 154-155
Morristown, 1-3, 98
Mount Holly, 9-10, 13, 84, 87, 114, 140, 159
Mountain Lakes, 33
Mountain View, 107
Mountainside, 12
Navesink, 148
Neptune, 55, 106, 135-136
Neptune Township, 55
Netcong, 126
New Brunswick, 11, 35, 48, 59, 99-101, 124, 163
Newark, 21-24, 27, 29-31, 38-39, 44-46, 61-64, 74-76, 80, 84-86, 97-98, 100-101, 111-112, 117, 124-125, 143, 147-148, 150-151, 155, 160-161, 170-171, 174-176
North Arlington, 127-128
Northfield, 5
Nutley, 119, 121-123, 161-162
Oakland, 118
Ocean County, 13
Ocean Grove, 56, 102
Ocean Township, 55
Orange, 43, 98, 147
Palisades, 14, 80
Passaic County, 134
Paterson, 59, 107
Paulsboro, 92
Pemberton, 141
Penns Grove, 95
Pennsauken, 40, 156
Perth Amboy, 8, 31, 147

Pitman, 52, 81
Plainfield, 138, 149
Pleasantville, 6
Rahway, 69-70, 100, 123, 160
Rancocas, 42
Red Bank, 29, 59, 91
Ridgefield Park, 16
Riverside, 7
Scotch Plains, 91, 109-110
Sea Bright, 137, 148
Sea Isle City, 139
Somerville, 106, 147
Sorrow, 31
South Vineland, 33, 35
Spring Lake, 20-21
Stockton, 126
Sussex County, 31, 150-151, 154
Teaneck, 117
Toms River, 13, 77
Totowa, 125
Trenton, 12-13, 16-18, 26, 28-30, 36, 38, 51, 71, 95, 103, 105-106, 108, 114
Union City, 99, 149
Ventnor, 6
Wall Township, 20, 99
West Berlin, 42
West Orange, 73-74, 105
Westfield, 48-49, 172
Westville, 46-47
Williamstown, 8
Woodbridge, 106-107, 124, 163-164
Woodbury, 29, 52
Woodland Township, 158
Woodstown, 78
New Jersey Chamber of Commerce, 131
New Jersey Federation of Women's Clubs, 81
New Jersey National Guard, 21, 149
New Jersey Natural Gas, 21
New Jersey State Assembly, 6
New Jersey State Hospital for the Insane, 11, 25
New Jersey State Police, 40, 82, 106, 107, 113, 147, 167
New Jersey State Police Museum, 106

New Jersey State Prison, 12, 43, 46, 51, 60, 71, 79, 101, 105, 119, 134, 142
New Jersey Women's Prison (Edna Mahan Correctional Facility for Women), 14, 36, 67, 116, 125, 166, 171
New York City Police Department, 86
New York Times, 7, 137, 144
New York University School of Law, 130
New York, NY, 2, 7, 12, 14-15, 33, 39, 45, 50, 52, 56, 65, 74, 76, 94-95, 107, 111, 132-133, 146, 156, 174
Newark City Hospital, 32, 112, 170-171
Newark Compressed Steel Company, 97
Newark Packard Company, 98
Newark Street Cleaning Department, 153
Newman, Alvin, 135
Nicholson, Edward, 67
Nixon, Richard, 148
Nixon-Nordlinger, Charlotte, 72
Nixon-Nordlinger, Fred, 72-73
Nixon-Nordlinger, Fred Jr., 72
Nokes, Nancy, 107
Nokes, Sam, 107
Northern Ohio Traction and Light Company, 26
Norway, ME, 129
O'Brien, Eugene, 14
O'Malley, Walter, 175
Odd Fellows Cemetery (Pemberton, NJ), 141
Sandusky, OH, 1
Old Smokey (electric chair), 46, 51, 101, 105-106, 164
Olde, Peter, 37-39
Operation Pastorius, 161
Orlando, Frank, 45
Osbeck, Florence, 143-144
Osborne, Ray, 82
Overbrook Hospital for the Insane, 25
Owens, Genevieve "Chip," 124-125
Panella, Louis, 74

Parker, Ellis, 7-9, 11-14, 42, 84, 88, 93-94, 113-114
Parker, Ellis Jr., 114-115
Parker, Irving, 37-38, 40
Parkston, William, 8
Passaic River, 107, 171
Paterson General Hospital, 134
Patterson, Betty, 5
Patterson, Melville, 5
Paul, Alice, 168-169
Pennel, William, 78
Penns Grove National Bank and Trust Company, 95-96
Pensendorfer, "Lifetime Jake," 41-42
Persiana, Anthony, 81
Persiana, Frank, 81
Persiana, Lena, 80-81
Petroski, Eugene, 43
Petroski, Eva, 42-43
Petroski, John, 43
Pettite, Dorothy, 106-07
Pfeiffer, Elizabeth, 89-90
Pfeiffer, Ernst William, 89
Philadelphia Bulletin, 7
Philadelphia Electric Corporation, 21
Philadelphia Toboggan Company, 57
Philadelphia, PA, 7, 10-11, 20-21, 34, 41-43, 45, 47, 49, 57, 59, 66, 70, 72, 75-78, 82-84, 95, 100, 103, 120-121, 139-140, 157, 160, 172-173
Phillips, Alan K., 74
Pinchot, Gov. Gifford, 41
Pine, Harry, 175
Pittsburgh, PA, 65-66, 152
Plainfield Courier-News, 138
Pleasure Bay Inn (Atlantic City, NJ), 156
Plunkett, T.B., 62
Pokomoke (sailing ship), 3-4
Pokomoke City, MD, 118
Pompton Lakes Gang, 107-109
Popola, John, 142
Poquette, Ramon, 170
Port Jervis, NY, 59
Powell, Charles M., 9-11
Powers, Ann, 170-171
Presbyterian Hospital, 98
"Pretty Boy" Floyd, 95
Prickett, Mrs. Charles A., 81-82

Pride, Dorothy, 122
Pride, James, 121-122
Pride, Lloyd, 123
Pride, Zelma, 122
prohibition, 4, 24, 61-63, 76, 78, 86-88, 111, 120, 143, 149
prostitution, 79, 120-121, 143
Public Enemy Act (1933), 108
Public Service Company, 74, 109
Public Service Coordinated Transport Company, 45
Pullman Car Company, 1
Pusey, Lloyd, 118-119
Pusey, Winnie, 118
Queens, NY, 58, 106, 176
Quick, Tom, 154
Quick, Tunis, 154-155
Quinn, John J., 54
racketeering, 62, 111, 157
radium girls, 43-44
radium jaw, 44
Rado, Joseph, 45-46
Ragtime, E.L. Doctrow, 66
Rahway Reformatory, 97, 100, 126
Rahway River, 97
Rahway State Prison, 158
Raritan Bay, 39
Rauber, Alfred, 107
Reade, Walter, 56
Reading, PA, 140
Redwood, Norman, 117-118
Reeves, Myra, 124
Reeves, Paul, 123-124
Regent Theater (East Orange), 64
The Register, 1
Reid, David, 45
Reid, Georgiana, 19
Repetto, Louis, 4, 34
Richmond, Joe, 13
Richmond, VA, 91
Rising Sun Brewery, 76
Roberts, Horace, 83-84
Roberts, Horace Sr., 84
Roberts, Margaret "Peggy," 28-29
Rocco, Joe "Joe Rock," 142
Rodia, Anna, 140
Rodia, Dominick, 140
Rogers, Ginger, 56
Rogers, Lena, 81

Rogers, Will, 11
Roland, Anna, 67
Romaine, Roslyn, 154
Romano, Braggio, 152
Roosevelt, Franklin D., 86, 91, 130
Rose Marie, 91
Rosen, Joseph, 112
Rosenkranz, Bernard "Lulu," 111
Rosenthal, Charles M., 74-75
Rosenthal, Margaret, 46
Rosoff, Joan, 118
Rosoff, Samuel, 117-118
Rosoff, Stephen, 118
Ross, Betsey, 77
Rost, Hildegarde, 99
Rost, Richard, 99-100
Roszanski, Adam, 163-164
Rowe, Thomas J., 170
Roy, Capt. J.A., 4
Runyan, Damon, 35
Ruscansky, Andrew, 145-146
Rushmore, Hazel, 139
Rushmore, Samuel, 138-139
Rusniak, Walter, 163
Russel Schwartz Cabinetmaking Company, 32
Russian National League of America, 151
Rutgers University, 55
Rutigliano, Nick, 75-76
Saint Catherine's Catholic Church (NJ), 21
Saint Michael's Cemetery (Hackensack, NJ), 175
San Francisco Giants, 176
Sanderson, Harry F., 36
Sansone, Joseph, 106
Saraga, Lou "Luger Mike," 118
Saranac Lake, NY, 15
Savitski, William, 8
Schofield, Lemuel B., 77
Schreiber, Alexander, 37-40
Schwartz, Edward, 96-97
Schwartz, Isadore, 97
Schwartz, Sigmund, 96-97
Schwartzkopf, Herbert Norman, 113
Scott, Alice, 163-164
Scott, Andrew, 170
Scott, Dorothy (Rowe), 170-171

INDEX

Scott, William, 103-104
Scranton, PA, 19, 21, 59
Scullion, Charles, 15-16
Scullion, Lawrence, 15
Securities Exchange Act of 1933, 149
Seippel, Benjamin, 42
Semenkewitz, Paul, 100-101
Shanley, Robert, 163
Shark River Inlet, 20
Sharp, Frank, 17
Shelters, Vernon D., 98-99
Sheridan, Anthony, 31-32
Shewchuck, Peter, 142-143
Shrewsbury River, 137
Siebert, Fred, 123
Siegfried, Frank, 37
Sileo, Albert "John Rocco," 75-76
Simmons, William J., 30
Simon, Benjamin, 95
Sims, Eddie, 67
Sinatra, Frank, 174
Sinclair Oil, 91
Sing Sing Correctional Facility, 50, 74, 76, 112
Sir Walter Hotel (Raleigh, NC), 70
Skale, Albert, 77
Smalley, Sarah D., 169
Smith, A.G., 23-24
Smith, Jack, 166-167
Smith, Violet (Martin), 23-25
Snowden, Woodbury B., 29
Sohl, Ethel "Bunny" Strouse, 124-126
Solly, John, 53
Somerset County, PA, 166
The Sopranos (TV series), 62, 175
South Hill, VA, 70
South Paris, ME, 127-128
Special Committee to Investigate Un-American Activities (Dies Committee), 150
Spindler, Charles, 20-21
Squire, Susan, 16
Stader, Phoebe, 69-70
Stafford, Bernard L., 134
Stahl, August, 145
Standard Oil Co., Inc., 38-40
Stark, Ruth Peggy, 74
Staten Island, NY, 74
Stein, Agnes, 121

Stein, Alfred A., 60
Stein, Louis, 121
Stein, Peggy, 121
Steinbach, Jacob Jr., 43
Stewart, David, 5
Stewart, Roy R., 102
Strader, Phoebe, 71
Strittmater, Louisa, 168-169
Studeman, William, 52-54
Sturm, Joseph, 146-147
Superior Manufacturing Company, 63
Supreme Court of New Jersey, 11, 25, 51, 71
Sussex County, PA, 29
Sweeney, Walter J., 137
Syracuse, NY, 74
Szathmary, Rev. Julius, 164
Szewczak, Arthur, 84-85
Taggart, Thomas T., 157
Talbot, Hazel, 128
Taylor, William Desmond, 7
Temple University, 125, 172
Tenerelli, Jean, 156-157
Tenerelli, Michael, 102-103, 156
Thaw, Evelyn (Nesbitt), 66
Thaw, Harry Kendall, 65-66
Thaw, Russell William, 66
Thornton, Alice, 15-16
Toner, Bernard, 58-60
Tortariello, Gene, 136-137
Town Topics, 2
Trenton Psychiatric Hospital, 134, 146, 173
Trenton Times, 28
Truchanociz, Mary, 100
Truman, Harry, 91, 115
Tryon, Jacob K., 52
Tyler, Elizabeth, 30
U.S. Soldiers' and Airmen's Home National Cemetery, 107
Ukrainian brown shirts, 151
Union County Court of Oyer and Terminer, 28, 60, 64
United States Census, 2, 11, 18, 25, 28, 43, 60, 76, 100, 107, 130, 134, 146, 156, 162
United States Penitentiary, Atlanta, 26
United States Penitentiary, Leavenworth, 133
United States Penitentiary, Lewisburg, 144

United States Radium Corporation, 43-45
United States Treasury Department, 26
University of Pittsburgh, 65
Unruh, Howard, 172-173
Van Dexter, Joseph, 67
Van Riper, Walter D., 64
Vergara, Lillian, 155
Verrier, Virginia, 19
Voelker, Franz, 72
Volstead Act (National Prohibition Act), 3, 86
voodoo, 57-58
Walden, NY, 69, 71
Walsh, Louise, 81
Warren, Frank "Bunk," 58-59
Warren, Whitney, 56
Wats, George, 16
Webb, Mamie, 141
Webb, Mary (Jobes), 140-141
Webb, Murrell, 140-141
Weequahic Park, 98
Weigand, Frank, 25-26
Weiss, Mendy, 111-112
Wendel, Paul, 113-115
Werner, Gus, 8
West Papoose Swamp, 88
Westervelt, Gladys (Johnson), 89
Westinghouse, George, 105
Wetmore, Charles, 56
Wexler, Irving "Waxey Gordon," 86-87
White, Stanford, 65
White-Slave Traffic Act (Mann Act), 120
Whitlock, George, 121
Wightman, Donald, 115-116
Wilentz, David, 114
Wilentz, William, 163
Wiley, Frank, 103
Wilkes Barre, PA, 19, 59
Wilson, Ruth, 83
Wilson, Thomas, 104
Winchell, Walter, 121
Woodlawn Cemetery (NY), 3
Woodward, Robert, 46
Woolbert, Roy, 6
Workman, Charley "The Bug", 111-112
World War I, 13, 27, 30-31, 39, 44, 63, 80-81, 89, 109, 130, 132-133, 146, 149, 151, 160

World War II, 31, 79, 151, 172
Wright, Hannah, 22
Wright, Martin, 21-22
Yenser, Irwin, 101
Yenser, Warren, 100-101
Yetman, Elizabeth, 135-136
Yonkers, NY, 37, 39
York, PA, 59
Zied, Charles, 103
Ziegler, Mary, 29
Ziegler, Rev. Roscoe Carl, 28-31
Zwillman, Abner "Longy," 61-62, 86, 143, 174

About the Author

JOSEPH G. BILBY received his BA and MA degrees in history from Seton Hall University and served as a lieutenant in the First Infantry Division in Vietnam in 1966-1967. He is Assistant Curator of the New Jersey National Guard and Militia Museum in Sea Girt, a board member of the New Jersey Civil War Heritage Association, a columnist for *The Civil War News* and *New Jersey Sportsmen News* and a freelance writer, historian and historical consultant. He is the author, editor, or co-author of over 400 articles and twenty-one books about New Jersey, including *Submarine Warfare along the New Jersey Shore*. His latest work is *New Jersey: A Military History*, the first comprehensive military history of the state ever published. Mr. Bilby has received the Jane Clayton award for contributions to Monmouth County (NJ) history, an award of merit from the New Jersey Historical Commission for his contributions to the state's military history and the New Jersey Meritorious Service Medal from the state's Division of Military and Veterans Affairs.

www.ingramcontent.com/pod-product-compliance
Lightning Source LLC
Chambersburg PA
CBHW070609170426
43200CB00012B/2633